Copyright © by Anna Tjumina, 2016
All Rights Reserved
ISBN 13: 978-94-92371-09-6
www.amsterdampublishers.com

To the Personally Awesome You

The New Generation Assistants series (Volume 1)

Six Essential Soft Skills of Indispensable Assistants

How PA personal development will secure your position

Anna Tjumina

Introduction

We are moving away from the knowledge age and entering the creativity era. A transition that will define a new world, bottom up. Are you fit and ready to face the transformation? Are you properly equipped to lay the groundwork for the next generation of Assistants to thrive?

This book is just the beginning!

The movement has started, waiting for new leaders to show how it's done. Taking the stage are the qualities of self-awareness, self-management and self-development. They will enforce your sense of self-belief and confidence. What matters most will have to come from who you are inside. Assistants have the image of being 'leaders from behind'. Becoming an equal partner at the leaders' table is our next move.

Multiple employers, economic struggles, a fast-moving digital world that has no international boundaries and cutthroat competition has made New Generation Assistants adapt to moving business structures, changing technical provisions, complex managerial duties, multilevel teams and 24/7 information flows.

Join the force and groom yourself to fit the role. Technical qualities never have been a challenge to us, if needed we can master anything. It's our ultimate service mind, our willingness to get things done and be there for others that determine our value. More than ever before, assistants are magicians of making things happen.

Introducing W.A.N.T.E.D. soft skills will make it all tangible for you to get started on this exciting journey. You will learn to acknowledge yourself first, find your Unique Super Powers and incorporate them in your daily routine. It's a soul-searching road of incredible discoveries and the source of new plans and ambitions.

When Assistants excel, others benefit!

Take the first step to find out what makes you a Personally Awesome Assistant and make it work in your favor. They say Assistants are dispensable, we know it's not true. If you are strong at core and master the W.A.N.T.E.D. skills you will become an indispensable Assistant to those that cherish and acknowledge your value. Be ready and willing to highlight what makes you look good.

What's your battle cry?

Your Personally Awesome Topics

Chapter 1. In the beginning

March 2014. I was attending the Executive Secretary Live (ESL) event in London. I remember being blown away by the attendants, and especially the numbers: over 250 PAs from 17 countries! I have never experienced so much PA power in one room. Just imagine the tasks we could have accomplished with all of us there right that moment! I get goosebumps just by thinking about it...

I could only attend one day of the conference, so I was soaking up every second. I will never forget that day, for one important reason. I saw the need to be together. With the will to learn together I realized we can achieve amazing things, and that our successes will pile up when we support each other in our intense and ever-changing profession.

This book builds on that inspiration. It is meant to collect and share knowledge of our beloved profession of being top-notch Assistants. Even more importantly, this book is born out of my own determined search to find ways to grow and develop. I want to be able to meet growing expectations, fulfill my responsibilities: basically, be able to cope with anything that life throws at me. There was something missing and I kept looking for answers until it hit me... I already possess everything I've been looking for, I just need to acknowledge my talents, and then reinforce them to become stronger.

My journey so far has made me a better PA, a better person. I believe this process is just beginning, and will evolve over years of experience, commitment and a lot of hard work. I feel strong and empowered and truly want to share this with every Assisting Professional out there.

Maybe you will find something here that can help you elevate your career, skills, and perhaps even your precious personal lives.

Pleasure to meet you

Let's exchange pleasantries first. I'll start by telling you something about me. My career developed in a rather unexpected way, as it usually does for PAs. I started off in the financial corner and throughout the years grew into this amazingly varied and rapidly expanding profession of Personal Assistant. I'm part of the so-called 'younger generation' of PAs, and my 14 years of experience began right after my graduation. Believe it or not — I couldn't wait to get a job, I was much more of a doer from the beginning. I worked in a Big Four accounting firm as a junior auditor and got to know the inner workings of various businesses in a relatively short amount of time. Soon I realized that being involved in different companies for only a few weeks at a time wasn't enough for me. I wanted to focus all my attention on one company, so I made my move to the internal finance department of one of the world's best known multinationals. From then on, my life took turns and leaps that helped me experience amazing new areas, and eventually led me to where I am right now — feeling proud and satisfied.

Along the way I turned out to be a good office manager and travelled extensively across Europe to manage offices, financial administrations and facilities. At some point, my executive was so happy with my results that I became his Assistant. All of a sudden I was a PA to a high-powered executive in the glamorous world of luxury yacht building. Here I developed a thirst for knowing my company inside and out and became more and more involved in different aspects of the business. I tried my hand at setting up companies, running overseas living facilities, organizing business and private matters of traveling expat employees, and I even had a taste of the commercial side of the business.

In addition, my Russian heritage came in handy when new business opportunities in Russia cropped up: I ended up in the middle of negotiations, new business developments and met some major players. Very exciting stuff!

After a while I decided to make a new move, and I soon found myself assisting a brilliant executive in a major Dutch live entertainment company with a strong international presence. This time my duties were focused on being a corporate PA, an Executive Assistant, for multiple busy executives with overwhelming schedules, frequent complex travel schemes and an extended international team. Even here I combined being an EA, running the office and assisting in legal mergers and acquisitions. As my dedication to this company grew, I tried to be involved in everything I could get my hands on, even things such as finance and business development. It was an incredible experience to work in such a dynamic and high-profile company. I had to be very flexible, sharp and quick. Soon I adopted the working hours of my executives — that was my big introduction to their extreme office lives and almost nonexistent personal time.

In search of more balance I decided to make yet another move. My next challenge was an incredible opportunity to combine my passion for architecture with my profession as a PA, working for the partners of an internationally renowned architecture firm. This was definitely mixing business with pleasure! The experience of working alongside the world's most admired architects was beyond anything I could imagine. I witnessed the creation, development and building processes of some astonishing architecture. Being on top of the world has a new meaning to me now!

As time passed, one specific recurring dilemma of the extremely busy professionals I was supporting caught my attention: they all had so little time after hours! In each case the work-life balance was brutally disturbed — obviously in favor of being so passionate and dedicated to their businesses.

As I have personally experienced such a time shortage, this phenomenon inspired me to become the Assistant that the PA profession intended to be all along — personal! And so I started my own business and became a private PA. At the heart of my company is being available to entrepreneurs, executives and solo professionals to ease their lives and make them as effective and efficient as possible. Being their private PA on demand, whenever they need it. Now, here is the point where you need to understand something crucial: in the Netherlands having a PA is not a common thing. It's a luxury (I like being a luxury product, don't you?).

So here I am, assisting successful entrepreneurs and professionals in business and in private and I'm loving every second of it. I enjoy the variety of my daily tasks: the intensity of different schedules, the power of amazing personalities, being involved in the workings and growth of various companies and being in the presence of true experts. Witnessing their results and seeing them excel makes me feel part of their success. You know what — everybody excels in these situations!

Turning point

Let me be honest here, my road was not always an easy one. There was one major moment in my PA career that changed my way of working upside down and inside out. It shook my very core in a very unpleasant way — but to this day, I can firmly state that it made me stronger and a bigger person.

The experience I'm talking about can perhaps best be described as follows: I was working in a company with the *The Devil Wears Prada* kind of executives, but you have to quadruple the character from the movie in order to begin to understand the magnitude of the force I was up against. To make the story short but vivid, I will tell you this: it was a very extreme working environment! It made you feel less valued than even the most insignificant animal, with no rights or freedom to have your own opinions or input, let alone a personality. I have never felt so small, humiliated, used, powerless...

That was definitely the lowest I have felt as a PA, but also as a person. It came close to being emotionally abused — every imaginable boundary was crossed ten times over. We worked in constant fear, up to a point where you actually felt physically incompetent to even move from your spot, trying to be as invisible as possible and hoping that it was just a very bad nightmare. And I say 'we' because there were a few PAs there experiencing exactly the same thing. You can imagine what this working environment did to the concept of teamwork. People on edge never make a good team to say the least. It was challenging on so many levels.

Specifics are not really important here, and I will mention some elements later in this book, but here is something to paint a picture for you: we frequently experienced flying stacks of papers, pens and coffee mugs, broken glass doors and visible footprints on the furniture, screaming, spit-talking, name-calling and threats. I found myself constantly comforting crying colleagues, all the while working ridiculously long hours and facing rejection. Well, you can imagine that all of that doesn't make it a great place to spend most of your waking hours. It leads to aggression, fear and backstabbing.

Instead of dwelling on this experience, however, I became determined to help others in some way, so that no one will ever feel the same way! It is my intention to prepare you for those situations: I will provide solutions and checklists which you can implement right away.

At one point, the harder I tried to incorporate any strategies the more miserable I got. I don't give up easily, so I kept trying to make it work. I worked harder to fulfill the expectations, which I did in every way possible, despite everything. And the crazy thing was that I was actually succeeding! My executives were content with me, and I supported them longer than any other PA up to that point.

Strangely enough you get used to that kind of treatment. You grow a thicker skin and you train your emotional immune system to work overtime! After hearing over and over again from my husband that the situation was not acceptable, I finally started to listen. But only after my physical health slowed me down, and when the tears were running down my face uncontrollably at the very thought of going to work. At that point I just snapped and walked away. It's not a solution to every difficult situation, but I know now that it is very important to not lose yourself. Looking back, I would have done one thing differently. I would have walked away much earlier.

Right after I left, I felt like a failure. PAs are supposed to overcome difficult personalities and make everything work, right? It took me almost a year to understand that, first of all, I'm not the only one that has experienced this, and, secondly, seeing it from a distance, it surely wasn't acceptable or normal. Sometimes executives do go too far and you need to stand up for your rights! And, most importantly, if you are not in perfect shape as a person, you cannot be a perfect PA. You have to look after and nourish yourself first.

This was the beginning of my quest to find ways to make my mind and spirit stronger. I needed to excel as a person first to become an amazing PA. I realized that we need to have a certain 'PA state of mind' to become those shiny Assisting Professionals. To be truly effective in every way and provide fitted assistance to our execs on their (usually) tough journeys, with huge responsibilities and pressure to perform. Right then I truly understood the saying 'love yourself first before you can love another'. Twist it around a little and you will understand the most profound lesson I have learned to date, one which I had to learn the hard way!

Now I can stay calm in every situation by being me, keeping my attention and problem-solving radars on without freaking out at the possibility of failure. I can predict actions and the ways in which people react because I truly care about them and know their personalities. I'm prepared to act accordingly, knowing upfront what they might think or ask of me because I'm committed to their lives. I get huge satisfaction by chasing the impossible tasks and I get grounded by doing the nitty-gritty errands.

I love what I do, because I see the bigger picture and at the same time I understand that I'm the hidden driving force behind all of this. I have found ways of actually having a life too, spending time with my family, raising my beautiful daughter and running a business.

Most of all, I feel centered, focused and secure about myself and my abilities. All those are not personality traits — those are skills that you can develop. Those are the exact abilities I want to share with you so you can be that empowered professional.

The know-how

Your story doesn't have to be anything like mine, or even remotely similar in any shape or form, for you to be able to benefit from what is written in this book. I actually assume that you have an incredible executive who treats you well and that your relationship and cooperation are up to everyone's expectations and satisfaction.

The techniques and programs I will reveal will be beneficial to any Assisting Professionals who love what they do. True professionals always look for ways to elevate their mindset, level of excellence and productivity. After all, that is the universal necessity to succeed in anything you do, business or personal!

One thing to note here. I often get asked, 'How can you work for such a difficult person?' The truth is that most execs are seen as difficult creatures, but there is a big difference between being difficult for the sake of being difficult and simply being highly demanding and result driven. This is how I always saw my execs; they are all qualified perfectionists, they aim for the highest standards and constantly tend to exceed them in everything they do. So yes, they are very demanding and they act from a different place in the hierarchy. And in addition to the pressure of their responsibilities they all have incredibly packed and demanding agendas, to the extent where you even have to schedule five-minute toilet breaks (true story!).

So it's not a big surprise that they can come across as rude in conversations with you: they are often very to the point in their thoughts and they frequently act on a tight schedule. Don't perceive that as difficult, but take it as a challenge and a sign of their faith in you.

Them being demanding of you is a sign that they think you are fit for the job! It's a hidden compliment people are usually not aware of. Think about it: would you waste your precious time and effort asking somebody you think is not good enough to accomplish anything important for you? No, you wouldn't! I will admit that it is challenging to live up to some requirements, but there are many roads to Rome. Find the one you can walk to the best of your abilities and be proud of the things you accomplish along the way. Again, it's a mindset and if you think from that perspective you will be a lot more effective and pleased with yourself.

Checkpoint

Let's go back to the event I attended in London. After speaking to a few participants (a special thank you to those amazing ladies at my table) my findings were confirmed, and actually matched the results of my interviews with over 50 top Assisting Professionals worldwide: we truly love what we do! This needs to be celebrated, treasured and become our main encouragement to grow and evolve our abilities and personalities.

Our community of Assisting Professionals is large but scattered. There is a big online presence, but you have to invest much time and effort to figure out which sources fit you best. There are a lot of similar questions asked, related problems discussed and issues shared. All this points to a need to be together and I hope to start a movement of focused attention on personal development.

In the last part of the book I will explain explicitly what I think we can do to get more focused, get tailored support and initiate effective sharing. We can organize complicated and impossible things because that is asked of us on the job, so let's organize some things for ourselves too. A wonderful example is the work of Victoria Darragh, who initiated internal PA networks at Hays UK and successfully translated them to external networks. Right now, she passionately pioneers this method across the United Kingdom. For all of us working in the private sector or representing single clients — we can do it too online! We just have to get our heads together. More on the importance and value of this topic is still to come, so stay tuned.

Hear hear

The main focus of everything you will read here is based on my strong conviction that you need to excel yourself first to be able to help others to excel too. True, simple and confrontational. We are not used to focusing on our own needs (at least I'm not), so that can be quite a challenge on its own. Please be patient and kind to yourself, respectful and loving, because it is especially those characteristics that will make you feel empowered, balanced, happy and accomplished. As Debbie Gross, celebrated EA to the CEO at Cisco, said in her presentation at ESL, top PAs are usually not expected to have a (personal) life. Sadly that's true, but I figured out a way to be that kind of PA and have a life! Sounds good right and no, it's not impossible!

We all know that you have to know the rules to play the game. In this book you will get my rules that help you to get ahead in our game. They will make you better equipped to face anything and everything, and act accordingly. I believe that our main power comes from our mindset. It determines our feelings, our thoughts, our actions and thus the inevitable outcome. It's that flow that we need to be aware of. If you have the knowledge and control that source, you will have the power of influence.

Magic beans

It all comes down to this: I believe that by incorporating a specific set of six core soft skills you can develop into a truly extraordinary Assisting Professional. Those skills are summarized in a fast forward formula: W.A.N.T.E.D. (I'll let you know what it stands for in the coming chapters). The important thing to realize is that these soft skills must be fully understood and internalized before they are put into action. I have to agree with Sheryl Sandberg (COO at Facebook, author of *Lean In*) that internalizing certain principles is a heavy duty but a necessary one.

We have a lot of convictions and beliefs stored deeply and firmly within us and we need to clear up that stash first before you can add anything new and daring. After ticking that off your list, you will need the sacred combination of preserving and acting on behalf of your authentic personality and leading a balanced lifestyle. Only then will you feel empowered, accomplished and truly content. I believe it's all about seeing and understanding the bigger picture, whether it's your life or the life of your executive. Our ability to master this will translate into direct results. Our willingness to notice those results and act upon them will determine our level of success. It's all up to us! We always have the choice to take control and responsibility for our actions. You reap what you sow, no hocus pocus there.

Again, please remember to be kind and patient with yourself on this journey, which will take time and effort. A truthful way of knowing if you're on track is very simple: check in with yourself — are you happy? If you feel grumpy today, adjust something if needed and move on in the desired direction. I can testify that the result is very satisfying!

Before I explain the next steps, I would like to take a moment and dig deeper into some terms and definitions that I will mention frequently in this book. Although they are commonly used I want to clarify the core basics and translate them to a PA's situation, the way I intend to use them. The meaning of these terms in our context might not be straightforward.

Hard skills vs soft skills

This book is primarily focused on the soft skills of Assisting Professionals. But let me state it loud and clear: this does not mean that you can succeed without the hard skills! You definitely need both. The main reason why I don't explore the practical abilities you need to perform at the highest level of being a top Assistant is because there is a significant amount of material already available: books, training, seminars, blogs and online forums. Of course you need to know how to take minutes, how to use Microsoft Office, how to use travel software and admin programs efficiently and effectively. But that's not the subject of this book.

On the topic of soft skills little has been published. There is no real sequence or program that specifically focuses on developing the soft skillset of Assisting Professionals.

Currently, there is no certificate in any of these soft skills (I would love to have an MBA in the 'Troubleshooter Mindset'). In fact, the only courses available are pure personal development courses (which most employers don't take seriously for us PAs). There are workshops out there, modules and many blogs, but no accredited institution willing to state that your mindset and soft skillset are up to a certain level of expertise. Don't you think that's strange?

I'm absolutely positive that none of us could succeed with excellent hard skills only. We need soft qualities and we need to master them at an all-time high level with continuous attention, effort, reminders and supporting tools. Most great PAs already have them and use them on a daily, no, hourly, basis. It's nothing new. However, we all need to focus a bit more on those qualities and cherish them. They determine our mindset and our mindset is a direct multiplier of our skills!

One small thing before we continue. I will use the word 'exec' as an abbreviation in reference to your employer, whether it is a business executive, a private individual, a group of people you assist or any other form of entrepreneur, professional or employer. I will also address the exec as 'him', but it may of course be a 'her' as well. It's nothing personal (I love working for female executives)! I will keep using the term 'PA', but it implies all variations of the title of being an Assistant.

Did you know there are over 150 title variations for what we do? Also, I will presume that the PA is a 'she' (how conventional) but I know from experience that the male population of Assisting Professionals is huge and growing. I love this trend, we can learn from gender-specific points of view and the way we do things. I better dig up more on this exciting distinction (goes on my to-do list).

From wanted to needed

There is a difference between being a *wanted* PA and being a *needed* PA.

Let's start with wanted. If you *want* to have something (unrelated to PAs) then your mind says: 'It would be really nice, good and useful to have it. But I don't want to spend too much effort, money or time on it.' If you don't end up pursuing the object of your affection you say: 'Too bad, but no harm done. Something else will come along or I will look for other options.'

Now presume you *need* something. That is the moment when your whole being is screaming that you simply can't do without it (think shoes!). It's something that will make the biggest difference to you and enable you to be, do, fulfill and have something that was missing. If you don't pursue that object of affection you will be truly devastated.

See the difference?

Let's translate this phenomenon to 'having a PA'. A lot of execs *want* a PA because they don't want to do their own scheduling, getting coffee, making copies, checking PowerPoints, running errands and calling all day long to make appointments. Now, if these execs do not get the PA they were hoping for it's no biggie. They will just keep on interviewing and change PAs as they go.

But, let's say you've found that special one who you just click with, she gets you, and does everything you ask of her the way you intend. Your partner loves her, your children adore her, your schedule never looked better, you get your stuff done and you talk to the people you need to at the required moments. Your fabulous vacations are taken care of and there is always a quick solution to any issue. She knows everything you ever ask and she actually helps you stay ahead and feel confident about your daily tasks. With this PA you feel at ease and you let her do more.

You trust her, you actually throw some of your ideas at her to see if they make sense and if there are any gaps you might have missed. At some point you even trust her to update you on 100-page reports in 15 minutes, you agree that she will represent you at some meetings so you can enjoy some quality family time, and you get to go to that 'ultra-difficult to get in' event you have been dying to attend for ages.

This list grows over time. You get to know each other on a personal level, she knows when to cheer you up and when to back down. She senses when you feel stressed out or when you're floating in a creative mode. Your mutual understanding is quick and subtle (her nudge of the head means your next appointment has arrived, you looking down at your watch means you are dying to be rescued from this meeting ASAP). She knows your every preference so everything runs smoothly etc. etc. etc.

At this point your PA has become almost irreplaceable. Your life will become hugely uncomfortable if she ever leaves her position for whatever reason. You would experience a moment of despair because you know A. it will take a while before you find anybody like that, B. the adjustment period will not be easy and C. you will keep comparing your new PA to the previous one — which will not make it easier for either party.

Some execs go a long way to keep their PAs for as long as possible, and are sometimes even willing to create new positions within the company for their PAs to grow. I know of cases where tears were shed when saying goodbye! They write a personal lengthy recommendation to the next employer, because they know it is a sign of trust and a stamp of approval. They know that this will make all the difference for their beloved PAs to get the next job of their choosing. Some relationships remain over time and friendships are made. There is even an internationally known case of including a longtime PA in a will! (James Gandolfini included his Personal Assistant and close friend Thomas Richardson and his secretary Trixie Flynn Bourne in his will, with each receiving $200,000, which demonstrates just how close the exec/PA relationship can be.) Now that is an extreme but pure form of appreciation, wouldn't you say?

I hope the picture I have tried to paint is clear. In conclusion, being a *needed* PA makes a lot of things easier for both PAs and their execs. Effective and efficient communication, speed of trust (a definition advocated by the renowned author Steven R. Covey), ease of information sharing, delegating and instant mutual understanding will make you a winning team!

And it's not a fairy tale. There are amazing tributes from high-profile execs on the internet praising their PAs and telling the world that their support makes them better, stronger and faster (just search for Sir

Richard Branson's LinkedIn blog post on his Assistants or John Paul DeJoria's video message to his valued EA Veronika Judish). Wouldn't it be nice to be that PA mentioned by name and with a personal note instead of being the third in a row of many?

Speed of trust

Let's take a closer look on the essential topic of trust. Strangely enough, trust is usually overestimated and underestimated at the same time. If all is good and jolly then the trust is there and thriving, but if something does not go to plan then it is damaged forever. Is trust that unreliable?

Trust is absolutely essential for the relationship between PAs and their execs, no doubt about it. Trust is a perfect measurement of the outcome of your efforts and can be used to predict the scalability of the relationship with your exec. I will mention it a lot in the upcoming chapters so it's important to be on the same page when it comes to what it actually means. The thing is, it is vulnerable and delicate.

How do we know it's there? How do we know when we still need to work for it? And if it is breached, is it really beyond repair?

The difficulty here is that it's a very personal issue and the answers vary with the person. Through the years our criteria change as we grow wiser (yes, it happens to some of us). I know some will disagree with me, but I compare trust with image. Your image is defining you, your positions, your family, your goals, your past and your future. You can build it, you can lose it, and it can be at an all-time high or low. The good thing about image is that we can control it! For some reason we tend to think of trust differently, it's there or it isn't. And that's just not true!

Trust is as elastic and manageable as image, you only need to know how to handle it. I believe that being honest, sincere and professional are key factors on the subject of trust. To make it more vivid I will illustrate trust in a wonderfully measurable equation later in the book (a big thank you to Charles H. Green, the founder of The Trust Equation) and we'll discuss different levels of trust, which will reassure you. Knowing this trust equation makes it so much easier for us PAs to find out where we stand when it comes to trust, where there's not enough so that we can poke and twitch and make it better. Or when to stay clear and move on, because without trust you cannot be a *needed* PA! When trust becomes a manageable concept we are a whole lot more in control of the most important element of our relationships, in control of the quality of our support. And we love anything manageable, right?

Here is one definition I would like to kick off with for now: the trust flow. It illustrates how trust is built and shows the whole flow of the concept. You can clearly see here that you have full control over it! It explains your part in it and makes it obvious why the six defined W.A.N.T.E.D. soft skills are so applicable to nurturing a trusting relationship with your executive.

This will turn you into their safe haven. Now that's a title I won't refuse!

You've got the power

I use words like power, control and influence with ease but, truth be told, they can be perceived as dirty words in business. Unfortunately, people have often misused their power to control circumstances in ways that have been devastating. The latest extreme example is the worldwide recession. Let me state that the purpose of the *needed* PA is to elevate others and let our execs excel in what they do. If these three magical words are used in relation to making something better, then I urge you to act on them fearlessly.

Here is a fitting description I have read somewhere and I think it's a great way of showing how we as Assisting Professionals have to act on those magical words:

Power is the capacity you possess, influencing is the way you are using that power. Be in control of those abilities to the best of your judgment and engage them in order to excel yourself so you will be able to elevate others.

This would be a great pledge for an Assistant!

Influence and being influenced mean being able to achieve our objectives by getting help, cooperation and commitment without formal authority. By using our strong soft skillset we can communicate and act without manipulation. Think about it, your habitual and automated actions can hurt your progress as they mean that you act unconsciously. You have to consciously control your actions in every situation while spicing them up with your soft skills magic. This will boost your effectiveness, professional impact and personal credibility.

Targeted use of our soft skills magnifies our ability to build and establish strong and sincere relationships. This is the right way to build the essential trust which is needed in order for us to be truly supportive.

The direct result of that trust translates into our 'PA power' to influence people, events and outcomes. It's a huge force to be reckoned with so use it wisely! Again, no hocus pocus here: trust is the foundation of it all. Keep in mind the above statements and you will see clearly why and how you can create trust and be in control of it when we examine Charles H. Green's magnificent formula of trust in chapter 5.

Keep your ears open and your mind alert

One of the most important abilities of a valued Assistant is understanding needs and acting on them. While it seems like a fairly simple and logical matter, it is an ability not often applied well. It begins and ends with our capacity to really and truly listen to what people are saying with the intention of actually hearing them.

Let's be honest here, Assistants often listen not only with the common devices called ears, but with a sixth sense. We use our multitasking skills to fit the received information with already existing knowledge of our execs. We know exactly through which lens we need to view the new data to understand what they really mean. In other words, we listen in

3D! The first dimension represents the actual words that are being communicated. The second dimension is understanding the context of when and how something has been said. The third dimension is being able to compare new data with past experiences, past intended reasons and achieved results. Are you still with me?

Let me simplify it through this smartly put together acronym:

L = Look interested, get interested, act interested with intention
I = Involve yourself in the conversation by responding thoughtfully
S = Stay focused on the target and topic
T = Test your understanding by reconfirming, comparing and asking questions
E = Evaluate the message in terms of content and timeline importance
N = Neutralize your emotions, but show compassion, understanding, support and resourcefulness

Need I say more?

Yes I do! There is one more element which is really important and can make all the difference, and that is the manner and execution of communication. Nowadays, I spend most of my time indulging in cyber communication and that makes things challenging at times. We all know that the actual words appearing on our BFF smartphones do not always reflect the core message or intention. Over time, we learn to recognize the little things that show us the state of mind of the typing hand.

What I'm trying to say is that we know how our execs communicate and it's important to use it to our advantage. So if you keep ending up with misunderstandings (online or offline) try to figure out what about the way your exec communicates doesn't get through to you.

I know that communication is a two-way street, but we are their Assistants for a reason. It's our job to make it easy for them to get things across, with us they can be less formal and at ease. *We* need to make communication work. *We* need to make it convenient for them, with no fuss.

What you resist... persists!

Last but definitely not least, I would like to mention resistance. Depending on your current situation, past experience, seniority of position or personal convictions you might feel various degrees of resistance to the things you'll read in this book. There is always a reason for that resistance and it's good to look closer at the areas where your resistance is strong. There is a space in the back of this book which I call The Resistance List. This is actually the first list of the workbook I created for you to track your findings and important insights (see the last pages in this book). Give it a go and fill it in on paper, in your head, or in an app and analyze your thinking processes and progression. You will work with most lists in the workbook later on, so it might be a great reference point on your journey to become the indispensable assistant you really are.

I would like to invite you to write down anything that comes up while going through the chapters. No judgment, just state the feelings and thoughts and move on. We will address them later in the book. I dare to promise you one thing — that list will give you the biggest insights! Furthermore, to be able to understand what is needed for us Assistants I would love to receive a summary of your Resistance List. Please see my contact info in the back. As you will find out shortly, there is something bigger cooking in my brain so I would love to hear any feedback, your current issues or anything else you might want to share with me or with our PA community. There is a method to my madness — just bear with me.

The pleasure is all mine

Before we begin the amazing journey into our PA minds (and it can be a scary place sometimes) let me express my deepest gratitude for you picking up this book and spending your precious time reading it. I truly hope I can support your mindset and give you tools that you can apply along the way, managing your busy schedule while juggling a thousand and one errands. I hope to help you deal with difficult conversations and challenging situations. I hope to make it possible for you to do all that with the ease and grace of an absolute top Assisting Professional who knows what needs to be done before it happens. To act fearlessly and decisively in any situation, to always remain professional but authentic. And most importantly, to grow in the desired direction, be proud, content and enjoy your life!

When PAs excel, others benefit! Let's go for it, let's get into that 'PA state of mind'!

Chapter 2. Spotlight on Hard Skills

Although this book is all about the importance of soft skills and mastering your mindset (which, unsurprisingly, directly impacts your attitude) I by no means want to devalue the importance of excellent hard skills. After all, those are the tools with which we actually deliver day in and day out. The technical skills are definitely crucial in themselves, especially because it is the way you use them that will make you even better and that will make you stand out. Sometimes it is the diversity of your skillset, sometimes it is an expertise in something special, sometimes it is about your ability to pick up new skills quickly and efficiently. It doesn't really matter in which form or version, hard skills are an important part of being a great Assisting Professional. Since this is a well-known fact, I will be brief.

Personally, I learned most technical skills on the job. I was thrown head first into company processes and administration that were seriously behind deadlines, chaotically organized offices and terrible ad-hoc environments. Some of my execs changed their minds every other day, floundering between opposite extremes, while some were very particular, forbidding and unrelenting. I had to be very flexible and quickly learn to accommodate whatever was needed at the time. I was never shy when it came to asking for help, and I made sure that I always had somebody around to guide me when conquering the unknown. I never had any formal secretarial education, as my background is heavily focused on finance and accounting. Either way, you'll have to learn the hard skills of being an Assistant — the way in which you learn them doesn't really matter!

There are countless institutions that provide an excellent education, and many courses and seminars on learning and mastering hard skills. I will let them do the talking on the specifics and the practicalities. In this chapter and those to come I want to briefly give you a few handy reminders, highlights and good theories on how to keep up the required level of your skills.

Divide and conquer

To begin with, it's good to be aware of the main differences between skills when you choose to polish up on one or more. I divide them into three categories: soft skills (which are more difficult to get a grip on because it's your inner core that needs a refresher), overall knowledge and general content (written or spoken information), and practical and technical skills. It's good to make three lists every once in a while and highlight any areas you want to update. Yearly reviews are good reminders and opportunities to reflect. The secret to every successful person on the planet is that he or she is a lifetime student. You truly should never stop learning. Even if you hold the same job for over two decades, the world doesn't stop changing.

So how are you certain to advance your learning and skillset? First of all, get in the habit of attending or buying/listening to at least one educational program every six months. But do so consciously. Not because somebody tells you to but because you want to! That is important.

Another major point — write things down. I guarantee that you will forget 60% of the content almost immediately if you don't write anything down. You don't even have to reread the written material: just by writing it once you will remember it on a much deeper level. Multiple scientific studies have proven that by writing things down you will achieve more, hold the information much longer, and effectively act on it by design.

My last piece of advice on how to preserve new information is to find the time to talk about it and educate others as soon as you are back in the office, at home or with your friends. It's the most amazing simple tool I discovered while following an intensive business training program. If you recount the information you've just heard to others, you will understand it much better, and it really sticks with you.

Unique vs commonality

For the lack of a more accurate description — every hard skill has a bipolar tendency! Although the practical execution of most hard skills is standardized, the environment it has to be executed in heavily influences the outcome. Therefore these outcomes or results can seem very different (or even opposite!) when compared. Just look into different outcomes per country, per sector, per company or even how your colleague is using the same skill, but in a totally different way.

Now, there is good news and bad news. The good news is that most hard skills are executed in the same way, which creates a familiarity. There is always something you are already familiar with, and, once mastered, can claim proficiency in. The bad news is that if you stick to your previous way of doing things you might find yourself at a disadvantage at some point. I'm sure you are a knowledgeable professional; just don't forget to reflect on your specific surroundings and their potential effects when something changes. Your expertise might also be a great addition or expansion to the new environment. Use the differences and commonalities wisely and to your advantage.

Another thing to keep in mind while assessing your hard skills: take into consideration how you arrived where you are right now. If you are a self-made professional, then it might be good to refresh a particular skill the official way. What you'll learn might surprise you. If you are a schooled professional, then try to learn a new skill in a less formal manner, on the run. You will discover a whole new side of yourself. Let's hope you'll like it! If you don't, don't be hard on yourself. Dealing with limitations is an amazing and certain way to grow.

To illustrate the essence of what I am trying to get across I would love to share the following quote from Gary Ryan Blair (aka The Goals Guy): *Don't limit your challenges, challenge your limits!* If your challenges are great enough, you will experience failure of some sort, guaranteed. It's the person you will become in the end, the one who conquers and wins, that is your main achievement. It's a humongous cherry on top of a cake which is very difficult to bake (and you'll know it because it is version number 57 that finally turned out the way it was supposed to!). In the end, it's all about the person you are. The things you do only outline who you really are inside.

By the way, any successful person will tell you that if you want to move forward, getting out of your comfort zone is the only way to do so. I always hated that, because it's called a comfort zone for a reason — it's nice, cozy and familiar. And you know what, staying there for a while is even mandatory in order to digest any freshly acquired material. In the chapter on 'me time' I will explain that having your own safe haven, your comfort zone, is an absolute must for any busy professional.

So, in a sense, you have to let go of some comfort to grow, but always know you have a sanctuary to come back to. We humans are creatures of habit by design. Habits keep up sane and secure, we need them like air and food. The great thing about habits is that you take them with you anywhere you go, and they will always serve you with the certainty of past experiences. Of course you also have the so-called unsupportive habits that you need to get rid of by replacing them with new ones. It's all about assisting resistance — but that's for a later chapter.

On the lookout

I want to share with you a few ways which help me deal with managing the increasing demands on my hard skills. There are two areas where I'm constantly challenged.

Fast-paced IT developments and industry-specific updates. It's absolutely mind blowing how many apps there are to achieve the same result. Back in the days when there were not so many options, and Windows ruled the world, I was on top of every update and new functionality. Soon after, however, it became impossible to know everything, let alone to have any experience of everything.

At some point I stopped being obsessed with keeping pace with IT developments and, as uncomfortable as it was in the beginning, I admitted I wasn't familiar with an app when my exec asked me about something he had just heard. And you know what — it turned out to be OK! What I need to do after such a question is to get familiar with the new app to form an opinion on its functionalities or start using it if my exec wants me to. It makes perfect sense to act this way, at least after some adjustment period.

Those apps are made to make life and work easier for us, not to stress us out, or complicate matters even more. So yes, you need to know the main IT applications of the environment you work in, but don't obsess about knowing everything. If I'm really stuck with something, or when something really takes too long to do, I have a habit of looking for apps that do in fact assist me. Or even better, I ask around if somebody knows a helpful tool — it just might work for you as well.

I will come back to industry updates in a later chapter as it is important to know what's going on. One piece of advice from my own experience: you don't have to understand every nitty-gritty detail of what you read. I worked in the insurance industry for a while and some terms and regulation amendments where really too much for me to handle. This is the time to find a person who deals with that information for a living, and to simply ask them to explain it to you in normal language that you can understand. I know that we Assistants are very proud creatures of whom a lot is expected, but sometimes you need to let that guard down. Better to be well informed than sitting on a high donkey pretending to be a horse.

And so, if you have decided to learn something new then here is what you do: make the effort, make it challenging if possible, master it to your best abilities, look for situations to apply it in practice and be very proud of your accomplishments. Learning something new is a great way to feel good about yourself, it is a fresh start and keeps you focused. You might find ways to combine new information and applications with old patterns in order to create amazing workarounds that will save you time, create better results and add more value in the process. All good!

Fly on the wall

I think I can be pretty certain that most of us already have a list of things to learn, courses to take, skills we know we could improve, but how on earth will you get to it if you don't even have time to deal with your daily to-do list?!

You know what (don't shoot the messenger): most impressions of a certain time deficiency only exist in your head! I imagine that after reading this, some of you are ready to close the book and go ask for a refund. Bear with me for a second, because I'm in that same 'overloaded' situation a lot. The thing we need to understand is that everything you do right this moment or plan to do ASAP has a sense of urgency attached to it! In a sense, you have the power to label something as urgent or not. Yes, of course your job dictates how you spend most of the time in your day, but believe me, if you really put your mind to it you can regain control of your own schedule and make it happen.

The sad thing is that most Assistants don't value themselves enough to turn the focus and the spotlight on themselves. And the surprising thing is that — and I hear this a lot from Assistants around me — if you tell your exec that you want to take course Y to get better at X, as long as he sees the added value, he turns out to be more than happy to fund you and give you time off to do what you suggested. Most execs are very fond of their PAs and they really want to see them shine, grow and be happy, especially when this benefits their business in the end! Yes, even the quietest execs are like that... So just give it a go!

If you do choose to undertake an educational endeavor, you can apply the following method to help ensure that it is carried out from start to finish. First of all, plan ahead so you, your colleagues, and your environment will have time to adjust and prepare if needed. Especially if it is difficult for you to find the drive to take the first step, give yourself a boost by telling others that you plan to take up learning a new skill or mastering a new course. Social pressure might motivate you to actually go through with your plan. And of course you can always find a buddy who will keep you on track and push you when needed. If you look for a buddy to push or sponsor you, ensure that you are exceedingly comfortable with that person, otherwise it can ruin your relationship in record time.

There is one last (and kind of funny) thing I discovered about PAs: we are quite comfortable moving in tribes. Meaning: we actually seek likeminded people, and need each other more than we might admit. That explains the growing number of events, seminars, social media groups and in-company PA networks. As mentioned earlier, Victoria Darragh from Hays in the UK is the godmother of the in-company PA networks. She founded and brought about recognition of in-company Assistants' networks. Just search for Victoria to find out more about what you can do within your company and the advantages it brings. Such an in-company network could easily advocate and provide educational budgets for training or possibilities to join amazing seminars — together!

In closing

So, what are the main take-aways of the last few pages? First, you are never too old or too educated to learn something! I hate it when people tell me that they missed the opportunity years ago. Or that there is more than enough time to think about it tomorrow. Scarlet O'Hara (the heroine from the classic *Gone with the Wind*) was wise to use that phrase to unleash herself from the troubles of today; however, that is not a way to think about your personal growth and new possibilities! Even if you're fine with where you are right now, there is always an abundance of things to learn, read, listen to or attend. You have the power of choice, use it! Make the decision to make your life awesome.

I also want to quickly mention a couple of 'non-logical' ways to identify how you can improve. First of all, ask Human Resources! It's not a very popular department in most companies, but they know exactly what skills are needed. As a result, they can likely advise you on areas you could focus on in your effort to be more valuable or inform you of any new educational developments as well as available courses. Embrace their power — you might be surprised by their assistance and knowledgeable feedback. You can also try to get in touch with head hunters and question them about trends and the 'most asked for' skills at the moment. For the same reason, don't reinvent the wheel, find somebody whose job it is to be up to date and informed about current developments and demands.

For example, there was a time when you had to know MS DOS, now there is never-ending demand for mastering every functionality of MS Office. Some companies live and breathe protocol, so their employees need to have excellent copywriting skills. There is always a demand for being able to take meeting minutes, but lately you need to be able to do that electronically. Writing shorthand or dictation is frequently requested by seasoned executives. Working in clouds and apps is a trend of younger execs... and the list goes on. You get the picture. Staying up to date and understanding which of the popular hard skills are required by your job are an important part of being a successful PA.

Last but not least: whether you are trying to find a new position, or just want to understand which skills are demanded by your current one, nose around local 'talent management agencies' — a fancy word for educational institutions. Subscribe to their newsletters and actually read them. You will be on top of new things coming up and new courses gaining popularity. You might find something that catches your attention and develop an appetite for more.

I want to leave this topic with the following battle cry: *There is always more to you*!

Make an effort to expand yourself. I hope you will make it your new mantra.

Chapter 3. Personal Branding

Let's continue with a subject out of the twilight zone — personal branding. Although branding claims to have very definite and set hard skills and prerequisites, it clearly also involves a fine mix of soft skills and perceptions. The great thing about branding is that it can be controlled. The question is: do you control your own branding, or do others control how you are perceived? Are you aware of how your environment affects your branding, or do you turn on autopilot and let your environment dictate the impression of you?

In general, we don't pay as much attention to personal branding as we should, even though we know it has quite a transformative power. Over the years, we have never seemed to get it right anyway, so it has been left as a sort of blind spot. However, in the last decade, branding has become increasingly prevalent — courses, workshops, books and TV shows are so often dedicated to personal branding.

Branding is a hot topic! It often goes as follows: first, we are faced with someone rather clueless, and then s/he gets transformed into somebody who looks completely different in no time. The crazy thing is that if we had first seen them after the transformation, we would have had a completely different impression to begin with. That's the deal with branding! It proves that personal branding cannot be overlooked.

On one particular TV show, a small jury was asked to say what they thought of the person in front of them. Luckily, that person was behind glass so s/he did not hear their opinions at first. The assignment was to critique the full appearance of the person 'on trial', not only looks but also any impression of what standards they may have, and even to suggest what they thought the person might do for a living. You can imagine that it was not a pretty story. It was incredibly demoralizing for the people behind the glass to hear what people really thought about them when they were 'themselves' at the end of the show. And that's the thing — usually we have no clue of the impact of our appearance on others, and how it may affect their opinion of us. Now, it is important to not become obsessed with others' initial impressions of you, but it's good to be aware of the process.

During that same TV show, the people had to face a new jury after the transformation. At that point, they got to hear all the flattering comments people made about them after they had been 'cleaned up'. And the incredible thing was that most of those super-duper comments weren't true either. The lesson learned is that you need to meet in the middle, but what is that middle?

Some shows actually revisit the transformed people after a while and it usually turns out that they have stuck to some aspects of their new appearance (and yes, they usually do look better now). But they never keep the whole shebang. And that's the trick — to know what to keep and of what to let go. I don't have a magic answer here: all I can recommend is to be aware of the power of first impressions, and to stay true to yourself and who you really are.

Personally, I see personal branding and image as a very complex matter, which is constantly in flux. Depending on the situation, you can alter and tweak your branding to fit expectations. Unfortunately, a truly sublime branding is only given to a few of us. Mostly, we choose a brand that fits for now — only to realize that after a while it fades away, becomes outdated, maybe does not represent recent changes in your personality or is seen as a scream for help. Whatever it is, everybody has those moments of confronting the reflection in the mirror.

That is exactly why I would suggest that you plan conscious dates with yourself to evaluate and revise your personal branding — work in need of revision.

Stamp of approval

You see, the reason we need the right image is because it says so much about us, and it does so even before we have an initial interaction with someone. Research states that we need four to eight seconds to form an opinion about someone we have just met (by the way, men need four seconds and women up to eight — I wonder why?!). The funny thing about image is that we tend to mention the existence of it when someone has an image that is good, attractive and representative. But we generally say that someone is lacking an image if the person does not appeal to us. Here is your social proof — expectations determine whether your image actually deserves the title.

I find it fascinating how preconditioned humans can be! Be aware of it, because some people really don't care about their personal branding. But if you do decide to engage in conversation with them anyway, you might find that they are the most incredible people you have ever met! No, I'm not labeling anyone (see how our opinionated mind works!). I'm just saying that most people don't have a clue about what to do about it. They follow the fashion trends, copy their friends or role models (which is a good thing to do if these people match your aspirations). Sometimes 'fake it till you make it' is a sure way to succeed; most sales professionals know this to be very true.

In our field of Assisting Professionals it's important to know your exec's branding as you are a representative of him. Your image has to match his message while being in the office and acting on his behalf. The great thing is that in your own time you can adopt a whole different image and that's fine, as long as the two don't clash in a single environment and are applied properly. Image matching is a fine line — the closer the required image is to you though, the easier it is to live it with conviction.

And... cut!

Here is another take on branding — think about it as role definition. A while ago I met a businessman, or at least that was his image, during the lunch break of a business training seminar. While talking to him, he briefly mentioned his military background, which I found very interesting since he didn't look anything like a military man (you see how our mind plays tricks on us?). When I kept asking about that side of his experience, it turned out that he had two current roles — being a very successful businessman, while being a high-ranking member of the military defense board. I was truly astonished, wondering how on earth he combined those two contradicting images. And then he told me the most amazingly simple trick that enables him to embody those extreme states simultaneously — the uniform! He explained to me that once he was all dressed up in his military uniform, stripes and all, he could easily let go of the business role and focus on national security and matters of a totally different order. How incredibly simple but effective!

That got me thinking. Every role in your life could have a uniform, fitted to its own tasks and purposes. It really felt like a breakthrough. And the uniform stands for a combination of physical appearance and a specific mindset, where the one enables the other to emerge.

So now, while being a PA, a student, a mother, a wife, a friend, a daughter (and the list goes on!), I have created a uniform for every role. It works like magic: as soon as I change my physical uniform, I am immediately in a different state of mind. It has a transformative power to be reckoned with, and you really want to master and fine-tune your ability to be in control of this process.

Jumping forward to the chapter on 'me time' — uniforms are the key to relaxing instantaneously. If I get home and have trouble relaxing, I quickly realize that while I'm in my working attire, I won't be able to leave my PA role. Changing into a comfy tracksuit (my 'wife' or 'mother' uniform) releases tensions immediately. Give it a try! I'm forever grateful to have met this man, who is wise on so many levels and has been a great support to me (knowing his background makes me take his advice more seriously — we are weirdly wired like that).

So, back to your branding at the office. You can recreate the sense of control and immediate focus in the office by applying the same 'state change' trick. The simplest thing to do is to wear office-appropriate shoes! Yes, you heard me right — shoes. It's not something you think about as a first step, but it usually does the trick, for an internal 'state change' as well as for external expectations. For some reason, shoes say a lot about a person (and I don't just say this because I'm a shoe freak).

Actually, ladies, it has been scientifically proven that wearing high heels hugely reinforces your confidence. There is nothing commercial about it; it has to do with the way your posture changes. The shoe theory applies to men as well. I will never forget a young fellow who showed up to a bankers' meeting in a very expensive Italian suit, wearing sneakers. I know it's fashionable to mix styles like that, but for some reason I partially lost confidence in him as a professional. I know it's wrong, but that's how things work unfortunately... It goes back to the power of first impressions.

You want your image to reinforce your role and invite a sense of trust and professionalism. It also works the other way around, whether you are dressed up or down you want your appearance to fit your purpose. It's not about standing out or blending in. It's about whether the picture makes sense. It is usually a fine and risky line, mostly determined by ultra-personal considerations. Human beings can have the most extreme opposite reactions to the same image. Again — we are weird like that.

It's a balance between fitting you, the purpose and the role you currently hold. Go figure! No wonder there are so many stylists around, so many fashion labels and a variety of everything in every direction imaginable. What really defines you is a mix of details. I would like to call this creature by another name — the style definition! Having a personal style makes things easier and more reliable. For one, matching the content of your closet to your intended internal style (which is way more than 'what's in fashion' and 'what do I really dig') creates your external brand. You see — it works the other way around.

Another bonus to having a reliable style: it creates a certain expectation from people around you that has a psychologically calming effect. It has to do with sense of recognition. Our sensors are always on the alert. And they get alarmed and start searching for explanations if you show up looking completely different. Let's face it, if someone changes his branding too quickly our first reaction tends to be: why?! Even if it's a wonderful transformation and a standing ovation is in order. What keeps us preoccupied is the fact that we no longer recognize the person and that makes us highly sensitive, waiting for him to reveal the hidden reason behind this sudden change.

Can we still trust his person when he is such a chameleon? Does his appearance say anything about his character? Or worse — is he a cheater, a show off? Does he lack confidence to the extent that he needs his appearance to do the talking? I guess that last one is an extreme, but we all think it. It's psychologically impossible to resist. The only point I'm trying to make here is this: if or when you consider changing your branding, be sure to leave something from 'the old you' intact! It's still you, but a better version of you. And for the same reason, your style has to have consistent elements or recurring features. Make sure to keep, create and accentuate those while trying something new. It will preserve the benefits of your previous image and make it easy for others to stay convinced that what they see is still the real you.

The topic of styling and branding is so very complex and important. As you see, it has a lot of underlying influence. As PAs, gatekeepers and frontrunners, we need to master this one and play with it skillfully. Combine the hard skills of this territory with the soft skills of fine-tuning the effects it has on yourself and others. With all of that said, I must admit that I'm not an image expert — so let's move on. Find an expert to learn more about this subject if you're intrigued.

En vogue with the enemy

Before going into some pointers on how to get comfortable with this area of complexity let me state a few things from which to stay away. I will just mention them briefly and really want to leave it at that — branding is a sure way to manipulate. For obvious reasons this word has a very negative ring to it, but it doesn't have to. I just can't seem to find a better substitute. Let's see: provoking, redirecting, convincing, transforming — they all have something controllable about them. We all know that and we've all experienced the good and the bad outcomes of being manipulated. So let's agree that an image, a brand or styling are difficult to put in a corner. The truth is if something works and is proven to be effective, then it is bound to be misused. Here is your proof that having a certain image is an effective tool! Be sincere and don't be ignorant about it. Keep in mind that it has to empower your message.

The other 'no-go' zone is peer pressure. I know it might be cool to fit in, but if it doesn't suit you and what you really stand for — make every attempt to be bigger and remove yourself from any unwanted influence. On the other hand, if the peers in question are the ones you aspire to be for very solid and valid reasons — please feel free to follow the lead. Just be conscious about it.

Adapting to a certain image can really boost your spirits, even if you have to switch back after a short while. Do find things that make you happy, try to discover style elements that fit the state of mind that you're going for and apply them whenever needed.

Tame that wild animal

As I mentioned, I am by no means a branding expert, I simply share with you experiences from my journey of creating a personal brand. It is a relatively new topic to me. The idea was actually triggered in me not too long ago when a few people around me started to say things like: 'It's so Anna' or 'this is what makes you, you' or 'if you need this or that — go to Anna, this is definitely her thing' etc. Branding is more than just style. It's the way you act, talk, do things, the way you look and what you stand for. The binding factor is consistency, even though things are always in flux. You're never 'finished', and everything can change in a second. It's fascinating that something that is so defining and important is also so fragile, untouchable and subject to public opinion at the same time.

In an attempt to stay positive, let me make a daring statement: I have actually found that this wild branding phenomenon is controllable and teachable. It comes in many variations and it can fit anyone. You just have to be conscious about it, be willing to admit that it's not up to your or others' expectations at times, and decide to do something about it when necessary. That's the good thing about control. You have a certain power to make changes, no matter the shape or form of your image today. There is always a way to improve or to adjust. So stay assured and confident that it's within your reach.

The second obvious key to a successful personal brand is to stay close to your own values. In order to do so, however, you need to know what your values are. Truth is, as cheesy as it sounds, very few of us can promptly recite our current ruling values.

Here is a striking example of us (human beings) being clueless, even those who run a multimillion-dollar organization: once, at a seminar, we were asked to come up with seven values we hold high. We all rushed into looking for answers right away. And we all came up with standard values, because hey — if you don't value the basics (trust, honesty, etc.) there must be something wrong with you. The next assignment was to go to page X of our workbooks and choose another seven values from an extended list of values, there were at least a hundred of them. And you know what — we all chose very different values than we had in the first round. The moral of this story? The second selection represented our inner core values much more clearly and profoundly. What we thought of initially were socially accepted convictions and beliefs instead of the values we truly associated with at our cores.

So, what does it say about us? To begin with, our prehistorical purpose is to survive. How do you do that? By adapting to the majority. The group element has always been important, because once you left your pack your chances of survival were close to zero. (We can't all be Robinson Crusoe after all!)

The story above of how we chose our values shows that we are still like that, only on a different level. We tend to adapt our beliefs and standards to the ruling majority. Of course you can scream: 'I'm not like that', but I dare you to examine that thought. No hard feelings please, because I know you won't like the outcome. This theory is actually based on scientific facts and data. And really — it's OK to have a few matching values, it just means that you are in a great group of likeminded people.

But, back to branding — it's important to know your own values and mind you, they change overtime. We'll get back to this in the chapters on the action plan and evaluation stage.

Another reason why I'm pushing your buttons is to make you aware that you've probably adopted a few values of the company you work for. Whether it's out of awareness or a sense of insecurity — it really doesn't matter. What matters is that it's pretty easy to define them, just look into the vision and mission statements of your organization. When you know what you're working with, you have the power to do something with it.

By knowing what comes from within, and how your environment contributes to your set of values, you'll have a pretty good picture of what's important to you. Once you have defined your message you can assemble associated style elements and create the right brand for yourself as an Assisting Professional. By the way, include the apparent values of your exec here. You need to be in sync with his values. This is assuming you love the job you are in, and the adopted values are close to your own. Don't forget: exactly that match makes you an incredibly persuasive, representative and effective Assistant.

Bring in the dress boy, please

Now that we have reviewed the guidelines, let's refine the execution. First of all, remember that your brand is the outer layer of your identity. You need to stay comfy while wearing it. No sticking pins to hold pieces together, as they will fall out at some point, or will irritate you so frequently that you will rip the whole thing off.

'Comfortable but appropriate' is what we need to go for. (You may have realized by now that clothing metaphors are great for branding, for no other reason than the fact that they make branding tangible.)

But we are not there yet. These are just the basics. Every fashion line has basics. Now we need to dress up your basics. Again, keep in mind the role you're in, because you may be able to stop here — sometimes basics are just fine!

Let's say you find it difficult to adapt to a new image, or to make alterations to update your style — in other words, let's say you are me! When I started reading books on personal branding and digging deeper into the overload of information on this topic, I was seriously lost. Everybody had different tips and tricks, different starting points, and sometimes contradicting manuals. The easiest thing for me to do was to imitate a role model. Choosing one is of crucial importance! Choose wisely, because you might end up being like one — be careful what you wish for. It can work miracles, as long as you keep your own basics and choose a few consistent brand elements. Please don't become a copycat — go the extra mile to make it your own.

I think you will find this to be a sneaky trick to explore the inner workings of a personal brand in a non-obvious way: find a person that seems to pull off an image or a certain style with ease, grace, respect and acceptance. Then, try to figure out what puts him or her in that position of expertise. Don't confuse this person with a role model — because his or her style doesn't have to match your aspirations. It's the skills of mastery you are looking for. Let's call them 'action role models'. You simply want to know how he or she pulls it off so naturally. Being and acting comfortable is usually the overlapping trait, keep that in mind.

By the way, this is always the best way to learn new things: find people to whom this comes naturally and genuinely. You won't find better teachers, because some skills you can learn and some not to perfection. If you struggle with the one that got away — try to come as close as possible and reside in the presence of an authentic master. It works like a disease. At some point you'll get a glimpse in yourself of that same skill or quality. I can't explain this process scientifically (although mirroring comes to mind), it just works!

A few last words on how to cut corners without being hit by a truck. It's no weird science really: make sure you are educated! Attend seminars or read a couple of books about personal branding. It is also important not to ignore cultural, country-specific, religious or industry-related standards and prerequisites. The easiest way to adopt those which are appropriate (while avoiding those that aren't) is to make them part of your basics. By integrating them into your basics, you make them a non-issue, and you can move on, dressing it up accordingly.

You have reached your destination

As I said, you never finish learning, but there is a sure way to know that you are on the right path and moving in the right direction. You'll not always like this frenemy, but personally, I grew to respect it: it's called feedback.

When people react to you in the desired fashion, if they comment on your appearance with consistency or even praise, if they talk about you to others in a similar and, again, desired manner (which you will probably hear about in the form of referrals), you'll know you're doing well. It really does take time and usually it comes unexpectedly, without even your active focus.

The latter is the true proof that you have mastered your brand, as it apparently comes from within, and appears with ease. Do pay attention to those comments, but don't get too excited when you hear them, especially if it happens sporadically. I have to admit, the first time you hear something along these lines, it is truly sensational. It's like winning a war nobody knew was being fought!

The pitfall here is to see it as a point of arrival. No way, this is just a sign that you're getting closer. Stay focused, play the part, fine-tune the mode for it to become customized to your daily doings. The point of no return is when you hear the same comment over and over again — consistent confirmation is your gold medal. Even bigger proof of authenticity is when others ask you how you do it. Remember what I said just a minute ago — look for 'action role models' who seem to pull it off naturally and effortlessly. Well, now others see you as the natural! That is the proof that you have mastered it. Be truly proud of yourself.

The next step of owning a personal brand is when you'll be able to choose a purpose or a message you stand for and carry it out there with ease, confidence and authenticity. Having that conviction that there is simply no other way about it and that you are the respected pioneer of your message. When you succeed in this endeavor, then you can truly call yourself the authority of your brand. You are the new role model! I'm not there yet — but I do have great role models to follow.

Sticky notes

A few last reminders before we move on to the doom and gloom of being an Assistant. Not the prettiest chapter, but so very necessary.

First: stay aware of differences between your business and personal roles. They might have different branding, although some basics will always remain. Actually, I know executives who make their personal and their professional brands as opposite as possible on purpose. That is their way of keeping their private life truly private and sacred — and I really admire that. It takes a lot of effort and attention!

And mind you — it is very challenging and demands precision, coordination and discipline. There are sure benefits to this method, although I still struggle to accomplish it. I do believe I'm getting there and yes, it does make a real difference. I'm really privileged to have worked for some amazingly wise people who have taught me well.

The next reminder is all about updating. Once mastered, branding is not a fast-moving creature, but it has a tendency to fade. You don't want to begin all over again, so remember to evaluate your image once in a while, and run an update if needed.

In closing

There are a couple of specific situations where you apply your brand purposefully. For some, this might be the very reason to build the brand, for others this is something you do to contribute to the bigger picture once done with your own.

The first applications are the situations where you deliberately choose to change your purpose and so your brand. Some blend in and wait till their new identity reaches its puberty; others shout from the rooftops that the baby is born. Both can work out fine, just prepare the look and feel of your new brand upfront and be ready to answer the difficult question: why? Don't be surprised by it, because that can undermine the newborn.

The second type is the situation where you have mastered your brand to the level of authority. You are ready to put it to good use and become an ambassador for a specific message. Choose your battles carefully. Your brand has to empower the message, but the real win/win is when it backs you up in return. Choose badly and it can end in disaster. We all know countless examples of public outings making the speaker go head first into the deep seas.

And last, but certainly not least, is the case where you are motivated to build a brand because you are aware of the power and influence a brand entails. You want to be appointed as its just and fair ruler! A strong personal brand is your greatest supporter if you plan to reinforce company regulations and message delivery with a soft hand. Again — no manipulation here, please! The power in this situation comes from a place of respect and acceptance.

I know an amazing senior EA, who is a kind, lovely and deeply admired lady. People listen to her, follow her and she is usually the one to communicate announcements of major changes. When she does so, not a single person objects, nor raises their tone of voice, becomes uncomfortable or is thrown off guard — no matter how bad the news are. She has this air of authority that comforts you, provides clarity and security, leaving you no choice but to accept the message and get on with it to the best of your ability. And believe me, her exec was a tough one to handle. She was always graceful, confident and amazingly effective with him. Her brand is unshakeable and I have seen her fertilizing it on a regular basis. Oh yes, she is definitely one of my role models when it comes to soft-handling PA authority! Not to mention, proof that a personal brand, once developed and matured, can actually be relatively unshakeable. Her consistent branding element – a pearl neckless.

Chapter 4. Downfalls

People often want to discuss what can go wrong when being an Assistant. Books, forums, social media and countless training sessions — you name it. All the things that make our profession tough, difficult and sometimes even unbearable are available to read about and assess. We all get stuck once in a while and we all have our bad days / weeks / months. Although we are masters in acting appropriately in uncomfortable situations, we might feel pretty desperate at times.

For example, the amazing book *Who Took My Pen ... Again?* (by Joan Burge, Nancy Fraze and Jasmine Freeman) contains all the core elements Assistants should know, think, do and live by. However, while reading it I had a feeling I was reading about a mystified superhero Assistant who is Ms. Perfect in every way, and I felt very insecure when I realized that I did not have all of the requirements, in fact, far from it. Yes, it is a super guide for EAs, PAs, AAs or whatever your title is. But it sounds really unattainable. And yes, I'm all for promoting and pioneering Assistants (which I'm gladly doing anyway), but this totality of qualities is not fair to ask of anyone.

I actually think it's the world around us that makes it so difficult sometimes. Or, let me rephrase that: we make it so easy for *them* (our execs) to be careless, leaving room for them to make a mess of it occasionally. They know there is a PA at their beck and call who will deal with anything and clean up everything! That is what we do... This is one of the longest chapters in the book, so bear with me — it just might be the most important one!

Assistants are human, thank god for that, and that means we also have our bad days. It usually goes like this: one moment you are on top of everything and doing your thing, working miracles, and dealing with piles of work when all of a sudden it hits you, you are in trouble! I find this to be the case time and time again. Strangely, it's the off switch we don't have any control over, but we do have the ability to turn things back on again. The moment you realize something isn't right is a doom and gloom experience. Usually you don't see it coming and it is usually right in the middle of a busy period. There is never a good moment for it and it never makes an appointment. So, let's look at some of these situations, in an effort to help you understand that you are not alone and that there are things you can do.

Red light district

No, not those red lights, but definitely ones to be aware off! Let's start with the most unusual one – your comfort zone. Say what? Yes, it's not good to stay in your comfort zone for too long. Let's examine it: I personally love the feeling of everything being familiar. You know all the team members. You comfortably answer and deal with any incoming phone calls.

You know your exec by heart and you're always prepared. You are one step ahead and tracking his movements and agenda with ease. You feel secure and confident. You deal with anything in a timely fashion and have the luxury of being able to plan ahead. And you actually enjoy your own life as you go along. All is fine and dandy! But then, suddenly there it is – you're stuck in a rut!

I have had that experience twice where I suddenly realized that it's all too smooth and I'm way too prepared for everything on the agenda a few days prior to the events. Colleagues seem less chatty (because you are less involved in the conversations). The office starts to look less attractive (because you haven't changed something small in the interior as you always tend to do, when seasons change or just because you feel like it). Emails seem less interesting (because there is nothing new there). Planning your heart out to get six execs with busy schedules together in the same room with your CEO doesn't seem like a challenge anymore (because people know you will accommodate everybody's preferences and do so perfectly).

The tricky thing is that on the outside, nothing has changed. You have hit a certain glass ceiling, and therefore lost a bit of your passion. Now, there is nothing wrong with this comfy place, but the way forward will determine whether it will stay this comfy. You have a choice: A. wake up, shake it up, relocate and reinforce your passion for this great place that you are so proud of B. realize you've reached the peak here and that you are ready to move on to conquer the next one. The downfall is that while you keep pondering rather than taking action, you start losing the grip since you know your surroundings like no one else. Eventually, you might slip and fall once, twice, too many times. People will notice you've checked out, and eventually you will become just another PA.

I actually sat across from one of those, doing her nails, chatting away with her stay-at-home-mom sister, having long lunches and constantly planning the next personal vacation. And she was actually a good PA: everything was super organized, she was on top of her duties and she completed every project that came her way. Only the load was low, projects where few and her exec was a pretty self-sufficient director. She complained occasionally about being bored and not really motivated, but that didn't move her to go and do something about it. So when the reorganization cuts came, guess who was out on the streets first...

Another more common situation is when you catch yourself walking on eggshells for so long that your toes hurt worse than after wearing your new eight-inch heels. You always have a choice about how to act — you just have to realize that and check in with your surroundings.

I made the mistake of going with the flow for too long once and found myself in an undesirable dead-end situation all too quickly. The one where I lost my drive and passion along the way, working mechanically and looking forward to go home. Surprisingly enough, I didn't see it then. Live and learn, right? Now I know when to pay attention, assess the situation and define what's external and what's internal. And yes, I'm certain things could have had a totally different outcome if I had just stayed close to my own values and convictions instead of following the course of that department. I'm forever grateful to my exec back then for being a great teacher by being self-sufficient, because not in a million years would I have learned that lesson so well (working in a too comfortable position) if I haven't been there myself, up to my ears in boredom.

Overload

Here is my favorite no-go zone. I'm a frequent trespasser when it comes to accepting work overload. However, by now I'm also a very experienced modifier and know when and how to correct it. Meet the state of being too eager, too involved and overly enthusiastic! Yes, that's my middle name, and I'm not ashamed to admit it: I love that state of mind. Truly, this is where I walk on air! Things happen, I love every second of it, it's contagious, you get everyone on board, my exec thinks I'm a freak of nature but lets me be because it's kind of cool to see someone going for it — it's like a circus act!

And then it all blows up — you realize you haven't seen your bed for four straight hours in the last few weeks, your diet has adopted a 'fast food only' policy, your energy levels are so low you will fall over if someone walks by too quickly, your desk is covered with post-it notes because you can't seem to remember your last name, and your 'to archive' pile is about to overshadow Mount Everest (come on — you can only archive when you are calm or want to become calm, it's at least my idea of a great therapy session!). You find yourself in a semi burnout, people around you don't laugh anymore but look annoyed and keep their distance, and your exec will happily use your 'on a roll' state to overload you with even more projects. Yet, again, it's up to you to decide what to do next. Considerably slowing down will absolutely raise questions about whether you are OK and fit for the job. You have raised your own bar when it comes to delivering fast results — can you keep that promise? So, what now?

First of all, if you have a tendency to leap into overload, then you should try to go 'Speedy Gonzales' in the privacy of your office or cubicle first. It is counterintuitive when your end goal is to show off your results, but, I can vouch for a 'time release' method if you're anything like me. The major downside is overdoing it. A solution is to assign your 'super-woman' powers to projects that have a definite end. I guess that is a skill that comes with maturity: 'Hi, I'm Anna. I am sane and sober and for a few years now I am doing better at tempering my workload.'

Before we move on: this mode does have one cool side effect and that's the art of being super creative. If you want to get in a creative mood, get yourself overexcited about something. You will see your mind go crazy and pull rabbits (and what else) out of hats (and what else)!

Middle ground

Below I want to outline the five attention areas that represent the highest risk of a downfall for Assistants. They are pretty self-explanatory, so I will not elaborate on them too much. I have found that it's crucial to have a clear and confirmed set of guidelines in all of them. It makes us so much more at ease and encourages us to act boldly. Of course, both parties have to be fair in keeping to and guarding the agreed proceedings. Bear in mind that life is changing. Be the first one to step up and ask the other party to the table to renegotiate. Try to come up with fitting middle-ground arrangements for both parties to coexist together in harmony and understanding.

To be honest, I only found these areas to be important subjects of negotiation after 'bleep' hit the fan. So be smart and don't let that happen to you. When you have established the ground rules and expectations in all of these areas, it will actually be OK to submerge yourself in your work completely. It will be OK to forget anything else even exists for the time being, coming up for air at some point, only because you know you will need to stick to the agreed promises in the end. And after that is done you can safely return to your madness and lose yourself in your task lists again.

Attention area one: your social life

No matter how close you are with your family, relatives and friends — these people will be a huge part of your professional life. No secret there. But did you know that most conflicts are based on misconceptions and unclear expectations? Realize that those people are important and that their roles are definitely here to stay. Be the first one to get to the negotiation summit. I know it doesn't seem loving and family-like, but if you are willing to do so anyway, the resulting talks will be far more productive and effective. Let your friends and family in on your career plans, warn them of a busy upcoming period, and stay open to their input and feedback.

It might surprise you how to-the-point and valuable their support and advice can be. In my case, I'm regularly surprised at how one sentence from my husband can turn the whole run of events around in my head — it's like I see the light! Outsiders have this strange power of being smarter than you are. Even my daughter of three, no taller than a smurf, has already given me some wonderfully supportive advice from the unwritten universe of simplicity.

Therefore, try to realize the importance of your social surroundings and commit to prioritizing spending time with them. And while being there, even if it's just for a short while because your exec needs you to finish that PowerPoint presentation before midnight, really truly be there in that moment! Even 15 conscious minutes with my daughter can be exhilarating if I'm really present in her world and give her my full attention. I'm not saying 15 minutes is enough to be a mother or enough for any other member of your social elite club, but you get my point.

Attention area two: their social life

This might not concern every Assistant, but I include this category anyway because most of us do have to interact with the friends and family of our execs. Let's start with partners, as it's probably the first person you will have any interaction with. As I will explain in upcoming chapters, it's important to discuss with your exec if this contact is desirable or not. I have had both extremes: a partner who actually called herself a 'package deal', and others who had partners that I was strictly forbidden to talk to. Once you know your code of conduct, set up a doc with all the details about your exec's partner you might need to know about. Make sure to note their agendas, preferences, likes and dislikes and need-to-knows. I call my doc the 'Emergency File', but it really contains anything and everything. It will not be filled up right away, nor will it ever really be complete. You will gather more info overtime, so be sure to update it regularly. You can use apps and any other software to keep it available to you at any time. I simply use a Word file, including attachments like passport copies etc. I usually keep it in a cloud-like environment.

For security reasons I will not mention the whole description of my storage facility, I'm sure you can think of a way to make yours safe, available and practical. OneNote or Evernote apps are great for quick access, just make sure you have an updated copy somewhere else. I lost a few docs like that when my phone or laptop crushed.

To mention the obvious, no matter how close you get to the friends and family of your exec, always make sure to stay professional, discreet, and keep your integrity standards high. Remember that you are still a representative of your exec. Consider notifying your exec of anything that bothers you or stands out about his social life. He might not have the luxury of time to be updated on everything that is going on in his inner circle. Obviously, be considerate of special dates and happenings. Your exec will probably mention them to you anyway. But if you notify him of an upcoming event upfront, asking him whether he wants you to arrange a fitting present or remind him to make that call, it makes you look good. Be the one who knows.

Attention area three: multiple Assistants

This subject has its pros and cons! Understanding a situation where multiple Assistants are present, involved, and considered is an important matter. There are two instances where this is of importance. First, the 'PA gardens', where a few Assistants of different execs sit in the same space or area. Second, 'PA families', that is when one exec has multiple Assistants to assist him (if you are not familiar with this, think *The Devil Wears Prada*).

I have been in both scenarios, and both have profound and possibly extreme differences. Both can work wonderfully or be an outright warzone. I've been in most of those variations — and learned a lot!

It will save you a lot of headache to know and agree upfront on tasks, priorities, roles and expectations. Just choose the ones that are applicable right now. When being part of a 'PA family', make sure to meet each other face-to-face once in a while. That especially applies to when one PA is working at the office and the other one at the private residence of the exec. Always make sure that you both understand that your goals and intentions are similar. Make sure everything is aboveboard, get to know each other as people (not merely as titles) and look for shared interests and common ground.

Easygoing 'PA gardens' are a blessing to work in. On the other hand, it's OK if you don't like the other PA (or can't stand her). It's good to express that, so there won't be any gossip about it. Give and respect each other's space.

In 'PA families', though, it is a prerequisite to be on the same page — so just find a way to make it work. Personally, I truly enjoyed being part of such a family. Mind you — I was the third PA and it was a well-oiled machine.

Attention area four: multiple execs

Once upon a time I was at a PA conference, and during the lunch break I got into an interesting conversation with a senior PA who obviously struggled with her new responsibility of not one but *three* executives. Before I go on with the story I need to share a saying that I heard a few years back.

'Question: What are the textbook first cuts in any reorganization? Answer: Reception flowers and PAs.'

I was really offended when I first heard this, but it's the unfortunate truth! So this lady, being the most senior PA in her company, ended up with three jobs and was slowly drowning. I too have worked for multiple execs and it was tough at times. The general advice is simple and straightforward — discuss what you can and can't do within a certain time frame with each exec. You can also divide your day into segments and dedicate specific hours to specific execs. Yep, in theory it should work. But try managing three execs with completely different agendas which change constantly and who all have different personalities, communication styles and specific manuals.

If you have ever been in a situation like this, you know that it takes some time to figure out this juggling act. It's not undoable, nothing is! Clarity and timely communication regarding your and their workload is essential. Don't make it too official though, just be open and honest if you are slammed with duties for Exec A and ask politely if the task for Exec B can wait until tomorrow. There will be a huge difference between your execs being on the same level or in different places in the hierarchy. The latter one is easier to handle, as urgent duties for the top exec always have priority. Either way, it is manageable, as long as you have set some guidelines, systemized the input and outgoing flows and clarified expectations.

Here are some of my tricks to make this work. Hopefully you'll find some (or all!) of them helpful and applicable to your situation:

✓ Get together with each exec individually and clarify expectations of your support. 'Just the usual PA stuff' doesn't cut it. You need to know exactly what needs to be done, so make a checklist and go over the tasks, preferably setting specific days or time frames for specific duties.

✓ Clarify to each of the execs that you have to split your time. Sometimes, even if they know you assist a party of three and their teams, they still have a tendency to claim your time exclusively. Just remind them by saying: 'Sure (that should be your standard answer anyway), let me finish Exec B's declaration forms and I'll get on this new thing for you.'

✓ Sometimes, the only thing they need to hear is that you know about the things that need to be done, that you're aware of the deadlines and that you have set aside time to get it all done.

✓ Then, chop your day into 30-minute blocks. I love working in blocks, not in tasks, and the reason is a method I call 'multi-tracking in mono-mode'.

'I would defend her to the last because she was a complete star in my life. I learned a lot from her, and I tried to do all I could for her. She taught me lots of things, including that you should only do one job at a time and concentrate completely. Whether she was writing a speech or tidying a drawer, it had her total concentration. She taught me that.'
'The Margaret Thatcher I knew', by her Personal Assistant.

Multi-tracking in mono-mode

Let me quickly explain this one, because it's something I came up with in order for me to be super productive and work in a focused way. It might work for you as well!

There are a few well-known tricks to get focused:
✓ Set a firm deadline
✓ Plan ahead for a task so your mind will prepare itself for doing it
✓ Remind yourself a short while beforehand that you are about to start it (that is your time in the morning when going through your daily agenda)
✓ Just before starting your duty block, imagine yourself as a *vehicle* that can physically only be on one track at the same time

That last point is very true mindset wise. You have to know that it is biologically impossible to think more than one thought at a time. You can jump between them like crazy, but it's always one at a time. Once you're installed in your 'task vehicle' — just go for it.

The second element of 'multitasking in mono-mode' is the importance of role distinction. As Assisting Professionals we have many roles: administrator, secretary, facility, finance, negotiator, peacemaker, (event) organizer, travel manager, mediator, HR consultant etc. Every role has its own mindset and characteristic. A sure way to get stressed out and lose overview is by doing all those roles at the same time. We sure try to, but we end up hopelessly hamstrung while doing so. Your mind works so much more efficiently and effectively if the things you have to do are regrouped as 'role specific' combos. Every role has its own tasks (aka tracks). If you combine multiple tracks per role (while staying in one mindset) you will go through them faster and get more things done. That is multitasking PA style!

And to make this practical I use the mentioned time blocks — those are the role-defined blocks! Give each role a block of 30 minutes at a time and select/operate the few tracks that have most priority at this moment. Working in one particular role mindset is an amazingly smart way to get really focused, as it triggers and activates all the right qualities and capacities needed within that role — it works like magic.

So, in the case of multiple execs, block out a designated time to execute specific tracks. The thing is to define those first, then to communicate, for example, that Thursday afternoons is his admin time, so any receipts he has have to be on your desk by Thursday lunchtime. Or something like: Friday morning is 'meeting minutes' time, so please try not to bug me then, but also know that by Friday afternoon you will need to review them.

These kinds of *routinesque* arrangements are not easy nor quick to incorporate, but believe me, they will make your job significantly easier. The human psychology behind it is described best through a quote from Alvin Toffler, who said in his revolutionary book *The Third Wave*:

*Individuals need life structure otherwise they suffer from personal powerlessness and pointlessness. People need a comprehensive structure and absence of such breeds breakdown. The core wisdom lies in **relatively predicted fixed points of reference** and we all need them! In other words... we get a sense of **security by having relative certainties of things to expect**. We get grounded by having expectations so we don't have to be in a flight or fight mode all the time.*

Another scientific fact in defense of 30-minute blocks is this: our minds cannot concentrate on one single task for more than 45 minutes at a time. Around that time, your body and mind need a mini break or a diversion. Pay close attention to your patterns, and you will see that you already do that on autopilot: you will grab another cup of coffee, go to the printer, switch to another task etc. Knowing that, 30 minutes is a very manageable time frame in which to be extremely focused on one block of various single-minded tracks. And mind you, almost anything can wait 30 minutes, so it's acceptable for others to give you some space to finish and wait for their turn. As long as they know that you will be there for them come the 31st minute!

One last thing you need to know about focusing is the psychological understanding of your mind. I recently read an article that stated with utmost certainly that focus was the main ingredient for any success in life! I could not agree more. Whether you are a crazy-busy PA, a high-ranking executive or a stay-at-home mom — we all need focus to get through the day in one piece and hopefully with a few items crossed off our to-do lists along the way.

One expert on the human brain is Ned Herrmann. Here is his theory on the brain quadrant and it describes how our intelligence and soft skills preferences translate into actual results. It basically says that we all have specific dominant brain sectors which we use to influence or create results. There are many versions of quadrant systems, but this was surely one of the first ones, outlined back in the 70s.

The reason why I'm telling you all this: once you understand the predispositions of your mind, you can use it more effectively and be more efficient with your resources.

I want to share with you my translation of the four brain sectors according to 'The Hermann Brain Dominance' quadrant, and I will apply these profoundly different areas of our brain to the subject of focus. There is IQ isolation, EQ strengthening and CQ stimulation which all result in PQ excellence (please don't quiz me on the details). I will also mention the Brain Dominance Quadrant in the chapter on evaluation. It's a very profound way of getting to know a person, his strengths and weaknesses, and how to approach and communicate with him effectively. It's the combination of intelligence, emotions, creativity and practical vantage points of any character.

Here is a quick summary on focusing tricks for your brain quadrants (neuroscience for dummies!).

IQ focus: Our intelligence/thinking IQ brain is the front area of your brain (including working memory which is crucial for you to be effective in life) and your execution/practical brain is the rest of your brain. The best way to get into your thinking mode and not be disturbed by things around you is to preoccupy and distract your practical brain. This was Einstein's trick!

Did you know that while coming up with and outlining his theories, Einstein kept a working vacuum cleaner next to him? The constant noise preoccupied his practical brain, and in doing so, isolated his frontal lobe. That is how he could exclusively use his IQ brain to think. So anything with a monotonous sound or closely related will do the trick. This is why sneaking off to a local Starbucks is actually a good idea sometimes to get productive. Surrounding noises will isolate your practical brain as if by magic. You can also use music, but it has to be instrumental, no singing. It's your front IQ brain's job to translate any lyrics into meaning and that is exactly what you don't want your brain to do while you focus on thinking.

CQ focus: The CQ stimulation is about creativity. And the magic potion for creative thinking is classical music, specifically of the baroque period (Google baroque music for learning). I don't particularly like classical music, but I gave it a try and it is scary how effective this little trick can be! Isolating your logic sense and asking the right questions are also superb creativity soldiers, but that requires quite some effort, discipline and time.

EQ focus: This is all about emotions. Your emotional center is buried deep in the center of your brain and it's like a vault. The key to the vault is alcohol, stress, fatigue or any other extreme situation. The more physically fit you are, the more grip you have on that vault, the more control you have over it. If you want to focus, you don't want your emotions to come out for a chat. Also, to keep that area fit you simply need fresh oxygen and a steady blood supply. You can guess that physical exercise is key here! Another important point: the fitter your

EQ is, the more efficient your IQ center will become. It has something to do with rationalizing the information and setting it in the right perspective. It's all very scientific, but it's a huge recent breakthrough discovery! Being emotionally in control has never been seen before as a supporter of intelligence. Our brain is so amazing and we only know so little about it — I find that fascinating.

PQ focus: This is our dear and beloved practical brain. To focus on things in real time you need to have strong interconnections in your brain, aka habits! I will explain the magic of interconnections in your brain in more detail a bit later (very cool stuff!). For now, though, I will disclose the following: the more you think and experience something, the stronger those connections get physically grounded in your brain.

A habit or a skill is always made, nurtured and kept in shape in your brain first. That's why the phrase 'you are what you think' is so true. It's a muscle, use it or lose it!

I do want to mention one additional thing very recently discovered by scientists in Asia. There was a common perception that humans were born with a certain amount of neuro brain cells (aka the thinking cells). With age, it is believed that the amount diminishes, and that there is nothing we can do about it. That is one of the reasons conditions like dementia and Asperger syndrome are not treatable. But now, recent studies show that through moderate exercise for 20 minutes a day there are actually new neuro cells being created in your brain. How cool is that? So you can get smarter and better by practicing the act of repetition and getting some moderate exercise. You have to love science.

OK, apologies for this slight detour — let's continue! Where were we? Dealing with work overload and multiple execs...

✓ After you have your blocks defined and duties clarified, you should start filling in a few recurring blocks which you are relatively certain won't change from week to week. I don't really like to make strict hour-to-hour schedules for myself, as generally I need to be prepared as things happen, and therefore my planning is constantly on the move. What I found to work brilliantly for me is this principle: I define at the end of the day (as mornings are usually hectic) what I need to finish the next day, aka my must-do tracks. Then I look for similar tracks on my list and group them together. After that is done, my mind is automatically searching for 30-minute gaps in the calendar and making a priority list of when to claim a block of 30 minutes to get on with it. I love this system! I get so much done and because it's all grouped it is not one big pile of all the different things, instead it is all broken down into chewable ready-for-action 'role specific' pieces. At best, it ticks off up to 25 things on my to-do list each day. How about that!

I want to leave this juggling topic with one last sneaky piece of advice on how to manage conflicting agendas of your execs — let *them* reach a compromise! If one is not happy with the time frame you can offer them or when two things need to happen at the same time, ask the two execs to talk to each other and then tell you what needs to be done first.

Sometimes just proposing this is enough to resolve the situation and moving the deadline to 30 minutes later is suddenly OK. I even had a situation once when after an extremely urgent request from Exec A, I had to tell him that I was busy with a task for Exec B for at least another hour or so. As by a stroke of magic, Exec A had a change of heart deciding that next week was good too. Go figure!

We all get caught up in certain thinking patterns so it's good to receive a wakeup call from time to time. Of course it doesn't mean that you are not working your socks off trying to accommodate everybody and maybe even calling in support troops for extra manpower.

Use your common sense and judgment. When people see you honestly devoted and working meticulously they are willing to cut you some slack. They know that by doing so, you will deliver on the things they ask of you! It's a win-win-win if you ask me.

Attention area five: reorganizations and layoff season

Unfortunately, a lot of us are in those nasty situations where companies have to reorganize and implement huge layoffs. There is a lot written on this subject so I will keep it short. It sucks, no doubt about it. Be ready to accept the news if it concerns your job. I'm all for positive thinking, but sometimes you need to be prepared so you won't be taken by surprise. Be honest about it, but not too depressed. No matter how crappy you feel, there is always an opportunity waiting around the corner. When one door closes, another one opens. I used to hate this saying, and think it such a cliché. It's very cheesy, but true.

You have every right to mourn, cry your eyes out and be sad or even angry if you are laid off, suddenly or not doesn't matter. Don't hold it in, express it (preferably in the comfort of your privacy or close friends or family). The five universal stages of dealing with loss and grief (denial, anger, bargaining, depression, acceptance) are well known. Let yourself go through them appropriately — otherwise it will haunt you somewhere down the line (what you resist, persists!).

A job for a true master PA, or any other Assistant for that matter, is usually more than just a place where we work. Sometimes it is even more meaningful than a relative. It's huge, it's important, it's our baby and our partner, it's our sanctuary and our second home (in some cases even first home). Give it some credit and realize the good, the bad and the impact it had on you.

And then slowly move on, baby steps! Realize that only you have 100% 'response-ability' for your own life, nobody owes you anything, and you always have the power of choice. It's your evolutionary right. Regain your focus on your strengths and maybe new areas that you want to conquer. It probably won't be a straight line to a new shiny position, it never is. Accept the turn of events, accept new stuff to happen and keep your eyes open. Only when you have dealt with your previous job (at least past the anger stage), can you reset to positive and forward thinking. You will be strong again and nothing will push you back or pull you down.

One thing, while interviewing for a new job, be honest about the reason for leaving your last position. In these times it's not uncommon and there might be a good reason you sit there. Again, there is a lot written on this subject so Google around for tips and tricks.

In case you are the one staying behind, you also have a tough job of improving the vibe in a daunting office. Stay close to yourself; refrain from being too involved in the terror and pain around you. You will probably be the one people go to for a good cry and understanding pep talk. Your most important job now is to motivate people to get through this period and move on. Don't get into psychoanalysis! I want to leave this topic with a few amazing quotes:

> *Today you create tomorrow!*
> *Don't let yesterday take too much of today!*
> *Tough situations don't make characters, they reveal them!*
> *If you are not having problems,*
> *you are missing an opportunity for growth!*

They might sound cheesy, but they might just boost the broken spirit.

Danger, danger

If you thought we were done with painful situations, think again. Here are three main danger zones and I will throw in a bonus no-go zone too before we'll talk about how to deal with them in general. Bear with me, the good stuff is still in the chapters to come — we simply need to get a few things out of the way first to have a clear vision into our mindsets. I will try to keep the danger zones short as they are all self-explanatory:

Danger zone one: gossip

There are three types of gossiping. How to deal with each one of them really depends on its nature.

✓ The first is the well-known 'personal' one: I'm bored out of my mind, nothing happens to me so I'll focus on others. Let's see how I can talk for ages without getting to any specific point. I need to kill some time, let's see how I can stall other people's lives etc. And any other overly detailed gossip, usually based on vague observations, partial information or expectations. It's a black hole —it's not relevant whatsoever so stay away from it. We PAs always have a good excuse in the form of a huge to-do list! An extensive gossip culture will lead to only one conclusion: project management! When people have time on their hands to gossip all the time a new project might keep them busy and focused. A great and effective remedy!

✓ Then there are the 'after echo' rumors. Those are usually born after a company meeting or an announcement which was not delivered clearly or openly enough, leaving room for speculation. It's good to be aware of those. You could let your exec know that more explanation or clarification might be needed before stories are made up and flies turned into elephants. Also, realize that certain people know a little more about company strategy and behind the scenes policy. If they connect any dots the wrong way, there might be an invisible underground rumor source that will be difficult to detect and correct.

✓ And then there is feedback lacking courage to take the stage so it's dressed up as easygoing gossip. People come to me sometimes starting a conversation with, 'Hey, I heard something going around...' followed by a very personal take on something. I get it, giving feedback is difficult! I try to figure out what the underlying reason might be and sometimes it's just very personal. Some people need a little extra attention or comforting. Use your common sense to determine how to handle this one. You might just thank the person and move on. By the way, being heard is a very important part of self-valuation, so don't be snappy here.

As you see, I have a lot of views on gossip. I don't agree with the commonly accepted perception that all gossip is 'the devil in the office'. Call me a pessimist, but I don't think gossip will ever be banished. People talk and will always do so. And the more office cultures disapprove of it or try to get rid of gossip, the more it will happen behind closed doors and after office hours. It's not the gossip you need to be worried about, it's the overall atmosphere in the office you need to address and cultivate. Focus on the positive vibe and the tweaking of business systems. Don't give people reason or time and space to even consider gossiping. If you focus on something, you only make it bigger — it works both ways!

If you feel the urge to address a nasty piece of gossip because it needs to stop ASAP there are two ways to do it. Firstly, never discuss or approach the gossiper in public. Arrange a meeting and just ask the reasons behind why this person is spreading gossip. In my opinion, it's not about the content but why it is going around. Alternatively, sometimes a group approach can be very effective. Talk about the subject of the gossip in a group meeting, give an option to ask questions, clarify where needed and highlight the damaging impact of this gossip on the person and the company. Most of all, urge all participants to stop this progression. Empower teamwork, state something cool that the company will have to face in the near future or recite some company goals and objectives for a mindset switch. Your goal here is to get everybody on board again. You don't have to be best friends, but don't be arch enemies. If the situation is too far below the freezing point, the best solution is to get rid of the biggest liability. Gossiping is never good for business. Appointing a confidentiality contact might also work, it is usually someone from HR. That should, however, be the last resort as you want the gossiping to stop and to not spend any more precious time on it.

PAs and other office Assistants will always be gathering points of such info streams. You need to have your own tactics when it comes to dealing with them. People seem to open up easily to us, because we act by 'confidential and secrecy' codes! We are a very comfortable place to go to if you need to get something off your chest! It's both good and bad.

It's a fine line, especially when you hear something that you think is important for your exec to be aware of. Now that is a tough judgment call. Before you even think about it, make a thorough analysis: can you predict with certainty how your exec will react and what he will do with the information? Is your relationship in a good place so that misconceptions won't be punished? Can you tell it in a way so that you won't be seen as gossiping? I'm talking in the light of a very painful experience here: I hadn't considered all the implications, had wrong assumptions regarding the reactions that followed and I didn't have a context for the message. It blew up in my face, big time! Lesson learned to tread carefully. Your own personal integrity should always be your guiding light: at least I got that one right.

Let's repeat some of the well-known advice out there on gossip: never start a rumor, stay away from gossiping where possible, know that some gossip is based on personal experience and just might be very personal expressions of discomfort. It's not a simple, nor is it an easy, subject, and luckily there is a lot written about it. Find your own way to deal with it and stick to company guidelines on this matter like a leech.

Keep in mind that not all 'he says, she says' talk is per definition gossip. Small talk has proved to be very necessary in an office environment. It can felicitate teamwork and be the so needed chill-out moment in the crazy business schedule. Small talk can easily turn into gossip, and everybody has a different definition of suitable subjects for small talk. One tip: keep small talk fun or entertaining for everybody involved (also for the people who are not there). As long as you stick to this rule you will be on the safe side.

Danger zone two: indiscretions

There are many variations on the topic of indiscretions. I am going to mention a few obvious ones, but I'm sure you can fill in the blanks. Anything in the area of lying, stealing, backstabbing, overly graphic verbalization of your discomfort, picking fights etc. How to deal with any of these indiscretions depends on the code of conduct of your company. Most companies have very strict regulations and procedures. Confide in and ask your HR department for guidance, they are trained to deal with it.

I do want to mention one specific area that I have to deal with frequently. Bad-mouthing! People are very honest with Assistants. If they don't like someone, they just might tell you all the juicy details about it. There is always this little phrase involved, which indicates that some nasty things are about to be said. Be aware of anything that comes after 'between you and me'. It's up to you how to deal with it. You can leave it at that or you can try to avoid people that tend to do that a lot.

Here is a dangerous statement — I do think those conversations can be useful. They can provide you with a sneak peek into underlying relationships and sometimes that information can come in handy. You will not seat two feuding people next to each other for a long meeting or on the same long-distance flight. Be aware that if your gut tells you that the information you hear is something really wrong and might hurt the image of the company or your executive or any department, you should consider discussing your worries with your exec. One huge point here: if your exec sees the behavior as threatening, make sure to discuss any actions forward *together*.

A straight-on confrontational approach usually doesn't work. First of all, your 'cover' is blown and most importantly, you will definitely end up in yes vs no game. Nobody is willing to admit they were doing bad things deliberately. You will reach an impasse in no time, experience a lot of discomfort and in the end the exec will have to rule with an iron hand to resolve this mess. Not the way to go! Try to figure out more politically correct ways of dealing with these issues.

To start with, focus on the action of misconduct itself. What does it tell you about the person's attitude, intentions and foremost, what is the impact of their actions on the surroundings and the company? Never focus on the content of the actions. It is too detailed, too personal or too circumstantial. There is always a way to solve any conflict without huge collateral damage if you take on the root of the problem. Again, an HR department or a good talk with your exec can do the trick. Just be sure you can predict the outcome with relative certainty.

Danger zone three: intimacy

This is a touchy subject. Let me first state this: in my opinion, you have to really care about your exec for you to become the needed Assistant.

Only from a place of caring will you pay more attention to the details, the bigger picture, the crossover between his personal and business life etc.

And sometimes, you will have to walk a fine line to stay professional while showing your care and devotion. Note, it's not what you think, but that others might see it differently.

I frequently have straightened the ties, buttoned up the shirts (even ironed them while my exec stood beside me impatiently watching my every move), straightened the hair, been the shoulder to cry on, dealt with personal hygiene issues etc. It's all part of the job if you care! No, it's not a prerequisite. Yes, most of the time I just mention what I think needs to be done without physical interference. At some point, when your relationship is mature and full of trust, things tend to get personal. Again, nothing out of the order, just more personal and human than the world tends to accept.

That is the thing, we live in a society where real human touch and contact are seen as 'not done'. What happened to us? Most people I have worked with are afraid to be harmed in some way, nobody fully trusts others and we are on constant lookout for backstabbers. The hard reality of this situation is that this conduct is based on experience. We all had too many of those and that shapes and conditions us. To have real and profound relationships you need to be vulnerable on some level. I have set aside a whole chapter on the topic of relationships, so let's move on for now.

Intimacy (not the romantic kind, because see, that is how our minds work) is a little creature that sneaks up on you. It's up to you to keep the boundaries professional and be in control of the circumstances, but you absolutely need to master this area. Yes, you can have intimate business relationships! And now stop for a second and realize what that sentence does to your imagination! That is the preconditioned nature of our world right there, unfortunately. The new trending Warm Leadership is all about that — but it basically means the same. What it all actually stands for is when the Assistant truly and deeply cares about the job and her exec. And the exec, in return, values his Assistant, supports her development and stands up for her rights when needed. It's a win-win, on a very personal level.

I do still prefer the word 'intimacy' because it reflects the true state of mind behind the actions that follow. There is a certain shift in the whole way of acting once you consider the intimate approach. That state change is the key to being personal as a PA. You are more in tune with your exec's feelings, gestures and body language and you immediately sense the intentions behind his actions.

You need to be aware of those intentions to fully assist somebody on that profound level. It translates into straightforward practical intelligence; you know which tie to give as a spare one, you know that tea is a better option now instead of the usual espresso, that you have to talk the CFO out of meeting your exec right now, you know when to close the door so your exec will have a quiet minute to finish something important etc. I call it assisting without command! It's when you can use a sixth sense to move faster, smarter and seamlessly.

Now let's quickly go over the obvious downfalls of intimacy. Actually just one — don't become the stereotype Assistant steeped in seductiveness, sensuality and that certain intent! That's all you need to watch out for. It's usually not a good idea and ruins more than it provides. We all know the stories. Time is the enemy here, so be smart and don't go there. The non-supportive thing here is the universal fact that most PAs are good-looking. It's astonishing when going through LinkedIn profiles of Assisting Professionals how many model lookalikes there are! I'm not discriminating, it really is a fact — do your research! I guess it comes with the territory. It is by definition the biological nature of human beings to be attracted to good-looking people, they get the benefit of the doubt and they are presumed to be more successful (research had proved this point time and again). For us it's not always a good thing. It's an extra layer in communication analysis we need to consider, an extra point to keep in mind for everything we do and how we present ourselves. Every rose has its thorns...

I do have to mention that I know a few 'original PA/exec' couples who actually got into romantic relationships, married, had children and lived happily ever after. It happens! It can work and it's actually a great way to really get to know your partner as you have full access to their lives and personality by order of your job description. It's tricky though and may cause one or both to change or leave their jobs eventually. Every office relationship has its pro and cons. The fact is that 30% of relationships ending in marriage begin on the work floor. And I am personally one of those who found my soulmate in a colleague (way before I became a PA). This too is a complex subject and I'm not an expert. Just be sure to always stay professional and follow the rules of integrity.

Big no-no

We're almost done with the pitfalls. To wrap up I want to share with you my top three *zero-tolerance* conducts that you need to have a rehearsed strategy for upfront, and regarding which you need to be well aware of the company regulations.

Discrimination. I don't care what kind, you just don't do it, don't tolerate it, always flag it and look for ways to deal and exterminate it.

Violence might seem straightforward but it's not. What one perceives as violent, the other might just see as a dispute gone bad. There is an absolute zero-tolerance for obvious acts of violence. Be especially cautious regarding mental abuse. We all read the stories of PAs under pressure. It all goes back to personal integrity, let that guide you while examining your experiences. Bonnie Low-Kramen (former celebrity Assistant) became a pioneer on the subject of office bullying within the Assistants' community. Her presentations are scary, as the numbers don't lie and they are huge! This disease seems to be spreading among offices (and not only among Assistants of course) and needs to be dealt with in a serious group effort.

The mildest version of the three is disrespect. Personally, I hate that quality, because it is usually performed with conscious intent and with a premeditated action plan. I'm unfortunate to have known a few people who are very proud of their ability to think of a plan to hurt others and disrespect them in the most hurtful and profound ways. But that too will always be a part of our world. You need to have a strategy to deal with those. The more successful you and/or your exec become the more of them you will notice creeping around.

The sneaky thing about those personalities is that they are quite often right there in the open. They act very publically and are sometimes even admired and esteemed by others. It's the adult version of 'mean girls' from the high school scene. And the worst thing is that when confronted with their behavior they can always turn it around. They can make it look like an accidental outcome, a misinterpretation, an unfortunate course of events. Those people are highly skilled in communication, manipulation and team spirit tactics.

There are libraries written on this subject, have a look at what is out there on how to deal with it. Yes, sometimes a straightforward confrontation would do the trick but because it's all one big game for them, they will play it well even when challenged or confronted. Getting rid of those people is the only definite solution and the designated exec has to make that decision. Let's all go for a well-oiled team machine where you want to excel personally but also pull others along. You always look taller with someone else on your shoulders! That is what we Assistants do best.

A shoulder to stand on

Talking about standing on shoulders — here is a perspective that we not often consider. Sometimes your exec is the one in a tough situation, personally or professionally, and you don't have a choice but to be a part of that. I don't mean getting involved in nitty-gritty details, although you most likely will have to deal with some of those. I'm talking about a specific state of mind that you need to adopt. It's more of a protective kind that includes elements of care and support. Tough times for your exec usually mean you need to show you care in a more intangible and remote way. It will look like allowing room for variations, more tolerance, flexibility, massive proactive planning, thinking ahead and enabling crossovers. If you sense you know something that can actually help — advise and act on it. If you know that staying later in the office and maybe even ordering in dinner will give some much needed human support — please do so.

Actually, these are the times when we have to be extra alert and focused on the little 'unimportant' things. In the bigger picture, some of those 'epic turned minors' can usually be addressed to seem less threatening, less epic or unmanageable. The secret is in the small details ('Don't worry, I'll handle this. You can stay focused on that meeting/report/email.'). And most importantly, stay human and stick to your standards of integrity. Your common sense might tell you easy ways out that are not logical because the rules dictate otherwise. Sometimes a human approach can solve the unsolvable. We PAs are good at that! I invite you to bring that personal excellence into the harsh business world we ended up living in.

Being humanly professional is another phrase that doesn't really make sense when you hear it the first time. But it is one that we absolutely need to adopt, ASAP!

Cold, warm, warmer — tropical heat

When you find yourself in a less than desirable situation here is what you can do:

✓ Take a snapshot of the situation and try to retrace your steps. You need to realize the process of its creation to know what can be done next. Try to step away from your own perception and consider other vantage points. It's not easy, because we all get stuck in our own way of thinking, especially when the going gets though. In crises and painful situations there is this strong survival mode we get into and it's the best guide we know. When you are serious about resolving a situation for the better (and you really need to have that intent close to heart) you better be able to step back to see the whole picture. Why? You need to read the extraordinary book called *Difficult Conversations* (by Douglas Stone, Bruce Patton and Sheila Heen). It's based on the research and findings of the legendary Harvard Negotiation Project and it will blow your socks off. I will come back to that one later — just order it in the meantime.

✓ T.A.L.K. – Take Action and Let others Know! The more you bottle up, the faster and the more furiously the top will fly off at the moment of surrender. It's actually a no-brainer. Know that your timing has to be good and convenient. The setting has to be supportive, personal and trusted (never go to Starbucks for a difficult conversation or a 'feelings' talk). And most importantly, don't wait too long to talk about something. The sooner it pops up, the smaller the issue is, the easier and faster it will be to resolve it. I have to admit, no matter how small the issue is, it's still a confrontation and I hate those! Now is the time to grow up and be professional. You need a strategy to deal with it. Define for yourself one or two ways of telling something uncomfortable and practice until it doesn't bug you anymore (*'Repetition of something difficult kills the difficult nature of it'* — Brian Tracy). Being forward about the issue in a direct, constructive way is an amazing skill that will absolutely benefit you and your career. I'm still working on it — I'll let you know when I'll master it. There are some great tactics in *Difficult Conversations* book that seem too easy to be true, but they work!

✓ And the last thing: read *Difficult Conversations*.

Don't hang up

In closing, I want to warn you about the extremes: don't throw in the towel too soon, and don't let it overcook and take over your life. Remember: 'If you don't experience problems, you are missing a lot of opportunities! 'Bleep' happens, things go wrong, we all get stressed out, we all have things to learn, and we tend to get ourselves in situations where it's possible to learn — by design. It is how the universe works and it does a great job. When the lessons are painful, it means you are learning the right thing and by being educated now you can conquer the next step and elevate your performance. It's the right time for a quantum leap! As the great personal and business development expert Brian Tracy says: *'Life is a sequence of seven problem waves, six small ones and one major crisis.'* Know it is coming, be prepared, suit up, and catch a wave!

Make a decision to make the best of any situation first, it's a resolution that snaps your mindset into a very specific positive, solution-seeking and team-working mode. Guard the premises of personal integrity and you will be fine. Learn to excel a little more with every difficulty coming your way. Become the magician of transformation. That is a cool title for an Assistant.

Chapter 5. Relationships

I believe that this is the single most important element we Assistants need to master. Our jobs are all about relationships, as we navigate in constant partnership with another person. We need to have excellent skills in knowing who we're dealing with so we can adjust the way we approach them, talk to them, consider things they might say in a specific way, be aware of different vantage points etc. It seems like too much complex psychoanalysis for a single phone call, and it really is. But we already do all that — on autopilot and all day long. I believe that any Assistant in this profession has an augmented sense of others, it's in our DNA. Yes, we do have a lot of manual handling and work with lifeless technologies, but that sixth sense of knowing who we are dealing with is always there. Even more to it, it has to be present and 'on' every minute of the day so in case your exec rushes in unexpectedly you can figure out his mood in a second.

I worked for a genius exec once who is super intelligent and who's thought processes were quick and even complex. But in times of stress he could only handle one of my questions at a time. Asking a second would mean he would go back to the first one, alter the outcome for some reason (changing his mind back to the first option in an hour or so) and make any detail seem big and crucial. Even if I only asked which flight to London he would prefer timewise, asking whether he needs a ride from the airport would make him switch from London Gatwick to London City (and back) and demand the overbooked flight to guarantee him a 3A seat. To avoid a long discussion and unnecessary work I learned to ask my questions separately. Just the way he works.

Additionally, he was on the move a lot throughout the office, which is another specific to deal with in an organized manner. When I would finally locate him (it takes some time to search through three huge office floors with three separate stairways), I had a pile of stacked propositions, questions or deliverables. Urgent ones on top — the rest of them would depend on his mood. The thing with super-intelligent professionals is that they are in a flow a lot, so you don't want to disturb that, believe me. After assessing his mood I would select the things to ask him in a split second and then quickly be on my way. It worked and we were both happy with the arrangement. And yes, every exec has his own manual like this one. I bet this sounds familiar to a lot of you! Get to know the manual for your exec, or just make one up.

Gut feeling

That's the thing with relationships: they're mostly based on your gut feeling and past experiences. You cannot rely on what others tell you about your exec, because he can and will be different with you if there is a click. There it is — the click! You have it or you don't! It's a creature you cannot control or nurture.

It always astonished me that most of my interviews with my execs where extremely short. After an extensive HR selection I was invited to a meeting with the exec and I was usually out the door in 25 minutes or less. While stepping out of those office buildings it scared the hell out of me. Was it that bad? (There is your preconditioned mindset of common knowledge.) But I always got the job, even got called back the same day to confirm the starting date. I got into the habit of asking every exec after a period of great cooperation why that meeting was so short. I always got the same answer: my gut feeling told me we could work together. And there is nothing airy-fairy about it — a lot of execs make important decisions based on their gut feeling and they are usually right! It's the strangest thing in business I have ever seen or read about!

Being good in the area of relationships will make you a creator of great connections, which will benefit both sides along the way. And here lies an important factor — for a great relationship it has to be a two-way stream. Not all of them have to be all that, but make sure your most important ones do have this incorporated.

Never-ending story

Relationships and your related skills never stand alone. Every new relationship will be measured against a past one. Based on your experience you will get into them with a certain attitude and manner of acting. There is just no other way to do that and that's totally fine. Once in a new relationship (whether it's a new exec, new supplier, new colleagues, new neighbor or a stranger on the street) your seventh social sense will automatically start tweaking and directing your actions. The more fitted your actions are towards the true nature of the person and that situation the more successful the relationship will be, no magic there. This seventh sense is definitely a maturity skill and all Assisting Professionals have this ability within them.

You need to realize what you're doing and do it consciously. Your experiences now will have a tremendous impact on your future similar relationships. It's a potential vicious cycle you need to be aware of. Let your past experiences guide you, but don't see what you have taken from them as set in stone. We live and learn. You will be surprised how some relationships fall apart for no apparent reason and can't be mended no matter what you try. Others will grow and develop surprisingly easy.

People will turn out to be totally different from what you initially thought and you will have the strongest relationships for years to come. We tend to attract certain people over time and that changes according to the skills we need to master. OK, this is a little airy-fairy but it's true. I adopted a guiding open-minded attitude and the combo of these subtle traffic lights works great for me. Find what works for you and tweak it to practical perfection!

By the way, I saw a quote from Steve Jobs which I loved from the very second I read it. It's about being a perfectionist (which is not a good thing at all), but his view turned it into a good thing with a twist:

Perfection is not attainable, but if we chase perfection we can catch excellence!

Whenever you are in a new environment there are a few things you can do to get familiar with the relationships you need to build. Scan through the job description and make a list of contact points. Add any names to that list while talking to the previous PA, enquiring about the things she did on a frequent basis. She might tell you some useful inside info about the points of contact. Hear her out, note the specifics but don't let it guide your judgment.

I have had many occasions where people acted very differently towards me than to my predecessor. Relationships are always personal and person specific. It's up to you to make them work or not. And your third source of instructions on important and needed relationships is your exec. Just ask directly what you need to know, with whom you need to establish contact and if there are any agendas to keep in mind. By the way, people say they avoid relationships with agendas — but they are all alike! It's naive to believe that some are not intentional on some level. So don't be misguided and make your own win-win agendas for every relationship you build, sustain or pay attention to.

Picture perfect

Before adding to that list you've made of all the relationships you need to establish or maintain, you need to know what your standards are in terms of relationships in general. Here is a checklist:

✓ To begin with, define for yourself your three to seven most important values (not practicalities) when it comes to relationships in general.

✓ Then describe the ideal core elements of every relationship on your list.

✓ Now comes the tricky part, but I really think it is a necessary one. State your previous specific/positive/negative experiences for each similar relationship. This will help you to know whether you are acting in a way enabling you to build or ruin a new connection. Negative experiences will impact new relationships more heavily, so be aware of them. Did you know that it takes up to five positive experiences to equal one single negative experience? Life sucks like that!

✓ So now, make a short checklist of things you need to keep in mind in every relationship on your list.

The great thing is that you only need to go through this process once and it will be anchored in your mind for a while, keeping you informed and aligned while establishing new connections.

The best way to approach new connections is with a neutrally positive attitude. Even if you know this person is not liked by most or difficult in some way. Don't be too optimistic as it might seem suspicious. Most people need time to adapt to new people. We all need time to get to know somebody and form an opinion regarding their intentions. Know that all people are 100% emotional! Be generous with the 'benefit of the doubt' in every new connection and you will be off to a great start.

If you want to revise your current relationships this checklist method works great too. It will provide you with clarity and maybe some pointers for improvement. You see, relationships are living creatures. They change, evolve and move along constantly. We take most of our relationships for granted until they start to fall apart. I don't have to tell you that every creature needs food, a pat on the shoulder or a slap on the head to snap out of something. That is exactly how you should look at your relationships. Some are born, some die, some turn 180, some will surprise you by their depth, and some will reveal their true face and scare the hell out of you. We all know and have all of them. They are all important, so let's treat them accordingly.

The recipe for…

The core ingredients for lasting and supportive relationships are pretty obvious. Of course there needs to be a trust element. The importance of that one will vary per each connection, but it has to be present. If you don't trust somebody as far as you can throw them, don't waste your precious time on them. If you have somebody on your list you don't seem to get along with there are two things you can do.

First, propose to start over and talk about the underlying expectations, emotions and possible misunderstandings.

I had a very difficult relationship with a colleague once. We started off great, but after a while we ended up on the opposite sides of a truly horrific battlefield. It was so uncomfortable that I actually considered leaving my beloved exec because I wasn't able to handle the situation appropriately. Luckily, I found a moment to briefly mention this to my exec and he turned out be aware of the reason why my colleague's attitude changed so drastically. It made perfect sense and I asked her to join me for dinner (public neutral ground where you need to keep the peace but are stuck with each other for at least the first course). We talked about everything and found some mutual ground. We didn't become best friends, but the tension was gone. We agreed to stay off each other's turf and everything was peaceful again.

That's the thing, you don't have to be friends with everyone, but sometimes you need certain arrangements to make it work for both sides and move on. I also had a case where we couldn't find any common ground at all and we agreed to stay as far away from each other as possible.

After her exec moved up the corporate ladder we became dependent on each other in some areas of our business. Again, we officially agreed to keep our communication brief and strictly professional, a win-win for both of us after all.

Your second option is to go MIA.

Unfortunately, leaving our beloved jobs due to a feud with other Assistants actually happens a lot, although we don't state that as the main reason. It's good to say no — as long you are not saying no to yourself. Very important lesson I have learned along the way.

How is your trust doing?

Charles H. Green provides us with a magical Trust Equation (www.trustedadvisor.com) and this makes this complex subject more defined and manageable. This is how it goes:

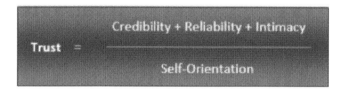

$$Trust = \frac{Credibility + Reliability + Intimacy}{Self\text{-}Orientation}$$

This equation is true in every relationship, so we need to translate this to a PA/exec situation. You can rate the values above the line from 1 to 10 (10 being 'hell yeah' and 1 being 'no freaking way') and the value below the line from 1 to 10 (10 being 'it's me, myself and I' and 1 being 'his wish is my command').

***Credibility (translates into words)*:** Do you believe and trust your exec's story, speech, appearance, professional skills and vice versa? This basically relates to authenticity and mutual respect.

***Reliability (translates into actions*):** Can you count on one another? This is an element of security resting on promised results and deliverables.

***Intimacy (translates into emotions)*:** Can you be truly honest and open with each other? Do you feel safe and secure expressing what's on your mind? This is a matter of confidentiality.

***Self-orientation (translates into motives)*:** How committed, willing, interested and involved are you in support to your exec? This is the level of your focus and you being sincerely into it!

You need all those factors in place to create trust! It's a complicated matter and you have to be honest while answering the questions. And in case it's not there yet, you have to be truly sincere about the missing elements in order to improve the situation.

Here is what you need to keep in mind:

- ✓ It is not so much the sum of values above the line divided by the value below the line. It's about the values *versus* each other. The rating will make it clear where you stand and will show you the direction in which to go in order to get where you want to be.

- ✓ Increasing the value of the elements above the line *increases* the value of trust. Increasing the value of the denominator, meaning a weak focus on your exec, *decreases* the value of trust way faster!

- ✓ It is possible to go negative above the line. That will only mean that you are positively diagnosed with a need to wake up and do something about it!

- ✓ Note that the state of your self-orientation is the *defining* variable in how you perceive and influence trust! That is a major thing to be aware of and it's an ultimate proof that your state of mind has 'make it or break it' power! The direction and strength of your focus are key elements to the success of your relationships. You have the responsibility and power to control and maintain it.

- ✓ This also shows that if one element is lacking it doesn't necessarily mean the whole equation is impossible, unworkable or unrepairable. We can influence our trust image by attending to ill areas. This just paints the picture of what is missing in your trust relationship and pinpoints what you have to do to fix it.

- ✓ Note: the mathematical rule of two minuses making a plus does not work here! The more negative ratings are in the numerators, the more negative impact they have on the level of trust.

- ✓ To state the evident: your goal is to get a high total above the line (but a few minor values will not make it impossible to work together) and strive to have a low value below the line. But please make sure to include a healthy dose of good balance for the sake of your private life. We'll get to it in a second!

So to sum up: trust = worthiness! Is this relationship worthy of your time, energy and effort?

Do the math...

With a sprinkle of...

Trust usually goes hand in hand with integrity, which we talked about in prior chapters. What I love about relationships is the fun and support factor. When you have a great connection with someone it is all about that small something that frees you up. It makes you smile when you see their number on your phone screen. It's that knowledge of assurance, optimism and 'result guaranteed' that makes it a bullseye for me to nourish and build relationships with everybody and anybody around me. You never know when you might have a great laugh while solving a super-challenging situation.

Because let's face it — we need each other. The gain is different but the common ground of reciprocity is very fulfilling and energizing.

I had the most amazing contact with one of our travel agents while preparing some extreme and complicated trips and itineraries. The impossible dates, the impossible directions, finding ways to make the impossible stopovers work and changing the same flight for the eighth time — it was so cool to see us cooperate, have amazing fun and make everybody happy. When I saw his number on my screen I would smile.

The same goes for receptionists. For some weird reason I always end up with great advice and tons of funny stories while talking to receptionists. They might seem invisible but you just can't do without them as a PA. The great thing about receptionists is you know that they will always pick up the phone and you know where to find them when you need them. They are the true meaning of 'predictable fixed points' of comfort and support!

Further, I love building great relationships with main suppliers, any team members who interact with my exec a lot, and especially facility people and HR people. I found HR teams the most difficult to connect with, but it's very rewarding to have great connections there. And you will find that they are usually just as isolated and 'feared' as we are. That is a weird but very real commonality.

Needless to say you need to build special relationships with other PAs and Assistants, but I don't really see them as team members. Those are more likely to resemble family members, you treat them differently! No matter your differences, we are all peas in a pie. Don't get offended — it's a great thing and a yummy pie!

The holy trinity

To complete the recipe for a great relationship here are my '3R' values:

Respect

Unfortunately, it's not a given nowadays! We all know the saying that you need to deserve and earn respect. The cool thing about respect is that it really makes our job a lot easier and fulfilling when we respect our exec. Nobody is perfect, but there is always something that stands out. I always found great things in my execs, business or personal. I was always proud to be their PA. That is a truly cool feeling. It's not human to be great at everything you do and sometimes even the best of us slip and slide. Yes, respect can be lost in a second, not to be ever found again. Handle it with care!

And don't forget that it goes both ways. I lately had an amazing experience where an executive openly admitted he respected my qualities. It was the first time ever I heard that in those words! I honestly thought I was lifted a few inches of the ground. Now I know what it does to people, so if they deserve it I will definitely return the favor!

Reminder: always start by giving the other the benefit of the doubt, even if you have heard rumors. Sometimes it's the excellence in one area that makes other areas suffer. And if you respect that shiny brilliant one you will find ways to forgive any shortcomings. We are all human — learn to cut others some slack and don't be too hard. It does wonders when you adopt an attitude grounded in respect. I know it works for me.

Responsibility

It's an obvious one, but not everybody gets it. It's all good and dandy until bleep hits the fan. Then we tend to catch the virus called 'excusitis' and easily end up in a blame game. A quick and sure remedy: adopt the belief of 100% responsibility! It doesn't matter what happened, you're in it so it's your responsibility in some way. Don't shoot me yet, because I'm not saying take the blame, pay the price for all, be the underdog or whatever you think you'll end up with if you say you are responsible. You decide things, you take on an attitude, your actions show, your thoughts or communication flow in a specific direction.

Be responsible for things that you affect. Also, be aware that you are in control of your every move, physical or mental. Take responsibility for that if that makes it easier to grasp.

Also, from a professional PA point of view, it's your responsibility to fix things, make things work and happen. Most of my execs couldn't care less what happened — they want to know what I'm going to do about it and when they can expect results, either way!

Taking responsibility is a great way to build good and lasting relationships. You have to know if you can count on each other. Proof of responsibility provides a relative certainty of expectations, which is why this is so important while in the process of creating trust!

Reliability

This one is closely related to the previous one, but there is a definite difference in timeline. Where counting on responsibility is a certainty for *after* actions, the act of being reliable is providing certainty to *beforehand* decisions. Think about it for a minute...

Reliability entails acting responsibly to achieve the set goals with set standards and provide defined deliverables. If you prove to be reliable with consistency, you will gain respect and trust. Proof is in the cookie, let's bake some according to this recipe!

Focus pocus

I found that a few things can change the course of any relationship as if by magic, sometimes making it difficult to continue as before. I'm sure there are many more examples, but I'm very familiar with these:

Hierarchy is always a topic to handle in a politically correct way. There are some standards that need to be respected. When you know about those hierarchy definitions at the beginning of a relationship you easily adjust to them. But there are times when you or the other person climb or descend the ladder and that tends to disrupt the great relationship you had before. It's not always the case, but it surely affects the way you communicate. The best way to deal with it is to do exactly that — keep on talking.

I once was very surprised that a person I frequently talked to and thought was some kind of professional equal turned out to be the president of the company. She just happened to be very involved and the first few times I called she was the one who picked up the phone to handle my requests. And so our relationship grew. When I shortly afterwards discovered her actual position I was truly embarrassed. I never talked to her again, ending up mainly talking to her PA via email. As a junior PA it was a very uncomfortable situation.

Actually, any kind of **change** can affect your relationships. Deals gone bad, restructuring, takeovers, personal issues, policy changes, gossip, career moves — the list is endless. Some changes are obvious, some are underground. If your relationship changes suddenly, look for any environmental, social, economic or structural changes first. There might be a reason you are not aware of. When that occurs it's up to you to be flexible and willing to talk to clarify the situation. And the sooner the better, at least if that relationship is important to you.

It's not always a negative reaction by the way. Sometimes people suddenly appear much more positively inclined towards you. The first thing we usually think then is, 'what does that person wants from me?' How preconditioned is that? And the worst thing is that it is usually true! It's up to you to handle that one professionally.

The most important one is of course the relationship with your exec. Be on the lookout for changes, because that might indicate an extra area in need of support and attention, or maybe a topic to talk about. It's good to have frequent talks anyway — but when things change, have one that is especially focused on the element of change. Make sure that you are aware of things going on, it will make your life so much easier and your support so much more valued and appropriate.

Stereotypes

In the PA world there seems to be a few over-publicized stereotypes of relationships. Some are common but not always what they appear to be from the outside.

The Devil Wears Prada connection

Yes, they do exist. They are extremely demanding, strictly result and quality driven with a diehard business focus. I've been very close to one of those and the movie is nothing compared to the real deal. I don't have to explain the specifics, I just want to point out that deep down below, those execs value their PAs tremendously!

And yes, most senior executives have some of those featured qualities and most Assistants do behave in that same manner. But most of us don't even mind that, because we are in the position we love! The level of accomplishment is astonishing and fulfilling. For sure, not everybody sees it that way.

It really makes you grow as a PA — in record time. Although making mistakes is not well tolerated, it drives you to perform close to perfection. That is a skill! No, that is not a job for a long period of time. But it's truly an experience that will mold you into shape as a PA in no time!

Doormat connection

This is the most disconnected one of all, but sometimes execs are really curt. It's not as degrading as it sounds. It's just a form of relationship where you don't have much say in any matter as an Assistant and you are truly a subject to your exec. Not ideal, but sometimes it's just what is needed and it can work fine for both parties if you don't crave a warm and fuzzy relationship with your exec. To be honest, it's good to have experienced such relationship at least once, if only just to know that it doesn't fit you and to appreciate other options at hand. Yes, I'm talking from experience, and it really makes me appreciate the things I'm doing now. Moreover, while being an interim Assistant and being equipped with that experience, I have reinforced more than a few PAs along the way by making them aware that their execs are not that bad compared to others. Usually they look really relieved after that statement and they move on a lot more confident and happy. So cool to see it!

Warm and fuzzy connection

Not an overly common one and not as cozy as it sounds. It's the one where you are very close to your exec, essentially glued to him wherever he goes. It's where you get cut a lot of slack, are never given a bad or critical review, have decent working hours and are very comfy in expressing what's on your mind. The easygoing relationship, exchanging personal Christmas gifts and having dinners together! They do exist...

Lovers' connection

This is the last one but surely the most popular stereotype. Again, it doesn't mean there is an actual love connection in a physical form. It's more something like a PA has a crush on her exec or the other way around. It's tricky, playful, uncomfortable and rarely lasts long. The cliché is out there, you get the picture!

I prefer to use this stereotype as a 'motherly affection' type of relationship. This helps you profoundly care about your exec without entering the twilight zone. I love this quote from Sheryl Sandberg from her book *Lean In* (you should absolutely read that one):

We cannot assume that interactions between men and women have a sexual component. Everyone needs to act professionally so they feel safe at all times.

And here is why, Sheryl just nails it:
Motivation comes from working on things we care about. To really care about others we have to understand them, their likes, dislikes, feelings and thoughts.

To implement that, I find it easy to assume a motherly point of view; a mother cares deeply because she wants to and needs to know her loved one to the bone.

Any Assistant role is a mix of the above. I'm not judging, just saying: be aware of the extremes! Every connection has its own characteristics and manuals. If you are looking for a job, these are actually good samples to decide what you want to end up with, steering your way in a certain direction. Mix and match to create your desirable personal profile. And if you realize that you have already found your perfect fit, congrats! Life can be generous!

Should I stay or should I go

I have mentioned that your personal integrity is key in choosing your way forward. Now let's say you are still on the safe side but it's not really working well.

By the way, I got a comment once, a very surprising one, that I'm too focused on the negatives. Ehm, well, it might look that way from a distance, but I am an extremely positive person. Many will testify to that! So how come? Well, unfortunately, my PA religion tells me that most of my actions derive from something that has tight deadlines and great expectations which usually entails many things don't go right or will derail without strict supervision.

As a PA, I'm constantly on the lookout for things to help along on their way forward, to tweak them to look better or perform faster. To smoothen situations that tend to be uncomfortable or undesirable. To avoid unnecessary mistakes or correct them before they land on my exec's desk etc. So yes, I'm focused on things that do not go according to plan or expectations because there is an implied action for me there. I do see and cheer the good, but that is just a short single moment of happy thoughts. They never make my to-do list extremely long, stressful or difficult. Yes, happy occasions need celebrating. But at the same time things get complicated and stressful and go awry while planning those celebrations. Does it make me a negative person? I hope not! So please excuse me if I bring you down with all the things that could go wrong. I just want you to be prepared and able to take action accordingly, with less stress and uncertainty.

So, back to the topic. Let's say there is something bothering you that is not extreme enough for you to consider parting ways. Here is what I tend to do, see if it works for you too.

First of all, I go back in time to before the creepy feeling came out of the shadows (yes, we're back to the negatives). Then I work backwards to see if I have missed any signals or alarm bells. Usually you will detect a few of those. Make a note of them and try to think what the real origin might be. The reason why I'm saying 'look for the real origin' is because it's usually not apparent and fades away after a while. Again — read *Difficult Conversations*! When you figure out why things got a little less than desirable you can do two things. Invest time and effort to attend to the root of the issue. And the second is T.A.L.K. (Take Action and Let others Know). Let them know you want this situation to get resolved and you want in on the action. Find mutual ground and come up with a plan.

It's important to act swiftly when you discover there is something wrong. Time is the enemy in these situations. Although, if you come to understand the origin and it's really something minor that only grew to be an elephant in your own head, then you need to adjust your translations, expectations, and definitions and move on. Remember this piece of wisdom (no, it's not mine): something has only the meaning you give it!

We have this tendency to label everything based on our past, our values and our assumptions. Those are often different from the truth and the perceptions of others. If you adopt the mindset of questioning your labels once in a while, you will see a totally different world out there! This is highly prequalified personal development stuff. To mention it in normal language: invest effort in placing yourself in someone else's shoes and you will get a picture that might be vastly different from yours. It's a skill you can develop and learn. Make an effort to master that one. It will enable you to make better, more educated and cooperative decisions. You could become the actual peacemaker which the book *Who Took My Pen … Again*! so beautifully describes. And again, read *Difficult Conversations*! There is a really easy method with a set of questions that you can apply right away to get the actual picture of any situation.

Have no illusions

Grass is always greener on the other side! Don't overstretch but do make a fair effort to build fruitful and fulfilling relationships. No, you don't have to be loved and liked by everybody. Everyone is unique and different. And you don't match with everybody, by design. If somebody seems to do that, then I can assure you that the person in question has no real personality and is a major 'go along'. Even the greatest people always have enemies! It's a law of nature. So relax, it's not a competition. The only thing that matters is that it has to work out for you and the others you choose to connect and cooperate with. Go for a win-win! Like I mentioned before, even in situations where you really can't find any commonalities you can always agree to disagree. Get into the habit of setting certain codes of conduct that both parties will feel comfortable with or at least accept. It's also a win–win, only not a traditional one. It's all about your mindset!

And yes, 'bleep' happens. Every relationship has its course of ups and downs. If those are acceptable to both sides and are in relative harmony (with a ratio of at least 5 to 1, remember) then you're good! Don't chase perfection, be satisfied with understanding and peace of mind and enjoy the power of clarity. Yes, going the extra mile to achieve a great relationship is very fulfilling. Just make sure it's a two-way street, otherwise the unevenness will mess it all up and all the good will be forgotten. That's the downside of our human nature. We believe in negatives easier than positives. Negatives leave a bigger mark. So try to focus on getting an overload of positive experiences to make the bad stuff seem small and meaningless.

Cheerios

The conclusion from the longest (75 years and ongoing), most expensive (20 million USD) and most extended scientific study about happiness (The Grant Study, named after its main funder), conducted by Harvard, was: the only great factor defining happiness in our lives is the quality of our relationships! Furthermore, another well-known study confirmed that although feeling happy is largely determined by our DNA (50%) we still have a huge power to influence our happiness by undertaking certain actions (40%). Only 10% of our happiness is determined by our environment.

So let's be smart and combine the two: surround yourself with great relationships and make the effort to nurture and cultivate those that really matter to you. That will make you a happy person, it's scientifically proven!

I don't have to explain the benefits of a great relationship with your exec. It will elevate your productivity, effectiveness and satisfaction. And it certainly works both ways, although most execs will not show it in an obvious way. Become a relationship master, make this skill your own, define ways that work for you and stick to your values. I believe that relationships are the single most important element in our PA profession. By definition, it entails 'personal' focus and 'assistant' literally means that someone is leaning on you to get ahead. All that makes me a very proud PA, and I'm sure I'm not the only one!

Chapter 6. PA's Journey

Let's explore the path of an Assistant by focusing on certain situations we seem to find ourselves in. I hope to paint a total picture so that each of the W.A.N.T.E.D. skills (which we will discuss in the following chapters) will make a little more sense and have a clear context. I will keep mentioning PAs, but I think that every Assisting Professional could benefit from knowing how to deal with similar situations. So here I am, with a brush, some water, as many colors as I could find, and a clean canvas...

Busy bees

Today's PA is (unfortunately) overly stressed a large proportion of the time. We're running around with our 100-mile long to-do lists, trying to consider everyone's preferences, personalities and agendas. I think it's safe to say that most PAs don't have a very balanced life... I even dare to state that we have a very cruel work/life balance.

That doesn't mean that we are unhappy all the time, though. We usually love what we do. Getting through the long days and getting things done, things others don't even seem to notice at times — that makes us happy. Debbie Gross described it very well at the 2014 SecLive in London: 'If you're working for a high-profile executive you don't have a private life.' It might be a harsh thing to say, but for most of us it's true. So here is what I think about it — I love being that busy bee and getting things done that seem impossible for a normal 9-5 employee. But I'm also positively sure we can do that and be happy and fulfilled at the same time. It's all about your mindset and your willingness to get there.

Are you making it easy for yourself or do your to-do lists and ever ringing phones dictate your existence? If the answer to the question is the latter, then try this one — are you willing to change it?

Before looking for answers, let's have a look why we get stuck in that rat race. The main source of this evil is the fact that things do go wrong and most deadlines we get are slightly unrealistic! There are many factors that contribute to an unbalanced, over-worked Assistant. And sometimes it's simply bad luck. Many PAs are living and working disconnectedly, some get stressed out by something simple, like having a bad hair day every Tuesday. Some are not happy in their jobs, which makes a small issue — like your cat having diarrhea — make your day even more aggravating. The problem is that, like Debbie mentioned in her presentation, we are perceived as machines who must act accordingly, errorless and considerate in every situation and to every person. Oh, and by the way, we are on duty 24/7.

When things go wrong or get stressful it directly translates to our relationships. Because let's face it, execs usually don't care about the motives or reasons when things do not go the way they expected. They are focused on the person closest to the situation and target them (forcefully) to come up with a solution. When it reaches this point, our most important relationship can be ruined if it happens too many times. And I don't really blame them for not being our Dr. Phil every time the printer gets jammed, or if they have to find their own cab because you forgot to get a driver, or when we are behind on a major deadline. It's our job to be extremely detail oriented, fast and forward thinking, problem-solving experts, and always at their beck-and-call, with a smiling McDonald's face where possible.

We have to put our A-game forward to prevent such a crack in the relationship. Nothing new. But let me step out and say that you have the power and capacity to be in control of those situations! To do that continuously you have to be grounded, clear-minded and focused.

We have an image to preserve, and each of us should strive to get the impossible done, or at the very least show that this misfortune is something you were prepared to deal with. It's not easy to be the one they count on day and night, but that's the name of the game. 'Bleep' happens, so get used to it. Let's focus on building our reputation, our image, and provide more than enough supporting evidence. In doing so, we will get the benefit of the doubt in times of crisis. Sometimes you will have to run a little faster after such an unlucky event, sometimes it just blows over. I recommend you to see the post-drama period as an extra opportunity to prove your worth.

Bad start

Let's say you are a fresh PA; you can usually expect to go through a tough trial period at the start of your employment. This is especially the case when you have been hired because your new exec had negative experiences with his former Assistants, or decided they weren't up to his standards for one reason or another. This also goes for Assistants who come from difficult prior employments. All there is to say: uncomfortable beginnings are not very unusual for us. You need to act professionally and don't let your previous experiences influence you, because this could potentially be the best job of your life! Be aware that a lack of trust always hinders yourself and others from being open and sincere: this is crucial when breaking new ground.

It's your job as a professional Assistant to make this transition as smooth and comfortable as possible for your exec, so take that responsibility. Of course you might still have mixed feelings regarding your past employment, but urge yourself to concentrate on the new relationship and the new results you want to achieve. Actually, the worse the experience your exec had with his prior Assistant, the greater the opportunity for you to prove you are the right person to be there. Problems motivate us, so embrace them.

Now let's turn it around — it's not always tough. How does an ideal trial period look? Although it never happened to me, I would picture it like this: you start with a pleasant introductory talk, share some personal stories, discuss the duties that are expected of you, the manner of execution and all the important things below the ice that you have to know before you even turn on your computer.

You mention a personal note here and there, and of course have a good laugh, because there is enough time to get to know each other. When an initial level of comfort is reached, you disclose what your strengths, work style and interests are, so your exec will know and be considerate of those. I truly hope that this sounds remotely familiar to some of you. My experiences, on the other hand, most resemble the metaphor 'sink or swim'...

The good thing is that the start of it all is not a defining moment in an Assistant's career. The way you will fix things, handle people and how you will manage to make your exec feel at ease with you, all that will truly show your abilities and win the trust and respect of your employer. So don't let a tough kickoff mark you for life. Just be aware of the things going on at that moment. Be attentive to details, they will tell you a lot about past experience, especially when it's still a very fresh memory. Be patient with your exec, their staff and yourself. Building relationships always takes time. And most importantly: always remain professional and neutrally positive.

One more piece of advice: when you take up a new position, adopt the skills of mirroring. You can find a lot about it online. While physical mirroring is the most well-known, don't forget to pay extra attention to verbal execution (meaning adopting some words, phrases or sentence constructions that you notice your exec uses a lot). There is nothing manipulative if this will make your new exec feel at ease, which is extremely beneficial for the first get-to-know-each-other period. The smoother this goes, the more you will be seen as a true professional.

Those damn expectations

A lack of clearly communicated expectations is the next thing that usually makes it hard to fulfill your exec's expectations (mainly because they are, for the most part, unknown to anyone else!). In big corporations it's up to HR departments to set up a profile for your position. They usually look for some standard requirements and then pad the profile out with what they think fits that position best. They might ask the exec what he needs — but how would he know? If he was lucky enough to have a great previous Assistant he will say: 'I want somebody like her.' If HR is on top of their stuff, they will follow that up by asking: 'How would you describe that in a job description and why do you prefer that style of execution?', to which he may or may not be able to give an answer.

On the other hand, you are in a very different situation if your predecessor wasn't the perfect fit for him. Job descriptions are usually not in tune with what the exec actually needs, so it's up to us to see how we'll make it work. And let's also consider that expectations change over time. If you have worked your way into his good graces, then your exec will expect much more of you. But if he changes PAs as often as he changes his shirts, then he won't expect much from you to begin with.

One more note: of course it's not only all about their expectations; your expectations are as important. Be aware of the conditions when you start, and how you will be expected to handle the handover with his former PA. Don't attach too much importance to her opinion if she was let go because he was not satisfied. The opposite can be even worse. It can be very difficult if the departing Assistant was close and comfortable with your new boss, and he was a terrific employer to her. You will have huge shoes to fill and your exec might not be very open to your appointment as he didn't wish for this switch. You have to stay neutral but enthusiastic, you are a different person and you will have to find your own way in this position.

It helps to know what the expectations are, but keep in mind that you have to make the role your own according to what your exec needs! Time will tell you what he really wants; you'll eventually learn how to respond to every nitty-gritty need in the right way.

The good thing to remember is that you were probably hired because there was some sort of a 'personality click'. That gives you the green light to start building a relationship based on a solid foundation.

The art of feedback

Next on the list of what's often lacking in the life of an Assistant: regular and direct feedback. I'm not talking about a shout-out when things go wrong, nor the very welcome 'thanks for doing this', nor the yearly evaluation and Personal Development Plan sittings (the notorious PDPs). We tend to get busy and lose track of spending 'quality time' with our execs. Make time to ask them real questions which could benefit your relationship, and enable both of you to be more effective and efficient. You plan their life, so plan a minute to do that! Remember — it's a habit, repeat it over time and it will become a routine.

It seems like a common sense to speak up when something is not working, and preferably immediately after the unpleasant event. But we do forget the importance of speaking up when things go well. I'm not asking you to recite a poem. Just quickly mention you are happy with the way things are now — sounds easy and logical, right? I will admit that I don't do that a lot, because usually I assume that if they don't speak up and I still have the job it's all good. I should though, point taken.

I know it has had a huge impact when I do exactly that. It forces you to slow down for a second and appreciate the situation. And by telling your exec that, you give him the opportunity for reflection as well. This makes a big difference and is a potentially satisfying moment. It's like a mini business moment of meditation! Strangely enough, giving positive feedback seems difficult to most execs, so make it easy for them and give the option to just agree with you! Reassurance and awareness make you stronger, give them a try.

Yes, it might also turn out there is something bothering you or your exec so it won't be such a euphoric experience. The sooner you know and talk about what's wrong, however, the sooner you'll be able to fix it. It's like asking Assistants: I have good news and bad news, which do you want to hear first? Spare us the precious time and always shout out the bad news first. If we need to fix something, we might need every second starting now.

Speaking up is important, we all know that. Here is a good reason to actually do it — speaking up about the inner workings of your daily doings will show that you care. That is a valuable quality, which will not go unseen.

Now, I want to stand still for second on the subject of feedback itself. There is a very frustrating saying about feedback (usually mentioned just before or after something negative is up) and it goes like this: 'It's business, nothing personal!' What the heck? Feedback is always personal! Let's examine this statement: a certain *person* is giving the feedback and another certain *person* receives it. The feedback is something the giver has experienced on a *personal* level and it might concern something the receiver has done *personally*. Do you see the irony?

It is true, though, that the content of the feedback itself doesn't have to say anything directly about the receiver. It is important to consider the setting in which the feedback is given. Both vantage points are important here (again – read Difficult Conversations!). The *when* and the *how* of the feedback will tell a story about the giver and paint a picture of the receiver's role, the one he actually didn't know he had or even what it had to be. Additionally, it's good to keep in mind the fact that the receiver triggered something within the giver that forced him to take action and deliver his feedback.

I can illustrate it with a simple example that I know we can all relate to. The companies I worked in usually worked on long-term projects or with constant tight deadlines, and I always received more feedback when deadlines approached. Logically, you need to notice the timeline stress! At one point I became well aware of this phenomenon so I reacted to these feedback sessions a bit differently, in a less personal way. And guess what: it made the feedback easier to hear, and infinitely more productive.

In other words — context is important. When you hear that saying just rephrase it in your mind, and decide not to take it personally *right away*. Analyze the situation and come up with an appropriate response. One point of advice here: always respond. Whether it's a 'Thank you, I'll consider it', 'Thank you, I didn't realize that', 'Thanks, although I don't see it like it. Can you elaborate?' or — and here the true attention to detail and insight come to light — 'Thanks! By the way, how are you? Is your father still sick? I am sure it must be weighing on you!'

Being a truly committed Assistant means we *see* people. Receiving feedback is a perfect tool for us to actually know what's going on with the giver of that feedback and connect with them.

But let's not forget, sometimes the feedback is truly to the point when you mess up. I personally love to get it because that will save me time and trouble along the way. Always be grateful and welcoming while receiving feedback. It's a mindset, and if you can master it, you'll see that feedback is useful in so many ways!

Here is another great pointer from Sheryl Sandberg especially applicable when it comes to communicating feedback:

Communication works best when we combine appropriateness with authenticity. Finding that sweet spot where opinions are not brutally honest but delicately honest. Speaking truthfully without hurting feelings.

I always admire people who can tell you something upsetting or uncomfortable in a way that you definitely get the point, but no feelings are hurt. You are actually grateful for the info and motivated to do better or fix it right away. Now, that's the true art of feedback!

It's time to evaluate

Mutual sharing is absolutely the main ingredient of the way periodical evaluations should be performed. Pick a time, set a date and make sure you are not disturbed. It doesn't have to be an hour. If you do regular feedback sessions, 30 minutes should be more than enough. And remember to see the context, it's not always a straightforward personality attack (just make sure your timing is right!). It's about the job you have to do to make them effective and efficient. We always keep fine-tuning our way of working as we go along, it never stays the same. I suggest you make sure you are learning something new at least once a year to keep yourself challenged and/or help you excel. And it would be really insightful to ask your exec where he thinks you might be able to improve. If you decide to upgrade your skills, you might find some courses within your company or external training. It doesn't even have to be directly related to your profession or industry, something like a personal development or marketing course could also give you an amazing boost to perform better at your job. Keep your exec in the loop of your development, he will appreciate your efforts!

Here is a tip to make you look good — always come to an evaluation with something you have thought of improving. This shows you care enough to look for ways to grow.

The best way to stay connected to the required level of assistance is to frequently ask about the way your exec wants things to be done and offer alternatives where possible. Usually your exec has a clear view of how he wants the end results to be and the manner of execution. Maybe not the very specifics, but there is always a preference (just get it done ASAP is also a preference!). They might also have ideas on how to improve things, but due to lack of time they won't have had the chance to let you know. If you force the continuation of those talks, there will be nothing left for the official evaluation moments and your performance will easily meet or exceed the requested standards.

Evaluation in the other direction is just as important. Give your feedback when *you* have any. Don't wait until the big evaluation moment, as small things tend to get bigger over time.

When your appraisal is on the agenda, the last tone you want to take is one of criticism! We see our execs operate from a distance daily, so we notice what can be improved in a heartbeat. We keep an eye on them, checking their every move, the way they do things and the amount of time they spend doing them.

That's our job anyway, so why not use that as a tool to nurture your mutual relationship and make it easy for you and your exec to be more effective and efficient?

Caught up in stereotypes

Breaking free from the common stereotypes of Assisting Professionals might just be your way to shine and grow. The typical image of an

Assistant was as follows: secretaries sitting at a table next to the boss looking coiffured but slightly messy. Nowadays, we are required to be well-rounded, 360°-skilled professionals with managerial duties, matching what is needed in any field or company. In fact, we have evolved so much that I cannot think of any other professional field exhibiting such forceful advancement. No matter what we are called these days — we can do anything our execs ask of us! And if we cannot fix it, then we'll find somebody who will. Let's agree that that is a profession in its own right.

Extremes seem to dominate common perception. Why, after all this time, are we still perceived as those madly typing types or high heels running *The Devil Wears Prada* kinds of Assistants? What can we do to shake off that image? Well, movies like that don't really help, although in the end Andy (the main character) does become the 'perfect PA' we strive for: fully in control and capable of doing anything asked of her before it has even been requested. So why is there such a gap in describing our position? My response is: no agreed standards. Every PA position is different and unique in its own way (which is by the way a great thing about being a PA if you ask me). Some companies still need original quick typists. Some need that but with a sprinkle of office management. Some need all-inclusive EAs, and in some extremes, if possible, a body double. Which flavor are you?

I would say, let's exploit it to our advantage: we can be whoever we want to be! We can make our own way into the lives of our execs, as long as they see that our presence helps them to excel.

Just a quick note here. Stereotypes are not only applicable to PAs, but as much so to execs. After a while, we always know 'who' they are and in which box they fit.

Some types need special attention or a specific type of approach. Some are easy to get along with, approachable and open for discussion. Some need a very detailed manual to even consider a phone call. It's nothing impersonal, but it gives us tools for catering to their needs better and more efficiently. I would suggest you to try and identify your exec's 'type' ASAP so you can start looking for ways to assist as best as you can.

What's in the name?

Apparently everything! Here comes the tricky part of titles. Down to the core, we are *assisting* and that is the only thing that really matters! In my opinion it really shouldn't matter what's in front of it, but the reality is different. This topic of titles appears to be very touchy and people tend to get emotional about it. I found out that your title means more to you than to anyone else. So what does the title mean to you? Try to actually answer this one. It's good to know how the definition of your title affects you.

Nowadays, there are many variations when it comes to describing what we are and what we do. Our responsibilities vary enormously per company, industry or country. There are no definite guidelines for the 'title versus job descriptions' issue. It's not surprising that people who work with us lose track of what we should be called. Sometimes you can even negotiate to change your title if you can defend the feeling that it doesn't represent you well enough. Despite the fact that I understand the urge of an appealing title I would say, be easy about what you are called, the only important thing is *to be called* if they need something done!

What else is in the name? Our ego! The funny thing is that we don't work for our egos, instead we focus most of our waking hours on the egos of our execs. So why is it so important for us to be called by the 'right' title? You might say it impacts your salary, it reflects your abilities, or your position in the company. But if you won't deliver what is expected of you, no name will save you! Focus on your duties and responsibilities first and foremost.

Your satisfaction should not come from what they call you, but from the fact that eventually they can't do without you and appreciate and cherish you being there and getting things done.

There is a quote from the great Martin Luther King which I love, so I bent it a little to fit this very purpose:

I have a dream, that one day we will not be judged by the titles we have but for the content of our character (and I would add to it) *and our abilities.*

And if you are still bothered about your title — get over it! You're wasting precious time and energy…

The journey of an Assistant

What's the most significant change for us Assisting Professionals over time? Speed, it's all about speed! Way back when offices were without PCs, mobile phones or instant messaging, you had a very clear agenda, simple and straightforward ways to get things done, and the right knowledge to do so. Fast forward to the twenty-first century, which brings us ever-evolving IT devices and software and, as a result, a noticeable growth in terms of responsibility. Suddenly we have a huge amount of information to digest, and the need to summarize it in preferably less than an hour. The need to be flexible to accommodate everyone's needs and timetables, and to always be up to date with the latest international news and economic forecasts. And please don't forget to keep your integrity and be discreet at all times. Did I miss anything? Just put it on my to-do list for tomorrow!

Sounds familiar, right? I bet a lot of you are nodding right now while reminiscing about your day today. How come it is expected of Assistants to know everything about anything at any moment of the day? It's because we evolved with the speed of light. Being an Assistant requires a very specific type of human being. Yes, we are a super breed! The ever curious one, who craves to be of service and in control, who wants to go beyond 'good' and prove that it can be even better. Impossible is just another task on our list to deal with before lunch! In some miraculous ways, we made all this possible and doable. We brought it on ourselves. Let's stick to it and enjoy the ride. Let's admit it, we love it!

You want me to do what?

Making decisions on our own is an example of something that has been added to our list of duties. Our execs trust us to have a full overview of what is important to them and the company so we can make well-informed decisions on their behalf. The level of this responsibility will of course depend on the kind of relationship you have with your exec, your seniority and your past record. To be able to act quickly and thoroughly, you need to master the skill of decision making, make it your own, and find ways that work for you.

Find a way to make fast comparisons, evaluate possible outcomes while keeping in mind financial instructions.

All that has to be done in a limited time frame and your exec trusts you to do it on your own authority and within the boundaries he gave you. Do that job right consistently, and he will raise the bar. If you are proven to be successful at this over time, he will even ask your opinion on bigger issues or entrust you with some delicate matters, saving him time and trouble.

Don't we all want to be in that position? Again, it is an evolutionary skill. I see more and more often that we are given tasks that are of an executive nature and our execs expect them to be handled quickly and professionally. We also tend to become their body doubles: attending meetings on their behalf, handling certain issues and communicating with their teams. Of course this will differ per company, industry or country, but we cannot deny this trend. In the next century we will probably need to have our own Assistants. What should their title be?

Now back to the (wo)man in charge

Simple but true — the better you know your exec the easier your job will be. Whether you have worked with this person for over a decade, or are just starting, you always have your radar on. Observing is our way of being out there and knowing everything. Truth be told, a huge internal and external network truly helps us being up to date. But our own observations and intuition give us the magical advantage of being well informed and prepared on levels that you cannot ask of others. Add to that the ability to ask the right questions at the right moment, and you have the formula for success as an Assisting Professionals.

As mentioned previously, it might help you to define the stereotype profile your exec belongs to. This is not an exact science and it can vary from 'verbal super intelligent loner' to 'creative Sagittarius number 7' (enneagrams). It doesn't really matter how you categorize the qualities of your execs, as long as it is clear to you how to communicate effectively with them, understand their needs better and whether or not you can predict their (re)actions. We all get to know the bigger outlines of their character pretty quickly and putting that on paper, giving it a name, and being able to analyze it will give you a huge advantage in your role.

Later on I will outline a few techniques on how to make your own and your exec's profile (3What Plan) and how this can help both of you to perform efficiently, successfully and comfortably. One point here: human beings tend to change over time due to our experiences, choices and ambitions (and recently our economy). This means that our profiles change with us, and in some extreme situations they can differ per day or per month. Don't get stuck on them, just use them as a guideline and always listen to the voice of your better judgment.

No lookalikes

Adapting to your job is never easy and some of us need to do so on a regular basis. The latest statistics show that we don't stay in our jobs even half as long as the generation before us did. This is of course not only specific to the field of Assisting Professionals. The necessity to master the art of adapting your skillset is more widely applicable, and for several reasons. Not only do we change companies, but it is common to change to a different sector, a different culture, a different country, a different setting (from corporate to private assistance) or even multiple employers simultaneously. Unfortunately, due to the current economy a lot of us have had to downgrade, level down, split or combine responsibilities with other team members. In the end, it's still the diversity of our abilities that matters the most.

We are used to adapting to new situations quickly, learning new skills, and doing whatever it takes to deliver the required assistance. Especially now, in these difficult times, we need to grow because others will need us not only for the practicalities but for much needed moral support. Our humanity is our way to stay real and connected.

We see people, we see their struggles and are the ones they can talk to. We relate to people and make them shine. Do not forget this honorable PA quality and we need to remember to incorporate it into our daily activities. We all perform better if we feel understood and valued, so we need to make an effort to empower others when possible. And foremost, we need to start empowering ourselves and each other as an *Assisting Professionals tribe*. It feels good and it will create an obvious win-win-win situation (teams will perform better — your exec will be pleased to see results — you will have a happier person to deal with).

Culture beat

As if all the above is not enough, there is still one more important element of being a fast-moving Assistant: while changing jobs, always be aware of any cultural change. It might be a different population culture of a specific country, a different religion, or just a strong underlying internal company belief system. Every culture has its own rules, customs, habits and, most importantly, expectations. Where possible, try to figure out the specifics upfront. Otherwise be extremely observant, search through past publications /minutes of team meetings, Google, examine the intranet or find someone to trust (the HR department is usually a good place to start) and ask a lot of questions.

It is important here to be a good receiver of information and create a safe environment for people to come and talk to you. If you do not seem interested, or appear reluctant, people will stop talking. Although it can be very desirable sometimes to shut out others for a while so you have a minute to do your thing — this is not that moment!

Needless to say, you always need to be respectful and protective of the current culture you are working in. Like anything else, you have to own it and take responsibility for it! There are some exceptions to this rule where a certain culture makes you miserable and unhappy in your role. In that case it's best for both sides to part ways. More about that later in the book.

There is one more method to this madness. Companies, like the humans employed by them, do change! Be attentive to any cultural shifts within a company, especially after a takeover, a merger or a change of board members. During those periods there are a lot of silent movements, delicate transitions and tense people. Be aware, make your exec aware if they aren't already and be prepared to handle anything that comes up. Looking surprised is not a good place to be. It doesn't mean you will per definition end up in that position, but it's better to be prepared. This is applicable to any situation we may encounter, so see this as an extra situation in which to practice your PA poker face.

So many choices, so little focus

So here you are, in the middle of things to do and it hits you — you need help! It might be something you don't have the answer to, or you realize you miss a skill which you need in order to do your new responsibilities justice. You start looking on the internet for blogs, magazines, books or training and hope to find something that will fit your criteria and has the right unbiased content. This is something I experienced more than once while looking long and hard for much-needed guidance on how to grow as a PA and expand my capacity.

As a matter of fact, I grew in my career quickly, and began to assist more senior executives before I knew it. Suddenly I ended up working for complicated people, and was thrown into the deep end without a raft on more than one occasion. It wasn't so much the practicalities where I stumbled (there are enough answers on the internet about those topics). Instead, I found that I desperately needed grounded and trustworthy advice on how to train myself to be able to assist those people (think personal development).

An example of such growing pains is the conversations I got myself into, because they became more complex, politically charged and every word I said required my full attention. Sometimes I had very limited time to get a difficult message out, get the feedback, quickly process it, and then find any flaws to address... And all that before my exec rushed to the next meeting or sprinted off to the airport.

Also, delivering unpleasant news to others became my responsibility more and more often. Even cases of participating in high-level board meetings where I ended up being the in-between person (because of a language barrier). I had to get the message across, taking into account the cultural conceptions and differences, understanding different points of view and incorporating all that into a different language so my executives would get the answer to their question. High performance pressure, an extremely packed agenda, conflicting interests and large teams where the reasons I had to evolve myself to a totally new level as a professional. *I needed a new mindset*! I needed to gain a new set of skills which went way beyond planning meetings, producing reports and making travel arrangement.

What's your framework?

What I quickly found out, sadly, is that there is not much out there specifically for Assistants on even the most crucial topics. There is a lot out there for business professionals in general, but I think you'll agree with me that an Assisting Professional has a very specific vantage point, considering our job requires us to be involved in business and personal relationships at the same time. I decided to go with personal development books from the world's business leaders and other well-known authors. I had to start somewhere! As it turned out, I found a lot of my answers in the area of soft skills development. I was relieved I had something to start with and so my awareness grew stronger. I began to see patterns, connections, cause-effect workings and it made me so much more effective, confident and, surprisingly, faster!

Before I share with you my revelations and key stepping stones to become a deeply connected, grounded and effective Assisting Professional, let me get one thing off my chest. This might not be the answer to all your issues. All I can say is that it worked for me, and it made me a better PA in terms of both a business and personal understanding of the people I work for. It might all sound silly to you as these key soft skills are not the practical nor measurable items you can subject to a trial. Soft skills tend to scare people at first because they mean that your personality and inner workings are examined and might be declared not fit for duty. That is scary and we easily shoot to defend when this happens!

Not only that, you might be told to change something that has been within you your whole life and served you well. Or maybe it's something you are strongly opposed to. Please relax, the choice is always yours and you decide whether you accept something and give it a go or not. No pressure whatsoever! To be honest, every true-blood Assistant already has these qualities, they are not foreign concepts. Unfortunately, we don't see them as such. We don't nourish them to grow and get stronger. That specific deed of supporting your already existing soft skills is exactly what I would love to achieve here in this book. Where attention flows, results show!

You might not get why these untouchable qualities will bring you the excellence that I predict they will. We Assisting Professionals tend to be stubborn about our qualities. We need a certain degree of self-assurance to survive and stand out in the tough surroundings we work in. I even think that's a quality to cherish. Please understand that because of your stubbornness, you might close yourself off from a possibility to grow. By changing or tweaking your intentions and your mindset your practical abilities will prevail. Your mindset is a hidden multiplier of your (hard) skills!

If you recognize yourself in the above description (I'm well aware of the fact that my own stubbornness is a tough cookie sometimes), then the only thing I ask of you is this: keep an open mind while you read on and give it one single try. You won't get worse and it really doesn't take a lot of time or effort. It only works if you are sincere about it and you recognize the necessity to acquire tools to grow in order to elevate yourself professionally.

To support this process of inner strengthening and growth I will share with you lots of theories, psychoanalytic models and methods. Something interesting happens to our thoughts and actions once we understand how a system, any system, works. Like a light switch — once you get the 'how' and the 'why' of it, you feel a weird certainty about the steps to take, things to say and plans to make. Additionally, we automatically believe it might work for us.

And here is why: *it's been said that 80% of success is psychology and only 20% is mechanics*! What is psychology? It's the knowledge of our psyche, not the practical therapy. Bottom line, it's all about the 'knowing'! That explains a lot! So, no matter what keeps us from acting consciously and thoughtfully (time deficiency, stress, ignorance, patterns or routines), sometimes it's good to take a second and ask yourself: Why? How come? What for? Where does it come from? What triggers it? What can I do with it? Can I influence it differently?

Hold this thought while reading through the chapters of this book.

That being said, now we can start. Although we Assistants are very practical creatures, we would not survive a week without strong soft skills. It is, unfortunately, an undervalued side of our qualities. You see, this 'soft' subject is not tangible, nor reliable. It's all in our minds. It is fluid, changeable, it can be influenced by unconscious elements and it can flip 180 degrees in a second. I really appreciate the trend for *Emotional Intelligence* and *Emotional Intelligence 2.0* in the last decade. At least we all recognize its powers now. I even dare to speculate that it all started with Dale Carnegie's masterpiece *How to Win Friends and Influence People* way back in 1936.

On my journey, I defined six main core soft skills. They are powerful, profound, and have the power to transform the way you perform to a level that will make you the Assistant that fits all the criteria your employer could ever want or need. Implementing these skills and incorporating them into your mindset will change the way you go about your day. The quality of your assistance will match, level up and even exceed any expectations. You will become the Assistant they just *need* to have! You will have the tools to become *indispensable*!

This soft skillset is combined in a fast forward formula: W.A.N.T.E.D.!

WILLING. AVAILABLE. NICE. TENACIOUS. EFFECTIVE. DEDICATED.

Chapter 7. Willing State of Mind

Results you will achieve...

✓ *Collect and preserve information, control and get an overview*
✓ *Reinforced sense of unity in your team*
✓ *Earn goodwill and trust from others*
✓ *It will profoundly benefit the quality of your relationships*

Let's go!

Soft skills are residents of your mind. They are born, nurtured and sometimes invented right in the squishy grey jelly cells of your brain. They are implanted into your character and you internalize them to be your second nature, in some cases maybe even your first. Sometimes, you are consciously digging through them deciding which one to use at a particular moment, but usually they are just the result of a fine-tuned autopilot. A little undervalued, but definitely not underused! They are the reason we are human, loving, intuitive, and emotional. They are the reason we can experience passion, anger, hate, love, pain and joy. Nobody will ever admit it, but they are often the main reason why we excel or fail.

The W.A.N.T.E.D. skills are meant to create and sustain a certain mindset. Being aware of it empowers you to get in control and enables you to benefit from it, impact people around you and influence situations.

To make it easier for you to digest the information, I will build the following chapters in a similar manner so the various factors will be clear and comparable. We'll start with why a specific skillset is important, followed by an explanation of what it entails, reminding you what to look out for, and then close with explaining how mastering it will benefit you.

To me this is all about personal development, and I want to point out that although this development usually goes along a particular path, I realize that everything might not be applicable or relevant for you at this very moment. Therefore, just take away things that linger with you immediately, the things that appeal to you right away. Leave the rest to a later stage or completely ignore it. Remember, if you are not open to a change then nothing will happen. If resistance plagues you, just write down a short description of it in the end of this book (or anywhere else you prefer) and move on. It's a process, it's a journey and the only thing that matters is that it will benefit you. That is what I truly wish for you, as it profoundly changed my way of being an Assistant and better positioned me in my professional and personal life.

One note before we dive in to the first skill. All W.A.N.T.E.D. skills intersect with each other in some areas. They depend on and empower one another. None of them is a standalone. Mixing them creates the perfect potion. Every ingredient has special powers and ultimately they are all part of one single Assistant state of mind. Let's start cooking up that mindset. May the mind power be with you!

State of mind

Your state of mind at any given moment enables you to act in a certain way. That is why it is so important to get that right first. This is your blueprint, which, once set, you will follow unconsciously and unconditionally. It's like preset settings you follow blindly once operating in a certain mode, like in your job. In the coming chapters,

I will extensively explain the inner workings of your mind that you need to be familiar with in order to be in control of your life.

It's a good thing that we don't have to rethink and analyze everything we do in our daily lives, but it's also good to stand still once in a while and evaluate where you are and if it is what you wished or planned for. Defining and tweaking your mindset is the key here. When your mindset is clear and defined, you will follow it to the letter without questioning. It's your hidden powerhouse and we need to be aware of who's in charge. It's all about your beautiful mind. It's a supreme skill multiplier by default!

So what is the targeted state of mind of this first *Willing* soft skill? Your target is to be truly open-minded and fearless while conquering new territories: to have a burning desire to assist and make things better, to get things done fast, and exceed expectations. Nothing is too small or too big for you and you are up for a challenge. Being willing also means that you won't mind dreadful tasks once in a while. You don't step back when asked to do something that is not officially on your list of duties.

Being willing means you will get creative in situations where you feel stuck, and won't give up easily. It also means you are willing to support others besides your exec as you have a desire to be involved and be part of the team. You are willing to invest your time to get to know the business you are in, the people in it and the processes involved in the bigger picture. Ultimately, it is the soft skill of being extremely result-driven but in a beneficial and pleasant manner.

Godly goods

On my path of going through training, I heard a fabulous expression from a very talented personal development trainer. It stuck with me before I had even understood its meaning. The law of G.O.D.S.!

When I heard that G.O.D.S. stands for 'Go On Do Something', it planted some seeds in my mind. I realized that if I ever feel down, lost or lazy, taking action is the mother of all success and achievement, so *do* something! It's the energy flow that will push you forward and transform your desire into tangible and measurable results.

Let's make 'action' visual (hot tip — people tend to understand and grab information better if they can see a picture of it). Try to imagine a pool of standing water and you will see a dirty, mossy, smelly thing. Now imagine a fast-flowing river that ends in a cascading waterfall and you will see freshness and movement everywhere you look. The water itself, the plants below the surface, leaves free-riding the current, insects dancing on it and glistering fish going in all directions. And then the powerful suction just moments before the waterfall reveals its cascading greatness, followed by the grand finale of white bubblicious foam extravaganza. The explosion of freshness and air of accomplished greatness! This is followed by peace and the steady continuation towards the next challenge while regrouping and slowing down but moving ever forward. I have a fascination with waterfalls, so I will use them to illustrate a few situations to come. Surprisingly, they're a great metaphor for businesses and life itself.

Unfortunately, we all suffer from procrastination. Although its intensity and recurrence seem to change, it's unfortunately always present behind the scenes. It's human, don't worry, you're not alone. There are always situations we try to avoid, tasks that seem to take forever to finish, small things that look huge in a pile of lookalikes, a lack of time, or a weekend that is so close you can taste it.

I have to admit that I too have a blacklist of daunting things. When I'm in the right mood, not feeling exhausted and I'm sure nobody will bug me for at least 30 minutes — only then do I dare to take on the tasks of that list. You see, the main recipe to handling those tasks is to strike when your mind is at ease, so that you have the ability to see that they're just a part of your big amazing job and you know that you will feel very relieved once you cross a particular task off your list. As soon as you do, a new task will surely follow, but for now you are a hero to yourself. That is a version of a planned G.O.D.S. action that works for me!

Sometimes, just starting a task will make its hairy image disappear.

Sometimes you will need to make it even hairier and bigger to force yourself to get on with it. In principal — you need to know what triggers your *Willingness* to act. Is it the deadline, the sense of urgency or the size of the task ahead? Know your inner motivator and apply it wisely!

What also helps is to make a small laminated note for yourself listing why you love what you do (that is, being an Assistant) and why this is exactly where you want to be in life (your current position) and why this is exactly what you want to be doing right now (being able to do anything). For this to work it needs to be written in a happy and satisfied state of mind. Preferably right after you have celebrated something huge and preferably something business related. Having done that I suggest you store it somewhere safe. You don't want others to find it as they might think you are a nutjob by loving filing, typing endless emails and making PowerPoints all day long. Let's say that most people just don't get it!

So now, when you feel those villain agents of procrastination closing in on you and your mind is working overtime trying to think of a good reason not to do anything from your list of daunting tasks, do the following: (...think waterfall metaphor)

Prelude. Slowly drag yourself to get a nice and warm cup of coffee (or whatever your poison is), take that last cookie, get back to your desk, take a bite and try to buzz off for about ten seconds. That's your cooling down moment from your previous task.

Now you have to *regroup for action*. Miraculously pull out your boost card, read it, sip your coffee and imagine how relieved you will be after completing those planned tasks from your blacklist.

Preferably, add an image of yourself doing the Macarena to celebrate crossing that finish line. You can't help but smiling, right? You know it's an embarrassing sight and that no one but yourself should ever see that in motion! That's your energy flow getting up to speed. Feel that suction right before the cascade of craziness.

Now it's *time for action*. Snap out of it, and GO ON DO SOMETHING! Anything to get in motion, just do it! Works like a charm and it is usually not as bad as you imagined it to be. Next!

Houston, we have a volunteer!

Having a *Willing* mindset alone is of course not enough. For a mindset to be effective you need to follow through and create new habits. Repetition is the key ingredient here! The following three things are necessary to act on in order to anchor this new habit. Let people know you are willing to help out where needed, be proactive, and don't forget to consistently deliver on what you have agreed to take on.

I know, I know… you are probably swamped with things to do already and telling others you are willing to help out might lead to an insurmountable workload. The trick is to expand gradually, which will only happen if you approach this in a smart manner. I usually start by offering assistance to other peer Assistants first. It's good to have a backup, so I always try to be the first to offer one. The favor is usually returned and it's a great way to nurture those relationships. If my workload is still manageable I descend to the lower management levels, filtering out the ones who don't have Assistants and selecting the ones who report to my exec most frequently. Usually it will be managers from the operations, sales or finance departments.

One obvious but important point here! Before you do all that, I suggest you start off the hunting season by asking your exec whether he has any additional duties for you. As stated in the previous chapter, job profiles are usually standardized. Due to lack of time (and interest) execs don't do any due diligence, and therefore don't have any idea when you might have spare time (or capacity) to maybe take something off their plate.

Pick the right moment, like your regular feedback sessions, or a Friday afternoon. Then tell him that you are up to speed with your outstanding things to do (please avoid telling him that you have nothing to do). Next, inform him that you could create some room for more duties if that would relieve him from anything daunting. A smart thing here is to be prepared! You know what your exec is up to so you might have a few ideas of your own on how to lighten his burden. Share with him your ideas on how you think you can handle ABC, ask if he agrees, or maybe if he can suggest any other things that he is willing to drop in your lap. It's a brilliant move no matter the outcome. Now he knows you are willing, involved and interested in his business.

And let's not forget, telling people you are willing to help out once and never repeating that offer again might not work. In extreme cases, it can even be perceived as a mere courtesy. When this happens, you are no longer guaranteed any bonus points. If you see people struggling with tight deadlines and you have a spare minute, be sure to jump in on this window of opportunity and offer to help out.

Most of the time others will not ask you to do anything because they know your position is bound to your exec. But here is a hidden magic trick! Sometimes even a single offer of a helping hand can speed up the process. This is what happens (again, let's picture it!). When you get offered help you are immediately forced to assess the situation. Often, by taking a step back to look at what can be done by someone else nothing appears to be that undoable and it becomes clear that you are almost there. So you thank the person for the offer of help and get on with your work feeling strangely empowered. This is how you speed up any process just by talking about it. It's a win-win, give it a try!

In case they do accept your helping hand, you have to hold your end of that bargain and be punctual and consistent. Your image is on the line now.

Offering a helping hand is tremendously good for your reputation, your in-depth understanding of the business, results, team building and trust. I strongly suggest that you engage in at least one extra curriculum-assisting job a month, and don't forget that repetition is the key.

You're in too deep

As a result of running to the rescue when help is needed, you'll find yourself in a very interesting place. A place called 'you may ask any questions'! If you get the importance of this part, you will have no problem being truly involved in any business or area of your choice. Normally, you meet others while getting much needed coffee or you bump into them while chasing that blue file your exec lost for the seventh time this morning. Being there you might ask things like 'How are you? How was your weekend? Any luck with that client?' and I'm pretty sure the answers will be short and polite. But if you are helping somebody with a deadline, a horrendously time-consuming task or delivering the completed task your chances of getting real answers just grew tenfold. People tend to be more sincere, open and willing to talk to you when you have done them a favor. Now, please don't get me wrong — it's not the reason why you help out! I only found out about this hidden truth from experience, helping anybody who crossed my desk.

This is a sure and honest way to build relationships too. Assistants are always very attentive to building, nurturing and sustaining durable and beneficial relationships. There are many ways to reach that sweet spot, and this is just one of them. You should be able to master a few techniques yourself, and it's good to be aware of the existence of all of the different ways of getting into people's circle of trust. Everyone has their own manual and their own equations through which they calculate whether they can trust you. Also, this is proven to be a good way to get to super-busy professionals who normally won't have a single second to slow down and truly engage in heartfelt chitchat.

As you can imagine, being able to ask real questions and getting honest answers gives you the opportunity to acquire a lot of information. Information that gives you explanations, and a deeper understanding, because it reveals the origin of ideas, issues, complications and achievements. Personally, I love being on the receiving end of that information exchange.

My life theory is as follows: I can only live once, my way, in my head, with my experiences, understanding, beliefs, convictions and truths. If you really think about it, it's pretty limiting. And believe me, it's more than enough most of the time. However, on some occasions I enjoy being invited into other worlds of perceptions, different areas of focus, surprising vantage points and fascinating thinking patterns. I sincerely recommend you to really listen to people around you from a neutral, observant and specifically non-judgmental position. You will be pleasantly surprised how much more there is out there. There are 6 billion lives to explore...

Now let's get back to the work environment. Being truly interested and asking questions is very important. We all know that. Be respectful if people don't respond to you with the honesty you expect. There might be something beneath the surface, some uncomfortable feelings (you are still a PA to their exec) or they might just not like you that much. Don't get offended, that's life! Just be very appreciative if you do get the interaction you are seeking. Be grateful for the information you get. No matter what that is, it will make you a better Assistant. This is only one of your tools for building relationships. And the great thing about it is that it's as valuable as a bottle of cool water in the attention-starved desert that we call our community in this day and age.

In plain sight

Yes, it's all about relationships when it comes to the true power of an Assistant. If you already understand the profound essence of this truth, and especially if you have already managed to master this skill, then you don't need to read any further. Everything that follows will come down to the manner of building and maintaining your relationships. Whether it's with your exec, your colleagues, your family and friends, strangers on the street, suppliers, receptionists, a grocery clerk or fancy restaurateur, cab driver or 'hard to get' stylist, hotel cleaning lady or president of the union, your partner, your goldfish and, let's not forget, yourself! It's all about the quality of every last relationship! The only way of prevailing in this area is to master your soft skillset. For those who will close this book in a second here's my last piece of advice: stay true to yourself! If you are still with me, you will love the next PA quality I'm about to dig in to.

For the brave souls out there, here it goes: one of the most undervalued skills of Assistants is fulfilling the role of a shrink. I told you it's a good one! Nobody will ever admit it's what so good about their Assistant, but I have had loads of experiences where my execs just needed somebody to talk to. I truly think it's one of the most valuable things you can achieve while being someone's Assistant. If your exec is comfortable enough with you that he can talk freely (and yes, there is a limit to that goodness) you can congratulate yourself for being in that position. That mental support is very important and very undervalued. Don't get any funny ideas for your next job review, this is not a negotiation point for a raise!

I keep coming back to the importance of trust and I believe that at this point, once your exec is at ease and talking freely with you, you have the ultimate proof that the trust is there! Savor this, be proud of this accomplishment, and be very protective of it. This is not something to gloat about to your colleagues or friends. This is between you two, and it's definitely under the protection of privacy and confidentiality codes of conduct.

And the next stop is...

Next in the process is the ability to think ahead while taking into consideration everything you know. Do you see things coming together? I'm sure everybody will agree that thinking ahead is one of the essential components of an Assistant's basic skillset. However, I do want to make a distinction here: there is logical thinking ahead, and then there is emotional thinking ahead.

The logical part is straightforward. When you are planning, you always work backwards, recalculating every step and any requirements needed to get to the end result fast, easily and efficiently.

Of course you need to incorporate any specific needs of the people involved, and try to foresee anything that can go wrong in the process, preparing solutions for the problems that have not even occurred yet. Nothing new here!

Very important: it is always a good idea to be prepared for anything that could happen along the way. In fact, sometimes it's not as much the things you need to prepare for upfront, it's the information you need to have at hand in case they happen! I once heard a story from a PA who always prepared two traveling routes for her exec because he was a magnet for 'bad stuff' happening along the way. Things happen, you need to know what to do when they happen. Don't be surprised, be prepared!

Now let's see what emotional thinking ahead means. Actually, I can be quick about it: it's all about a vantage point — try to envision yourself being in someone's shoes executing the itinerary you have prepared or implementing the agenda you so carefully constructed and planned. Try to remember to switch positions especially when the bleep hits the fan. We often assume others can be collected and cool while acting on our instructions over a bad phone connection, or remain peaceful and graceful while being in a room full of infuriated suits. No, it doesn't work like that unfortunately. There is a saying that fits perfectly: '*Difficult times don't form a character, they show its true nature.*' Oh so true! So make sure you know the character you have to deal with.

You also need to know if there is anything special going on. The good, the bad and the uncomfortable. For example, is he celebrating an anniversary or a birthday? He may not be fully into a day of intense meetings then. Or maybe he is coming down with a cold, or had a fight with his neighbor, maybe he is stressed out about a doctor's appointment the following week. On the flip side, if the financial audit was just finalized, he will probably be able to relax a bit.

Whatever the situation, Assistants might be perceived as machines that operate on 100% capacity the whole time, but in reality, that is also something we have in common with our execs (although obviously on a different level with a significant extra burden of responsibility). We respond to our context, whether consciously or subconsciously. No matter the circumstances, we need to make our exec look 100%! Therefore it's good to know his overall emotional state, because it's our job to make it look like he is in optimal shape, prepared, and attentive, no matter what.

Next to being considerate of the inner workings of your exec, there are tons of people around you and they all have that complicated thing called feelings. Here is where the quality of your relationships can come in handy: Assistants do have the power to plan things around those tricky areas of mixed, hurt, vulnerable, exploding, confused or damaged feelings. It's good to know when people are in conflict so you won't seat them at the same table for a four-hour gala dinner. Or maybe it's a good idea to reschedule the yearly review with the CFO to next week so he can mourn the loss of a tennis match to your CEO. A manager's sick child might influence the timing of his report, a lavish company party on Sunday can turn a team meeting on Monday morning into a less effective get-together. I can go on forever, but you get the point!

Sometimes executives are inconsiderate of those internal circumstances as their focus is always on results and business attitude. In some cases they are right, sometimes you need to explain your reasoning, and sometimes it's up to you to make that judgment call. It's not always simple. The burden of integrity is not an easy thing to deal with. I'm not advocating that you please everybody all the time. Just be considerate where you see fit. I'm sure you will find your ways of making it work — Assistants always do, it's supernatural!

Return on investment

One of the key ingredients of implementing the *Willing* skill into your routine is being willing to invest: specifically, to be willing to invest time and attention, and to do that regularly. Assistants are master planners, so plan some time for small projects, reports you intend to read through, or lunch with selected colleagues. Maybe you need to schedule time to visit a department of your company where you have never been before, or get a box of cream bagels for the mailroom and, this might sound weird to some, call your exec's partner for a chat.

I found it both interesting and rewarding to talk to the partners of my execs. The cold hard truth is that you probably know more about your exec and his doings than their partners. If this is the case, they will most likely benefit more than you think from your call! Sometimes it's just asking how their vacation was. Sometimes it's a 'Congratulations!' on their kid's birthday. And sometimes it's a really heartwarming chat about what they are up to. In almost all cases, it's a forgotten relationship, and it's good to pay some attention to it. Those time investments usually pay off, as you will often receive information that will help you to be a better Assistant and to have a better understanding of your exec's nature. Women love to talk, no surprise there!

Please note that I don't insist on you being friends! I have even assisted execs who specifically asked me not to be in touch with their partners. When this happens, it's important not to argue.

Attention does not only concern people. Attention to detail is extremely important, no secret there. And no, it's not an automated skill. You need to train yourself to switch your view to smaller elements and then back to the bigger picture – back and forth. This needs to be your core value and it has to be executed regularly, quickly, and in a timely manner. Preferably, you need to do so consciously. Only then will you be able to claim you have mastered this skill.

Another option for investing your attention is to make every effort to stay up-to-date about your company's doings and whereabouts. Read the newsletters and go to open feedback sessions. Talk to people on the sales side to know what the future looks like. Talk to people on the production side to know the present. Dig through old archives to know the past. Industry news might be very insightful to read, but be careful not to lose yourself in the huge amount of information and terminology. Remember — it's about gathering small details to see the bigger picture!

Life is an ever-moving stream, things are changing and so does your company. Invest your time and attention and it will inspire you, motivate you and give you a deeper understanding of processes, interdependencies and relationships. You never know what might be useful one day! Be aware though — you might like what you find so much you will want more...

A surprising benefit of knowing your company inside and out is that talking about it will often motivate and inspire others. I have a little system that works like a charm: I select a few things from the current business developments that I think are particularly interesting. Then, after I clear with my exec what I'm allowed to talk about (you want to be certain of what you can and cannot discuss), I introduce the hot topics into my chitchats with colleagues.

You see, not everybody reads company news as people are usually swamped with work. Nowadays people are too focused on their own few square feet of the business empire they call their cubicle. They simply don't have time or space in their overstuffed brains to nose around and be informed of where the company is actually heading. Being a cheerleader for the exciting developments to come I often find it really motivates and cheers people up. It's like a disease and you want it to spread fast!

Being attentive also means you carefully scan the environment you are in and you do so consciously. Again, we tend to get trapped in our own little worlds so it's something you need to train yourself to take on. Being attentive pays off, trust me. Picking up a vibe and acting on it can prevent misunderstandings and release pressure. And if you are really good, you can create a certain vibe that will benefit your cause. There is so much more to being an Assistant. We really need to get a grip on the power we hold.

Now, it might all sound very overwhelming. All the elements we have to pay attention to and the required investment of time. You might even call me crazy: 'Don't you get it that I need a second brain for my current things before even thinking about all this and preferably a third set of grey matter preparing for next week?'

Yes, I get it! I'm in there with you! So here is a magic trick that makes it all very doable and easy — all you need is to care, really truly care! If you care about something, your attention automatically flows in the right direction, and your actions are smoothly coordinated with your intentions to benefit the subject of your care. You need to love and care about where you are, what you do and the people you work with. If you love doing something the execution comes naturally, just give it a hand by realizing its impact.

Not yet

Here is a topic which, again, won't be new or refreshing, but it remains extremely urgent. I simply need to catch your mindset on this one: trust me, I am trying to make you look good!

It's about the importance of actively learning new things, especially when it comes to electronics! We have all had talks with our execs going something like this: 'Hey, I have heard of this new app and it's supposed to be fantastic. I have my notes right here from the last few days and apparently you can make beautiful reports with this app and systemize them in a snap. Do you know this app? Can you set it up for me?' And of course you try not to look panicked. Inevitably, based on the speed at which things are changing, your exec will request a new app or software every other month. As soon as you become familiar with one, he will immediately find something even more appealing in his app store next week. So, the answer I would encourage you to give is: '*Not yet!*' And off you go! Don't worry, your effort will show on your scorecard somewhere along the way.

By now, it's kind of standard and accepted to work online with 1001 apps and software programs, so most assistants have to be pretty IT savvy . But there is a constant flow of new technology, and there is no way we can be up to date with all of it. How do you keep up? I often feel overwhelmed by new technologies, especially if I work for multiple execs with different preferences (which means I have to be good at three times the number of apps). Luckily, most of them are still 'old-fashioned' and a simple paper notebook is still a very respected and appreciated tool!

So yes, you need to get familiar with the software your exec is using. Let's face it, if he gets stuck, he'll call you! How you will get the answers to his issue is not his problem. You better have people on speed dial who know software better than their mothers. And no, you don't have to know everything out there, unless of course it's the area of your company's expertise.

Education 101

If you are really *Willing* to be involved and acquire relevant knowledge, then being able to actively learn new things fast is a prerequisite. You have to be a quick learner in our 24/7 and 100-miles-an-hour society. Here is a way to be good at this.

First of all, if you want to learn a new thing fast and be good at it yesterday you have to practice this skill extensively.

The good thing is that quick learning is something you can train. The best way to practice that skill is to regularly learn something completely alien to your interests. It's like flexing a muscle you just discover you have had all your life!

You will see that you will actually develop your own system to adapt to this skill of quick learning: the more you read, study or practice new 'alien' stuff, the quicker you will adapt.

Start by making a list of small subjects you may not currently know anything about (like greeting rituals in Japan or the Norwegian health care system, the inner workings of an electric car or the energy-saving system of LED lamps, for example). Now try to Google and learn as much as you can in 30 minutes. Try to do that at least once a month.

You see, when you don't have any affiliation with the topic of your study you will work very systematically to find the needed information. You will develop a measuring system to test whether what you found is current, applicable and sufficient enough.

When you become good at that, then finding information on a subject you are interested in won't be a problem. Your search will be targeted, fast and you will actually remember everything you read. A great thing about discovering alien territory is that it can also be a source of amazing new ideas and fabulous insights for you to implement in your daily doings or current projects. It's a very cool process!

Brain science for dummies

For those info-maniacs out there, here is the mental theory on how learning and the creation of habits are managed in your brain: you can apply it to everything you want to master, and you will understand why everything needs upkeep, especially your new habits and skills.

First of all, it's not entirely true that we only use 10% of our brain. This fable originates from the number of thinking cells in our brain. Only 10% of the whole mass represents the thinking ability, the rest of your brain (the remaining 90%) contains crucial fluids and connectors. The clue to learning and developing new habits lies in the creation and quality of those connectors between the thinking cells. The more connectors, and the thicker they are, the better the skill and the force of our memory.

By learning something new, you will establish new interconnections between your thinking cells and therefore your memory. The more often you think about a new topic, the better those interconnections will become and the faster you will able to access the stored knowledge. The less often you think of them the thinner they will become. It's not necessarily a case of the connections disappearing altogether, but they will become so thin, it will be hard to access the desired information. Et voila! The neuro secret of being smart!

Be aware, your brain is lazy — it won't maintain the existing connections by itself. You actively need to do the upkeep regularly. Physical repetition is even better for anchoring memories and makes the interconnections grow stronger. That's why they say that practice makes perfect. Your brain preferably surfs only the bigger connections, so size does matter here and it's even of crucial importance!

Now you know you have the power to control the most extraordinary and still relatively unknown matter in this whole universe — your untouchable mind and your safely protected brain! This is complicated science made simple, so don't pin me down on details. For more on this subject I suggest you read the book *Brain Rules* written by the developmental molecular biologist Dr. John J. Medina. He is a true genius when it comes to explaining our grey matter in plain language.

There are also cool YouTube summary videos of his books. Highly recommended!

The last thing I would like to add on the willingness to improve is to ask advice from other people, preferably ones you adore, admire and respect. If you have a mentor, you are truly blessed! Otherwise just step out of your comfort zone and bluntly ask anybody for advice on anything that bothers you. As mentioned earlier, we tend to get stuck in our own ways of thinking and sometimes we end up running around in loops. A fresh perspective can really elevate your way of thinking instantaneously.

And the great thing is that most people will gladly empty their reservoir of good advice for you without even blinking. It's an ego-boosting thing (for them)! Always thank the person giving you the advice or feedback. Suck it all up, and filter the information later when you have a second of me time. The latter is important, as we usually need time to process new information: it tends to only start making sense (or not) after a while. Don't dismiss anything right away, there is a reason why you haven't had that thought on your own. It may even be that an alternative version of that contradicting thought will bring you the answer you seek. Your mind works in mysterious ways! Give it some time to digest and if it really doesn't fit you, then move to the next thought in line. I bet there is a huge line waiting to be served.

Your wish is my command

A great quality of something can simultaneously be a bad thing, don't you agree? That twilight subject is definitely the variety of chores for Assistants. The level of superiority, sense of urgency, range of time investment, extremes of personal vs business focus — you name it. Usually I love this part of being an Assistant. The dynamic is refreshing, at times even exciting and it keeps you sharp and focused.

Welcome into my brain: OK, let me finish this board meeting PowerPoint. Then I have to run to get cat food and order some extra markers. Then I'll have an hour to do some Google research on that public speaker who will be in town next month. Oh, and I have to remember to file the paperwork for my exec's travel visa before 4pm. And I absolutely have to call the driver for an early pickup to the airport tomorrow before I confirm reservations to the opera. And shoot — for when was that HR meeting scheduled, the one where I promised to take notes?!

The sense of accomplishment is incredible! Brian Tracy, the personal and business development guru, says that 'The Act of Accomplishment' is one of most powerful emotions of human behavior. And hallelujah — he is right about that one!

There is one big but. Sometimes (frequently) there are things that you don't really want to do as they are 'below' your level of authority. Or it's too personal, too complicated, too time-consuming or whatever — there are just too many toos. This is where the true nature of a great Assistant will prove itself. I'm not judging, but if it's within the borders of your self-respect and dignity, you just do it. No ifs, ands, or buts.

This is what potentially makes us *indispensable*: your willingness to step up and fix anything. This can make you that Assistant they *need*. It's the reassurance that you will be there for them whenever they need you. The fact that you will make everything 'fine and dandy', no matter what needs to be done. It's exactly that willingness that will elevate your value — it's the end result that usually counts. If you are the one that can make something possible (against all odds), then those 'little' and uncomfortable things might just make you indispensable.

Here is one tip if you really have a hard time digesting doing something uncomfortable — often nobody sees you doing it! And usually you don't even have to tell someone what you have to do to get it done. If that's the case, then relax, get it over with and do something glamorous and inspiring next. It's all in your mind and you have control over it. Use this ability wisely and you will excel.

Caution! Bumpy road ahead

A note of caution here: if those 'little' things make your workload unbearable and you can't remember when you had your last meal or sleep, then there are two things you can do: delegate or delegate! You need to be in top condition to fulfill your role, and where possible exceed expectations (we will get to this later and I will urge you to get yourself in that top condition). Any bump in that road will have a direct impact on your exec. You need to be aware of it and he needs to be aware of it, or at least the possible origin of it.

Make your overload known and discuss it (remember that timing is everything). Please don't just complain! Describe the situation, make it obvious it's not working for you while doing everything possible to fix it and come up with solutions (yes, multiple) so your exec can make a quick choice. Knowing you and your capacity well, I assume he will agree with you and you will find a good way out. If not, and I unfortunately have some firsthand experience here, then it's up to you to decide whether this is the way you want to move forward. No hard feelings, but if it's killing you softly then nobody will benefit. Remember — your wellbeing is important.

Also, be aware of the repetition and amplitude of uncomfortable tasks. One thing once in a while might be acceptable, but if you continuously have to deal with situations that freak you out, rethink your strategy. It's rarely worth all the trouble, be good to yourself!

We all have certain personal boundaries, and while it's important to be flexible and allow some to stretch more than others, it's even more important to maintain these boundaries at all costs. Be clear to yourself and to others about what's acceptable to you and what your limits are. These boundaries differ per person. If there is anything tough and uncomfortable that is essential to the job then there will always be somebody else who won't mind doing it. It sounds very obvious, but once caught up in the moment you might not notice the struggle. I do have to confess that even when you do find a way to establish clear boundaries, they tend to stretch overtime when you rub against them for too long. The good thing is that life will kick you if you go too far! But let's try to not end up in that position...

Relax, I'm not talking about absurd things you might hear stories about on TV (yes, those are usually from celebrity PAs). It can be something like cleaning up after a pet's chronic diarrhea emergencies, doing laundry, ordering specific personal services/groceries, being available daily from 5am when you're not a morning person, accompanying your exec on business trips twice a week while being the mother of demanding twins etc. It can also be something like accepting strong language, shouting, disrespectful behavior, people forever forgetting to inform you about a change of plans, ignorance or even dealing with uncommon/violent behavior. No, it's not OK! You don't have to do anything remotely that uncomfortable over and over again. Inevitably, you will hate that part of your job. It might overshadow the great job you have in a bigger sense and that would be a pity.

Always stay professional and respectful to others but especially to yourself! It can get tough and there are ways to deal with some things. Like we talked about before, sometimes your exec is not aware of the impact something has on you or others. That kind of talk is absolutely from the category 'difficult conversations', but it is a very necessary one. It often helps to understand that most things like that will be based on unintended and unconscious behavioral patterns. It will benefit your relationship if you resolve those matters through talks and cooperation.

If none of your approaches help the situation and you find yourself stuck, then the answer should be obvious. I cannot urge you enough: be clear to yourself on what is acceptable to you and be good to yourself! Even the current economy should not be a factor for you to stay in a place you don't like. I understand the implications, but the damage to your person will have a way bigger impact on your future without you even knowing it.

And the verdict is...

Although there is way more depth to the *Willing* skill, and therefore much more I could say, I will let your imagination take over now. And it's not even about all the practicalities I tried to describe above, those are merely illustrations of the outcome. Try to focus on your state of mind while being *Willing* — you will instantaneously feel a difference in your point of view, a certain urge to sprint into action and discover a newfound love for what you do.

As a conclusion to this chapter I would like to point out that there are major results waiting for you if you implement the *Willing* mindset, I guarantee you!

Being an Assistant, there are always two main areas of concern: yours and your exec's perception vs reality. Thinking about it, it can surely be applied to any relationship arena. Let's start with the good stuff for you:

First of all, being *Willing* to become a deeply committed partner to your company on multiple levels — personally, emotionally and practically — will provide you with a clear overview. This overview will make your job a lot easier. It will give you time to prepare and act accordingly. It will give you opportunity to find your own way of being a part of it in a considered fashion and you won't feel rushed into situations or events. You will own your spot and everything around it. Believe me, once you are there, you'll recognize that comfy feeling I'm talking about. It will become your kingdom!

In addition to being in control of your environment, you will also be much more productive. This is where the fulfillment will encourage you to keep on moving. The amazing sense of accomplishment will make you super attentive and content with yourself and the people around you. This will contribute to the unity I always strive to reinforce in the companies I work for. You will be empowered to be the glue of the teams which is quite an extraordinary feeling. Things will happen smoothly and successfully, with you being the secret driving force behind the machinery. And it is not for you to blow your own horn, because the power lies in staying 'secret'. Only a skillful Assistant knows which underwater currents need to be adjusted to get people to face the same direction and get everybody to do their thing at the right time and pace. I bet all of you have at least one example of difficult situations that turned out successful as a result of a lot of 'secret' tweaking on your part. It's a feeling only we know exists!

Now let's see what the effect of all this will be on your exec. Believe it or not, especially your emotional intelligence will create the most goodwill for you. It's about knowing when and how to approach people and situations. It's about being able to adjust the manner of execution according to any demands. The level of your commitment will set your exec at ease in trusting you to be on top of everything. Needless to say, it will benefit your relationship in a profound way.

The verdict:

**Mastering the skill of *Willingness*
will enable you and your exec to excel
by reaching more goals and being a better team together!**

Take-away notes

 ACT

✓ Remember the law of G.O.D.S.: 'Go On Do Something' when you feel stuck
✓ Invest your time and attention consciously on preset topics
✓ Be truly interested, ask real questions and really L.I.S.T.E.N.
✓ Really truly care about your job, your exec and your company
✓ Practice fast learning and repetition of new skills

 BE

✓ Be open-minded and willing by choice
✓ Be clear about your boundaries
✓ Be personal, non-judgmental and respectful to others and yourself
✓ Be good to yourself!
✓ Be aware that you can influence teamwork and
good atmosphere in the office

 THINK

✓ Practice 'ε.........' thinking ahead
✓ Keep in mind that helping others is a branding and
positioning tool for you
✓ Envision a waterfall to energize before attacking
blacklist tasks or anything daunting
✓ Use the power of your mindset to create the blue
print that will guide your actions
✓ Create new 'thinking' patterns and habits by
consistent practicing, enforce interconnections

Chapter 8. Available State of Mind

Results you will achieve...

✓ *Get more fulfillment out of your daily duties*
✓ *Realize the need for your services and qualities*
✓ *Advocate and pioneer your superpower for ultimate positioning*
✓ *Become a valued go-to person*
✓ *Create an informed helicopter view*

To understand the true meaning of the skill of having an *Available* state of mind we need to dig deeper into the origin of having Assistants. Nowadays it's a mere commodity. When you reach a certain executive or wealth level you just get an Assistant. But let's go back in the process, why should you have an Assistant? What was the purpose of creating that position?

The whole existence of our profession was born out of necessity. Executives wanted somebody else to run the practicalities of their lives so they would be freed up to do the actual management. They wanted to live easier lives and let the Assistants take care of time-consuming and daunting tasks the execs didn't like to do anyway.

This is important to understand — an Assistant is a necessity! Being there for others because they need us is the essence of our profession. To be there, available to perform tasks and duties to free up others. To be there when support is needed. This is a core value of being an Assistant. So there is no point in getting annoyed the next time your exec calls you late at night because there is a semi emergency consisting of checking the details of his travel schedule for the next day for the third time, although he can find this information in at least four different ways and versions (written, printed, in his phone agenda and on his tablet summary).

He needs you to remind him because he trusts you to tell him everything the right way and in his language saving him the time and effort of looking it up. He needs your availability and so you need to provide it! Even so, if you are a top PA you will be able to predict his conduct and have the necessary things ready with you at all times. Especially the day before a packed day as he might call you to verify something or to make last minute changes. It's all part of the game.

It's true that most people don't see it this way. To understand the reasoning behind this behavior you need to have a true service-minded personality. It makes perfect sense to us! Let's look at it in black and white: if he doesn't need you to remind him about those details, if he would love to make his own travel arrangements and if it wouldn't be a problem for him to do his own check-in in the middle of the night to get the best seat, then he doesn't need you and you won't have a job!

I hear a lot of you protesting right now that there are norms and standards, legal regulations and stipulated working hours, signed contracts and role descriptions. Yes, there is all that. But if you want to be a *needed* Assistant you will see all of that as mere guidelines. If your exec needs you in the middle of the night because his car broke down on his way back from a family dinner, no questions asked you will assist him in getting home safely and arranging someone to tow away the car. It's what we do, because we are their PERSONAL ASSISTANTS! We are called that for a reason.

Of course not every Assistant has to deal with these kinds of situations, being on standby 24/7 and luckily most of us have pretty normal 9 to 5 jobs. I just want to emphasize the profound truth: to be great you need to be available — by design!

Superwoman

Here is a cool fact, no two Assistants are the same! Everyone is special, everyone has their own super strength. See it as an X-Men community among the Assistants. What is your super power? What is it that you are absolutely the best at? I actually would like you to answer this one, it's not a rhetorical question. It's good for self-evaluation, but the main reason I want you to define this answer for yourself is because it's your ultimate marketing tool! My what? Yes, you heard me correctly.

Every Assistant should have their own marketable quality, something that makes you special. And of course we all have similar strengths, but the level of their superiority is different. Can you deal with difficult people well? Are you the PowerPoint expert? Are your language skills so extremely good that you can take minutes in six languages and flawlessly translate them on the spot? Are you a happy single which means you can travel around the world with your exec without causing issues at home? Can you handle tough male-dominated working environments? Are you so detail-oriented that the whole office is sending you documents for proofreading? There are limitless opportunities for Assistants to shine. What is your star quality?

Once you have defined that you need to become your own sales team and make the most of it. Sometimes it will lead to leaving the position of being someone's Assistant behind and becoming a professional in that certain area of expertise. I know that in the US this is a standard way of professional growth. You choose a 'mentor' in a certain profession whom you want to emulate and apply to be his/her Assistant. Through the experience, hard work and good examples you will end up where you want to be. Great, more power to you! It's not always like this, but it's a common way of ascending the business ladder.

In the rest of the world, and please don't shoot the messenger, being an Assistant is a chosen profession. There is no end goal upfront or any wanting to take the place of your executive. Make sure you know exactly where you stand. Clarity is important here, because it defines your 'marketing' strategy.

I'm here

Advocating your super power does not specifically mean that you're aiming for a promotion. It is focused on letting others know what you are good at so you can be of super assistance to them in those areas. This is a sure way to position yourself and earn some karma cookies! It's also important for task accumulation and distribution. And it is especially useful in teams with multiple Assistants. Clarity on what is expected of you is very liberating, wouldn't you agree? And things you're good at are done way faster, better and easier! That's why pointing out your strengths is good for work optimization.

Every company strives for teams with various areas of expertise so everything will be done at the highest standard possible. Why shouldn't we do the same?! That's why it's important to know what your super power is. Also, when you look for jobs and market yourself, you better end up doing a lot of what you're good at. It makes your life more pleasant and it makes you way more successful.

In addition, it is also important to know the things you are not good at. You can train yourself to become good at them if it's something crucial. Otherwise find ways to delegate or outsource such things if it's within your means. And it doesn't even have to be to another person. In these times you have an amazing number of apps and software programs that can help you out, just dig around.

One last piece of advice here. If you shout from the rooftops that you're good at something, you better have a track record to prove it! The times when you could make your resume look nicer than it actually should are over. You will be challenged on everything stated on your resume. You need to be professional and make it worth their while. Let's face it, if you get an assignment which is supposedly in your area of expertise demanding a result ASAP, you will have a painful problem delivering it. You will make it hard for yourself. You'll start walking on eggshells and that would not be beneficial for anybody involved.

In the end, it's your responsibility to get things done. Take that responsibility and own it. It's the sense of accomplishment that will make you flourish. And life is a funny thing, when you focus on certain things, you will get them. So focus on your strengths and you will end up doing more of what you are good at. How great is that?

On this topic, the next publication in this *New Generation Assistants series* (volume 2) will be all about personal positioning, resume profiling and your awesomeness branding. So stay tuned for every nitty-gritty detail you need to know about marketing yourself flawlessly and effectively. You will get a step-by-step plan from me on how to position yourself, create an undeniable brand and make it work hard for you. It will make you confident, proud and indispensable within your area of personal and business excellence!

So now what?

OK, you know your super power and it feels good. Now if you do not use it, you lose it. Not in the physical sense, but you forfeit your advantage if you don't advocate this strength in your working environment. Here is a crash course in how to make sure you represent your strengths so that they can actually get you somewhere.

First, make a list of tasks and duties within your company or department where you can implement your super skills. Try to be creative here if nothing really pops up but the obvious. Let's say that you are a super duper minute taker. The obvious tasks would be attending department meetings and quickly delivering well-edited reports. Never stop at one solution or a problem (a very effective lesson from business guru Brian Tracy)! Always ask yourself what else can go wrong, what else can be a solution and what else can be done. This way you can come up with chairing some meetings or taking charge of some points on the agenda, for example. You could also ask if other departments without a direct administrative assistance need minutes taken of their meetings etc.

This is a sure way of getting noticed! Your name will be featured on way more documents and you will get to know a lot more about the environment you work in, which can be incredibly motivating. Seeing the bigger picture is a very cool tool for an Assistant. It will make you look involved and people will see you as somebody who is dedicated.

They might even ask you for some advice or insight. You never know how you can connect the dots by knowing the logistics of different departments. It can actually be very useful and informative for your exec too.

Let's see how creative thinking can get you noticed by your superiors for a second. We'll use the same 'minute-taking' super power. I would think of something like sitting in on conference calls, offering to take minutes at out-of-office meetings, making a library of minutes and tagging similar subjects to make a timeline and log long-term developments. Try to see if you can make 'minutes' into an interactive conversation. You can come up with a design which will make the team actually want to read the minutes. The sad fact is that minutes are largely made as a reminder, but they can be a starting point for something new. You can become the queen of topics and the center of the conversation. But only if you desire that position of course...

Once upon a list

Moving on. Now you have a list with tasks that involves the practical translation of your super power. The reason you actually need a list instead of having those ideas in your head is that you will remember them way better once actually written down on paper. You need to be able to act quickly if somebody comes up with an emergency or a problem where your skills might come in handy. You will be able to shout out the magic words: 'I can do that!' Or you could think quickly about a similar version of what is needed that is closely related to your super power and be of help.

Everybody remembers a savior and it's very cool to actually be one! And yes, Assistants fulfill the role of savior a lot. Unfortunately, it's usually behind closed doors (nobody needs to know that your exec spilled coffee on his tie for the third time this week). Coming to the rescue might be a great confidence booster if you can actually do it 'in public'. You need to be prepared to blow your own horn. I know it's difficult for some Assistants as that is just not our thing. But admit it, we are humans too and we want some admiration once in a while.

Your availability in a crisis situation is always important — it strengthens your position. We are usually very good at finding solutions by attracting exterior elements to solve problems. But if we can show that we can solve stuff on our own by using our own qualities it makes us look even better! Serve yourself by serving others!

Let me also mention the less obvious way of cultivating your super power. If you are not comfortable with showing off your strengths, or at least not yet, start working on building a track record by doing small things and testing the ground. You are good at that particular something anyway! Looking for new ways of implementing your super power will make you feel good. Do it for yourself, it will make you glow a little and in the end, others will notice. By practicing it over time you will build a reputation and people will start finding their way to you.

Whatever you do, choose the way that fits your personality. Any skill can be made very cool, useful and available to others. Tailor your super powers to fit your exec — that will make you a needed Assistant. Also, by seeing how creative you can be, he might ask you for some advice from time to time in cases where there is no straightforward solution at hand.

That, I must admit, is a very special moment. The first time it happened to me it really caught me off guard. I actually asked him: 'Do you really expect an answer from me? Yes, looking back I know it was not a smart thing to say, but he knew I saw it as a huge compliment. We actually came to a very surprising solution together by talking about it. Things like that make your connection so much stronger! Don't get too cocky though, because it might never happen again if you do.

Lights, camera, shortcuts

Here is a very direct way of being *Available*. Assistants are usually not very present in the office environment. They follow directions, run around with countless reports, answer endless phone calls (did you ever experience times when people seemed to line up on the other side of the line and call a few seconds apart from each other, for hours in a row?), firefight through lunch breaks, battle through afternoons of meetings and try to catch their breath during dinner organizing stuff for tomorrow. Now you might say: 'How more available do you want me to get?!' True, it's not something you have to do or want to pursue on a daily basis. We all have enough stuff to do anyway and there is even more stuff to be achieved if you dare to look in that closet in the back of the room.

So here are some shortcuts to being available without sacrificing too much time. First of all, try to answer questions for information when asked — in real time. Personally, I used to write questions down in hectic times. The downside of that is that at the end of the day I had a huge extra to-do list I really didn't want to have. The thing is, it's not the time to look up the answers but it's the time it takes to communicate it back to the person that makes it so time consuming. If it takes you 20 seconds to look up the answer then you can just shout it back to whoever asked and move on with your day. If you do it afterwards you have to look up a phone number and have a conversation or type out an email — either way it takes much more time and effort.

Immediate answers only work if the questions are short, and they usually are. It will require some 'switch-tasking', but it will pay off in the end. So, answer short incoming questions immediately if possible. Set a time frame of one minute to deal with a question, if it takes more like five minutes then do a quick prequalifying scan to see whether you actually have those five minutes to spare right now. If you do, go for it. Anything longer than five minutes will have to wait and go onto that extra to-do list. That same procedure with a slight variation applies to acting on requests. If there is a specific action required on your part and its quick, then do it straight away.

By the way, the official productivity rule of the renowned David Allen (in his book *Getting Things Done)* dictates two-minute tasks for quick actions. But the thing is, we can way easier predict the timeframes of one-minute and five-minute periods without looking at the watch. And if something like this happens better automatically — it will work even better when applied on purpose!

The third way of actively showing your availability is asking for 'detail' feedback. Yes, it's a tricky one but asking for feedback on a given task will definitely show you being available. It's actually quite simple, if you ask for more detailed feedback ('Can you explain what you mean by this exactly?') it means you have cleared time for that person to work on his or her request. I have frequent situations where my exec mentions something on the run that he would want me to do or get something done by others in a 'but it's not urgent so just have a look at it if you have time' kind of context.

Now, if he knows me well he will know that A. I will not have a spare minute in the coming six months and B. I will find time if this non-urgent thing becomes urgent (as often happens the next day). By definition, it goes on my to-do list and will stay there until it's done and can be crossed off. It's true that some tasks were mentioned a while ago or maybe in a hurry. It's up to you to ask for feedback on some details in order to complete a task or to verify that it is still outstanding and actual. If you bring something up, it means you are on it. A very obvious and effective tool to show people you are engaged.

Those points above are really the quick wins when it comes to showing you are there for others. The actual execution of them will show your worthiness and will make you look good. It's a win-win!

Of course there is this old-fashioned way of just asking if you can be of help with something. I have this habit of always asking my exec if there is anything else I can do for him before I go home — always!

And there were times when I really regretted asking that. When the office is getting quiet after 7pm, they suddenly have the time and space to think about everything that still needs to be done before tomorrow morning or even that same evening. But exactly that, asking for something else, is a very important part of being *Available.* Do realize that you might get unwanted things on your hands and the chances of that happening are pretty big! That brings us to the next point...

Danger, danger — here comes a whole load of work!

If you successfully advocate your qualities and your availability to help out you will most definitely become a victim of your own success. Meaning, you will have a lot to do! Here is where you will be tested, because it's an absolute no-go to complain about your workload now. You will need to buckle up, plan your heart out and get on with it. Keep in mind that this will make you a better Assistant.

You will be more involved in different projects and departments. You will understand your company better. You will understand your exec better. You will know why and how he is running the business and most of all, you'll be able to stay on top of developments and actually be part of them. Personally, I love being in the middle of it all! It makes my mundane tasks a lot more bearable at times when I actually start counting how many cups of coffee people at those banking meetings consume and I Google negative effects of too much caffeine at 10am on a Friday. You know what I mean...

There is another aspect which you should be aware of if you decide to put yourself out there — you have to switch to on-mode in a snap. In hectic times that is not difficult to accomplish, that is, when you operate in a sort of 'twilight' mode. Your hands are completing one task, your feet are running to the next office and your head is calculating time left to finish your list before your exec rushes off to the next meeting. And then there is this weird sixth sense that controls and tracks the whole area around you. You are super conscious about everything that happens in your proximity and you are actually multitasking — that thing they say it's impossible to do. Well, we know it is possible because we do that at least once a day!

There are also times when you are in the safety of a few hours alone or few days without your exec in the office. Then we enjoy the well-deserved 'normal' pace of the work and it takes us a moment to physically switch our attention to the person who has apparently been standing next to us for the last minute or so. These moments are pretty important! If you are visibly not as sharp with other people as with your exec, it may tint their impression of you. Or imagine this, times when your exec magically appeared back in the office earlier because his meeting ended 35 minutes earlier than planned. You don't want him to see you slightly out of it. Although it does happen (we are humans after all) you don't want that to happen frequently.

To snap back into on-mode here is a neat little trick: try to summarize the stuff you did hear or repeat the question. This will give you time to think and the other person will most definitely repeat the information. In case you're really in a state of slow motion (and it's OK to be there too) tell them that you want to help them but you are really in the middle of something and ask them to email you about it or come back later.

'No' is a perfectly good answer

Now, let's talk about saying no. There are three kinds of nos. No, you can't help them. No, you don't have time. No, you don't want to help them. The first two are alright to handle, just make sure you give alternatives if possible. The third one is tricky but does happen and you need to be good at communicating it well.

You see, some people are very good at exploiting Assistants. We all know those types and every office has them. Some of them are really sleek and find ways to say it's on behalf of your exec (while you most definitely know it's not). If it's not too much of a burden or if it's the first time, just be the bigger person and do it. It creates goodwill! If it really reeks of misuse try to make a joke about it. Something like: 'If you want me to be your Assistant just double my pay and I'll move under your command.'

I actually had to use this 'financial overpayment' method by offering the 'sneaky' person 20 Euros to do the task themselves — he got the message and never came back again. But I'll admit it won't work with everybody. In serious cases of intimidation (like: 'If I won't get it by noon your exec will hear about it.') you can always suggest discussing the tight time frame with your exec first. In case your exec confirms the urgency of this new matter and insists on you taking care of it right away you will gladly help out. It's perfectly professional and polite. And in case your sensors were right about their wrongful intentions - you can guess how this will play out...

It's also OK to say no if you are really squeezed, just be honest about it. And if that is not an option then I suggest you ask your own fallback resources to help you out. In a company with several Assistants it shouldn't be an issue. If you are alone then you just have to learn to say no once in a while. Sometimes it's difficult for us to say no, it's not in our nature. Start by practicing this 'art of saying no' with little things. Practice how you say it and whether it helps to give an alternative. Sometimes things are really not doable, there is a limit to us too!

Timing is everything

An Assistant knows that timing is everything. We manage time, we spend time, we save time, we win time, we stall time, mostly we hate the lack of it and the pace of it, we lose time, we buy time, we cheat time and yes, we even invent time. I know that time management experts will start lecturing me on how all of that is not possible. Well, they haven't been a 24/7 PA so they don't have a solid ground to stand on when it comes to this one! For the purpose of this topic I want to mention a few situations where specific time elements are of the essence.

Let's start with the obvious. If you agree to do something and there is an agreed time frame, you have to play by the rules and deliver. Don't act differently in different situations, whether it's for your own exec or somebody from his management team or another Assistant. Your integrity and punctuality are important here and these are simple situations that can have huge impact on your image.

The second situation is when you get a request during your off time. Now, this usually comes from your exec and rarely from anybody else. Here is where I differ from others. I know there are a lot of PAs like me and I don't say that acting differently is by any means not good. In my experience, if my exec calls me, or reaches out to me otherwise, in my time off then there's got to be a good reason for it. Usually, it's not really urgent but simply a continuation of him being on the job 24/7 too.

I always hear out the request or call back. Whenever needed I complete the task or act on the request (I'm on it anyway so I can easily spend another few minutes). If it is possible to postpone taking action I will inform my exec of that decision. Again, your availability is the reason you have a job in the first place. I tend to be available 24/7 and sometimes it makes all the difference. Even more so, I encourage my exec to call me or let me know of anything that can remotely be considered my duty the moment it comes up in his head. That can potentially save me actual time and resources, depending on the situation. And sometimes, just leaving it on your plate will bring him peace of mind! Also (a really powerful productivity trick), by knowing what I will have to do in a while will prepare me unconsciously so when I decide it's time to act I will have a plan ready. Now, that gives me peace of mind!

Nowadays, while assisting multiple crazy busy entrepreneurs I urge them to call, email, text, WhatsApp, Skype or whatever else possible communication wise. And preferably as soon as they think of something. The reason is this (as David Allen says): your mind is meant for creating ideas, not for holding them! Your mind is not designed as a storage facility and my execs need that precious real estate in their heads for more important stuff than to-dos and things to remember. Another reason for their speedy communication is the fact that the info at the beginning of the thought process is usually the most correct and pure. It gives me a better insight into what they need me to do.

That is why I'm assisting them, so they can bug me anytime they want. Remember that in the end it's up to you whether you act on something now or later. And it's important to keep in mind that your exec reaches out to you because he trusts and counts on you. This is a very touchy topic as some Assistants will insist on not being available from the time they leave the office. In my opinion, if you want to be needed, then you just have to be flexible about this issue.

I can be very quick about times of emergencies — no question, you have to be available! Sometimes there won't be much you can do personally to ease the situation, but there might be a lot of organizing to do or just hearing out the trouble (yes, shrink duty is sometimes the answer).

There is nothing really remarkably different to these situations: get the facts, act on them, and get it fixed!

Try not to use these occurrences as a way to remind your exec of your value. You were available at a crazy hour, trust me, he will remember that! Also, don't always expect a grand gesture as a thank you. Some will see being on call as part of your job description and won't even thank you. Don't be sad about it, know when to walk away if this 'total absence of any gratitude whatsoever' continues and bugs you too much.

Call yourself lucky if your exec is grateful for your time and effort. But also know that the closer they get to the top, the more difficult it is to say 'thank you' for some reason. And especially saying it loud and clear. It's great when execs do say 'thank you' a lot. They know the power their 'thank you' carries. The fact is, some execs might see that as a sign of weakness. It's a well-known phenomenon.

You'll know when a short and quick 'thank you' is sincere. I've worked for some amazing execs who never really said 'thank you'. But when they did, oh boy, I knew it was very special and from the bottom of their heart. I have also worked for execs who sent flowers and really showed their gratefulness in obvious ways. And the truth is, both are equally special and fulfilling!

Window dressing

Here are more things you can do that will make you look good. It's all about having the answers before you even get the questions. You can copy/paste this whenever assisting anybody, but it works best within your own responsibilities. The only thing is that it will require some prep time and detailed knowledge about upcoming situations. Logically, there are four things you can do that will set you apart and make you look involved, dedicated, skillful and, for lack of a better word, useful.

First of all, when you do research for a business trip, a new project or any other topic that requires extensive Google time and multiple phone calls, make sure you write everything that seems remotely useful down. Also, make sure you keep this information for an extensive period after the event, project or occurrence. The times that my execs came back to me months after a business trip asking if I remembered the hotel manager's name, alternative dates for that venue or that other desk I found while redecorating his office are countless. And keep your notes well organized as well, because looking through a massive stash of post-its in the presence of your impatient exec is not good for your ego.

Include different flows of events in your prep work so you can plan for different outcomes. You have time to look for options and alternatives now, whereas you won't have much time and peace in your head when bleep hits the fan and you have to come up with an alternative on the spot. It won't be needed much of the time but (if it's not too much trouble) try to come up with at least one divergent situation while accommodating the usual preferences and ways of your exec.

Some call it planning ahead, others call it Plan B. I call it divergent research! Simply because usual planning does not include my exec changing his mind to dining at an exclusive restaurant in London with a party of eight on a weekend night. Or him deciding to catch an earlier flight home to catch his son's soccer game. Or needing a new shirt because the person he will be negotiating with has the exact same one. Or forgetting his passport in a hotel lobby for the second time this month. You just never know when you need a friend in the Russian embassy who's willing to come in at 3am on a Sunday to get you an emergency visa so your exec can pass customs without experiencing interrogation methods he would most definitely remember forever!

The next thing might seem obvious, but it saved me huge amount of time on more than a few occasions. Knowing my exec's preferences I print everything, even if he says that he'll have internet access to look it up when needed. For example, every time my exec would travel I would write, paint, highlight, draw, mark, arrow and circle everything he might need around his hotel or meeting location on a printed map. In case he would need something I know he would call me anyways, but then I would only have to point out that it's there on the printout (circled, marked yellow and with B on top). He would track it down while on the line with me. At some point, he knew to look for the printout in this travel pack and he didn't even bother to call me. So cool to experience that your artistic qualities are being used well! Oh yes, hell broke loose the one time I forgot to put it in his itinerary pack because he had been on that trip a dozen times before. We are truly creatures of habit!

And then there is this. Some execs will not comply or answer you, but it's always good to ask how the trip/meeting/vacation/dinner etc. went shortly after the event. Don't wait too long! In some cases asking for feedback on Tuesday afternoon about something that took place on Monday morning is too long after the fact — too many things have happened since then.

You'll know when you've hit that 'belated' bullseye. You will notice that by asking for feedback you are stalling his thought process and he might get frustrated and ignore you. (By the way: some execs would rather ignore you then engage in a conversation where they need to be politically correct. No biggie, just know what it means and move on). You know him and his schedule best, so show your interest in outcomes once in a while when the timing is right. In most cases that feedback is a huge source of intel. Not only the hard data but the vibe, the subtleties and the little details might be crucial for the way you will act from there onwards and the things you will have to consider in the future.

Here is a funny fact I discovered by conducting these 'shortly-after' feedback sessions. Often, things my execs state as their longtime preference or the preferred way of doing things don't work out. Not a biggie to me, but most execs would not admit it on their own. At least not right after it occurred. In the end, they asked for it and you made it happen. The sneaky trick is that you can easily make it less uncomfortable for them to tell you about 'things gone wrong' right after they happen by adding this sentence: 'OK, too bad. So how do you want it next time?'

If you wait a while or don't bother to ask at all, it will bite and haunt you next time you have to work with that preference. Imagine you don't know that it's not working anymore and the next time you act in that old preferred way or book the same preferred hotel he asks you to change it last minute, remembering how it went last time. That will cause unneeded stress for both of you. Actually, even more for you because you will question yourself if you missed something the last time and so on. So, ask for feedback in a timely way!

Personal loopholes

All of the above were external factors that can help you look more in control of a situation. Now let's see which internal tools you have to make it easier for yourself. Face it, it's you who have to deal with anything that comes along, so please don't forget to make things easy for yourself where possible.

Just as I have a habit of asking my exec if there is anything else I can do for him before heading home, I also frequently ask what the plans are for the near future. Here is the paradox: we usually have the most up-close-and-personal relationship with our execs, but company development wise we are often only involved in processes last minute. And everything last minute is more time sensitive, urgent and stressful.

By knowing what's coming, you can prepare better. Being up to speed will make times where your involvement is needed ASAP much smoother and communication more efficient and accurate. Less explaining, more doing! So, ask once every few weeks if there is anything planned for the upcoming month or so that you need to be aware of. Yes, you usually know the big plans, but most of the time the planning itself says nothing about the amount of work it might generate for you an hour before the meeting. Better 'early' save, than 'later' stressed and sorry!

Before I state the next point, here is my confession about something that tends to make my life more difficult than it needs to be. Please excuse me, as I'm not good at 'walking my talk' on this one: you don't have to know everything and do everything right away and by yourself!

This is actually the advice that I hear regularly from more seasoned Assistants when I share my worries or they catch me in the act. There is this very wise senior EA that taught me a great deal about delegating and saying no.

I do understand the meaning of it and I hope you do too. But on some level, it's against my beliefs of how a truly excellent PA should be. Maybe it's my (relatively young) age and I do really look forward to the times when I can ease up a bit. For now, try to apply it when you feel overwhelmed. It will force you to rethink your current ways of action and give you a different perspective. If something is really bugging me and I'm running out of time, I ask myself three things:

A. Is this really that important and urgent? What caused me to deal with it to begin with and can't it wait until tomorrow?

You will be surprised how often we wander off on a path that leads nowhere, usually related to petty issues, costing you your precious evening time off. The answers will be way closer to you in the morning when you are fresh and recharged, when other people are on duty to answer the phone and get you the winning answer.

B. Who can help me to get it fixed and won't mind doing so?

That last addition saved me from a few embarrassing moments. Try to find somebody who is not involved in the same situation or stands a bit further from your ideal support troops.

C. Would it be my problem if I hadn't heard about it through the hallway system (aka gossip)?

Sometimes that info is supportive and grants a subtle solution to a problem. Sometimes it causes more damage than good. I have experienced both variations in multiple forms. It's your judgment call!

The answers to these questions do ease the trouble and help me to get through things quickly and without too much pain. Sometimes there's an obvious solution that we can only see from a distance. And the moment you question status quo, you create that magical distance. Voila! The last element to consider is the different ways of communication. Apart from different communication styles, which is an important and extensive subject, you have to keep in mind that communication tools might alter the information and the message in the process.

As a professional PA you have to get to know the communication style of your executive as one of the first things you do. It makes a lot of things more effective and definitely more efficient.

While doing that don't forget to find out how your exec prefers to communicate, specific time frames, whether to use abbreviations, phone over email, full text or bullet points, print outs or post-its... Even things like before or after lunch, 30 minutes or five minutes before a meeting, right before/after or during a vacation. We all have a specific manual, get to know the communication manual of your exec by heart ASAP! And if you are in doubt about something, ask to confirm it. It's for his benefit so he better cooperate.

You are approaching your limit

I'm sure that by now the facts and the theory of being and acting *Available* to your exec and his close team are obvious to most of you. But we all have limitations and, although not everybody is willing to accept them, it's largely up to you to guard and protect your 'Yes sir, of course sir, right away sir' zone. This is where senior Assistants are very good and I keep telling myself that they learned it the hard way. So let's cover three exceptional situations where you just have to say no to something that is asked of you in addition to your daily and agreed tasks:

'Too much' area

This is where you literally could not add another thought in your head without wanting to jump head first into the Grand Canyon. And yes, sometimes we do exactly that and still on our way down we manage to make a few phone calls confirming dinner reservations and order new printer cartridges as your freshly ordered supply seems to have vanished yesterday in the middle of a huge printing job, as always.

You could make a 'limited' to-do list for your regular things and anything that comes as extra will have to go on your list for the next month. Or this one, which works even better — I have a 'maybe' to-do list! That is a list of things I haven't promised or confirmed to be due on a specific date. I only look at it if I have a spare minute or whenever I do a 'spring cleanup' of my to-dos (there are also a 'Thank god it's Christmas' cleanup, a 'Where did summer go' cleanup and a 'Whoa it's cold outside' cleanup somewhere near the end of October).

My 'maybe' to-do list is actually very nice because those tasks are usually kind of exciting but very extensive. And it's not because of their nature but because it would be very cool if I would be able to do that and still manage everything else on my 'limited' list. So, when you are really stretched on time and energy and something new comes along you have a few options of how to decline:

- ✓ Say no nicely: 'Sorry, I would really want to help you out on this one but I absolutely don't have a free second for the next three weeks.'

- ✓ Offer a long term solution: 'If you want I can give you a call/remind you in a few weeks to see if it's still outstanding.'

- ✓ Whenever possible offer to help look for other ways of getting something done, by someone else preferably!

'No thank you' area

This might not apply to every Assistant but what I have experienced is that we are asked a lot to join new projects, internal/external communities (so we can do the organizational part of it) or even brainstorming HR sessions. Now, being involved in HR-related projects is always good, but to a reasonable extent. Again, make it easy and manageable for yourself! If you can estimate the time needed for participating, and you can see it won't work, then just don't do it.
Here are your options:

- ✓ Say no nicely, don't forget to thank them for thinking of you and ask them to keep you updated (only if you are actually interested in that project).

✓ If you cannot estimate the proposed time investment right away then ask them to come back on this later. Maybe ask for some additional information and what will be expected of you including a list of clear deliverables.

✓ If you are really interested in that project but simply don't see how you can be a beneficial contributor with only five minutes to spare every day (which you can put to better use by taking longer 'meditation' bathroom breaks) ask if you can be involved in a satellite position. Maybe something like commenting on meeting minutes or coming up with suggestions during the run of updates. Usually there will be something you can do to be a 'mini' part of it.

'Eager beaver' area

The third area is not that simple to explain. It can be very politically and culturally sensitive. On its own it should say enough: it's the area of 'don't appear to be too eager'. For some reason people don't like others who are jumping on every request and are always available. Maybe it reminds them of their own reserved state of mind. Anyway, people seem to view it as suspicious.

We live in a strange world where doing good without wanting anything in return is not always appreciated or valued. Keep that in mind and find your own ways of accepting new requests. Of course it differs whether the new requests come from your own exec or others.

Here is a simple something I say a lot which is kind of in the middle of being too eager and too dismissing: 'I'll put it on my list. When do you want it to be done? I'll let you know what is possible.' Works well for yourself and others!

And the verdict is...

Being *Available* is a crucial skill for Assistants to master! It's not only for the benefit of the people we work for since, most importantly, we need to make it fit with our own personalities. Even here there is an element of inner qualities. It has to be already within you and it works better if you have chosen this profession to be the one you want to excel in. Some elements can be learned, but the drive behind it has to come from within.

One of the most significant results of you being there when you are needed is building trust and accountability. Again, trust is hugely important but it's a slippery creature. Even having missed one tiny time of not being there for your exec might scratch the surface of your carefully constructed trust masterpiece. Be aware of it, but not too aware. Remember that you are a human being with needs too and you physically can't comply with every need and situation. We certainly try and I do believe true Assistants are superhuman in that sense — we go a long way to do our jobs well! Be proud of it!

This skill also shows the quality of your involvement, which is secretly one of the most important indictors our execs are looking for in their staff. I've heard more than once that someone got the job or was saved from reorganizational cutoffs because he/she was very committed and involved in the company. The reason why this is so hugely important is because this skill makes us work harder, work more passionately and put in more effort towards the targeted goals. It's that inner drive that makes companies great. It shines through to the outside world and makes companies human, attractive and successful.

Another less obvious reason to cultivate this skill is to use it to explore the ways things are happening around you, the various ways people think and do things in the company. If somebody asks you to help out there is a certain trust-elevated sense of a comfort zone. I love it! Sometimes it's your chance to get closer to something unknown. Something new and possibly something very exciting. People often surprise me during project times like this. That's why I love to help out — it brings people together, makes teams stronger and that all benefits the company as a whole.

And let's not forget that sometimes the fact that somebody asks you to do something is because that person believes in your ability to actually complete that task to the necessary standards. It's a huge compliment we tend to overlook. It's an extra opportunity for you to grow, get boosted by the accomplishment and flourish by the 'thank you' you'll get by delivering the task to satisfaction. See — it's all about how you perceive things. It's up to you to make things great and worthwhile!

Now here is how this will affect your exec. I already mentioned trust — if he can trust you to be there for him when he needs you it will give him a certain peace of mind which is very valuable. It releases him from taking time to think about logistics and practicalities. On some level, execs will always think about that kind of stuff and maybe even give you a hard time, reminding you not to forget something.

Even a high-ranking CEO can be very tenacious when it comes to certain small details, which is really funny to experience. Actually, that signals to me that this specific situation is really important to him and I better make it spotless! If all goes well, you'll earn yourself some more karma trust points. If you do deliver excellence constantly you might even get cut some slack if something goes wrong occasionally. And trust me, it will! This kind of trust is a strong supporter of your relationship and will give you the benefit of the doubt in the long run.

Also, this skill of being *Available* hugely supports the skill of being *Willing*. Remember – they are all tied together in your beautiful PA mindset!

The verdict:

**Mastering the skill of *Availability*
will enable you and your exec to excel by being more
productive in terms of time, speed and resources!**

Take-away notes

 ACT

✓ *In everything you do, act from the mindset of a service-minded professional*
✓ *Get clarity on what you are really good at, try to delegate the rest to others*
✓ *Create a shortlist of things you are good at including practical applications*
✓ *Ask for more (duties, tasks, problems to solve)*
✓ *Do have a 'limited' to-do list and a 'maybe' to-do list*

 BE

✓ *Be personal while assisting, your service is intended for*
one specific person at a time, always!
✓ *Being Available is the reason we have a profession*
✓ *Be prepared to work hard to earn the position of a go-to person*
✓ *Don't complain about the workload*
✓ *Find ways to deal with workload or solutions to shrink it*
✓ *Be on the lookout for projects to join, it's a true team builder*

 THINK

✓ *Remember: having you as an Assistant is a necessity!*
✓ *Never stop thinking about creative possibilities: how can I improve,*
get more done, foresee what's coming, prepare
better, make people more comfortable?
✓ *Have prepared statements in your head when you want to say no*
✓ *Remember to motivate your exec to communicate*
with you as often as possible.
✓ *If he reaches out to you it's because they trust you and count on you*
✓ *Remember to make it manageable for yourself,*
it's you who has to do the job!

Chapter 9. Nice State of Mind

Results you will achieve:

✓ *Be perceived as a successful professional*
✓ *Effortlessly show your sincere respect*
✓ *Make your relationships better and make them work in your favor*
✓ *Become effective at conflict solving in a gentle way*
✓ *Become confident as a byproduct*

Being *Nice* is a very controversial quality. Soft skills are often under-valued as they are not something that will directly result in a raise. It is, however, one of the most important core qualities an Assistant possesses! I don't mean airy-fairy *Nice* as that will indeed not get you any serious credit. Maybe it's better to rephrase it as polite, kind, considerate, cooperative, calming and welcoming. It's the thought behind the action that counts. It's the mindset behind the gesture. How you deal with difficult situations. How you are perceived in an unguarded moment.

The thing that bothers me a lot is that due to our hectic schedules we forget to take the effort to be all that. Why is it that this quality is becoming a rarity? Why cannot being *Nice* go together with highly professional, result oriented and extremely driven? Is it the image of those harsh business professionals in the media that makes it impossible for the two to coexist?

Here is a funny but oh-so-true fact. There was a huge study on successful people and what makes them that way. One of the questions was: 'How would you describe a successful person?' And the most given answer was: 'Nice!'

Wait a second... what just happened?!

It sometimes surprises me how different a person becomes when you take the first step by being truly nice and considerate. Almost in a snap the vibe changes, conversation flows smoothly and the will to cooperate increases instantaneously. Sometimes a cup of coffee can change things around if delivered with attention and sincere politeness. I think it's all about a hidden respect element or even a glimpse of recognition. We all know that the worst thing you can do to any individual is to ignore them or disregard their presence. We human beings value our existence, we flourish if people remember our names and especially if anything else personal can be recalled.

Funny how we tend to consciously stay in the moment when someone is truly kind to us. It's like waking up from a fussy dream. How crazy is it that there are millions of YouTube videos about kind and selfless deeds? And that they always feature subscripts along the lines of we need to remind ourselves to be like that, let's not forget what it's all about, where did the personal attention go?

Assistants meet a lot of people, we speak to even more and we have to deal nonstop with social events and occurrences. We are the professionals that are expected to be focused on others so let's not disappoint them! But be aware, if it's not sincere, people will smell it in a split second. It's like a gas leak. Once you smell it you think it stays there for a while, even if you are in a totally different time and space.

It's a well-known fact that we only need three to four seconds to form an opinion about someone. Every second counts. One extraordinary thing I noticed in every job is that men trust their gut feeling even more than women. They will not make a show of it, but won't deny it either. It's a tool we use a lot, whether it's during decision making or just a coffee date — it's always there.

The beauty within

I admit that it comes easier to some of us as I truly believe it is a character feature. Luckily, it usually goes hand in hand with service-minded qualities which Assisting Professionals largely and abundantly possess. I never actually met anyone who didn't have it, although some have it deeply hidden under lots of layers and usually there is a very good reason for that.

I would also state that you can learn to be nice but you do have to be strongly motivated to cultivate it and be good at it. The right motivation will make you shine and excelerate if you consciously choose to behave that way. It's like a light switch that you can turn on. It's a mindset that you can control. One of the things that enables you to have that control is your willingness to be professional. Because let's face it, being professional always goes hand in hand with manners. And most manners are based on politeness, which is a sure form of being nice.

Let me tell you what being nice means to me. First of all, it's a real emotion and you just feel it in your bones: it comes with ease. If someone is truly a kind and considerate person it's radiating for miles. It's the attractive circle that you so want to be a part of and stay in for a while to be pampered. As I said, nowadays we just don't have the time to take a moment and be in that 'nice' state. So when you do come into contact with such a pure emotion, you notice it and you pause in that moment to enjoy it.

There are certain people who just ooze ease the higher they rise on the corporate ladder. It's those execs who are very approachable and you can actually tell about your weekend because it feels right and easy. For some reason, being nice and showing that you care are bound together. And if you care you also respect the other. And so the circle of personal greatness is complete! That's the thing: this quality makes it easy to be around those people. I so admire these individuals!

There is something about the togetherness of their character that takes nothing away from being respected and honored professionally.

Furthermore, those execs are usually very strict on agreed deliverables and you better comply with what is expected. And it's in no way in a negative sense. You just want to work harder for those people. Funny that the common perception of a boss is the total opposite, that harshness makes people comply.

Yes, it does, but the results and vibes in those offices are way different. So what does being nice mean to you? Answer that question and you will see it will motivate you to act more like it!

Use it wisely

Here are a few reasons why we should pay more attention to this 'underdog' soft skill. The obvious one is the fact that it supports cooperation. Even more so, lasting cooperation. It implies that you have to express your pleasantness and sincerity in the future as well and not only in the first few moments of a current emergency where you need the other person to help you out. I know it sounds very pedantic, but it frequently bugs me. Some people totally ignore and even forget you when they meet you for the second time when there are no catastrophes that they need you to deal with. It says a lot, but all the wrong things.

Then there is the result that derives from being nice, the grand ripple effect! It spreads around you like a disease you desperately want to catch. It breeds ease, a certain atmosphere that relaxes and strengthens everybody within this sacred circle. Enough said — you get my point, being nice is not rocket science after all.

When things are so simple and obvious there is always a catch, and here it is overdoing it. We all know those people who try to be extremely nice but for some reason we know it is one big Muppet Show. Sometimes we do so because we're desperate. Sometimes we're not aware of it and you only realize when you notice that you are the only one who is smiling in a room full of gloominess. If it's too hard to break through those walls of negativity then just don't. Be professional and move on. Not every situation is meant to be fixed or eased with politeness and a heartfelt emotion. Things don't always go right and sometimes that's fine. You don't want to cross the road to 'Faketown', it sends the wrong message even if you don't intend it that way.

And here is a reason why, in my opinion, this is a very crucial skill. When something is abused it only proves its power and effectiveness! In this case, I'm talking about manipulation. Unfortunately, this method is a very common and trusted double agent. And sadly, I have to admit I've been a victim of it a few times. Every time I was extremely disappointed in the person who played me so skillfully. Yes, being nice will give you results. But please, be nice to people because it's who you are and not because it's a tool you use to get things done. Keep your integrity.

You hate it when it happens to you, so don't act in a similar manner towards others. Again, not every situation is meant to be dealt with in a nice way. Sometimes you need to be straightforward, which can come across as harsh to the receiver. Honesty is the best policy. Even if it means you have to work harder to get something done. Believe me, manipulation will bite you somewhere along the way and it usually chooses all the undesirable moments for it to happen.

The tricky part is the moment that you realize that you are being played and it's your turn to move. Sometimes, it is better to play along so not to hurt other people's feelings. You play nice in order to move to a win-win outcome smoothly and skillfully. It's like talking to a kid who is obviously lying. It's a minor harmless something and you try to guide the conversation to a place where the poor thing can semi confess. In the end he will even be rewarded for being honest. Sometimes it's good to be the bigger person and play this game.

In other cases, where there is no win-win option ahead, it's better to confront the trickery. Now, this can get ugly if you falsely interpret the other side's intentions. Here is a way out: start by expressing your discomfort at how things are moving along. Mention that you don't want this situation to be based on assumptions that are not beneficial for either of you. The other person will get the message and this will give you the option to be more persistent in defending your ground if needed. This creates a space where you can safely state your suspicions but also gives you an opportunity to turn this thing around into a win-

win situation. If it becomes too complicated, just cut your losses. There is a limit to politically correct behavior.

Lookalikes

I already mentioned that 'nice' is merely a compilation of the soft skillset. There are many more similar qualities. Overall you can conclude that being nice equals being personal. The way you approach being personal in your role is totally up to you.

I would like to pinpoint a few specific affiliates just to make it clear that this soft skill is very diverse and you can make any of its components your own. The choice is yours, be certain that every variation works equally well. I have found three lookalikes that are special in times you're in a hurry, in a bad mood or if you're not a naturally cheery person which, don't get me wrong, is not a bad thing at all. If you are like that, then it can make this topic a little more challenging for you, that's it. So here is what you can do to make it your own if all of the above seems like too much effort.

When you analyze what makes somebody be perceived as 'nice', the first things that probably pop up are situations where people help each other out. Whether you asked for it or someone just hurried to your aid spontaneously. What's the first thing you say? 'How nice of you!' And this is, to begin with, the easiest thing you can do when starting to practice this skill consciously. You might say that a smile would be easier, but try to smile when you're sweating and running around with piles of papers, editing Word documents in between and tracking every five-minute break your exec has in-between meetings. Yes, a smile is a very fast indicator, but actions speak louder than 'nonverbal' smiles.

Then there are manners. If you continuously display good manners, that will be sufficient to be perceived as nice. Having good manners usually means you are considerate of the situation and the largely accepted ways of dealing with social encounters. Apply your manners and you will be on your way just fine.

And this third one is an even more distant, but nevertheless important, part of being perceived as nice. It is your image! This is a very extensive topic, as we have discussed earlier on. Image might mean different things to different people. Try to only focus on a few things like building a track record so in hard times people will cut you some slack. Focus on continuity in your actions while dealing with certain issues and situations.

Remember that communication style is also a huge part of our image. To make it your own you can use some specific 'nice' elements in your communication and add your 'signature' wherever it fits. Usually that translates to being personal next to being professional in your communication. If the receiver feels like he/she is being heard, appreciated or just noticed then you have achieved your goal. Nothing new, we all know and do that — it's just a reminder.

Practicalities

Implementing this skill will make you think about relationships on a totally different level. You will actually explore their inner workings. This can be exciting and frustrating at the same time. Now, this is a topic close to my heart as I love psychology. An extensive knowledge of people is something Assisting Professionals simply need, but it doesn't really have to be your hobby.

In case it's definitely not your hobby then here is an easy way to make this skill work for you. Have a few role models in mind and mirror their conduct in times where it is difficult for you to find fitting ways to act on your own. It's like a magic spell that transforms your understanding of the situation and lifts your consciousness to new levels. It changes your behavior automatically. 'Fake it till you make it' is a good one to remember.

The cool thing is that the way we choose our role models has everything to do with *who we are* deep inside. The theory says that the reason we like and admire somebody is because there is a certain resonance between the skills, the character or the qualities that is attractive to us. So if you see somebody as a role model, it doesn't only mean you want to be like them, but that you actually are *already* like them! You just need to bring it to the surface and practice it out in the open. Practice makes perfect!

There are times when I'm really clueless about how to act. I'll admit I'm not perfect. I misread people sometimes and then acting all nice and polite makes a certain situation even more awkward. In those cases I just admit I don't know what I'm doing and openly ask for feedback or guidance. Lowering your guard and being human and personal can be a way out, or just a way...

Whatever comes next always clarifies the situation and provides clues on what is really going on. It can save a relationship and even make it stronger. If you have those situations with your exec don't be afraid to do just that. Stay close to yourself and your core qualities.

Remember, this skill is most importantly about being personal. Even if it sometimes means going out of your comfort zone to grow. Success lies beyond your comfort zone, they say.

In some cases you will actually very consciously choose this skill to turn things around. Above all, implementation of these qualities is applied to conflict or problem-solving situations.

It might be a difficult relationship that keeps bugging you and makes your job a lot more challenging. Or maybe it's the unhappy vibe in your department during a period of reorganization. Or anything like long-standing issues and problems that cannot seem to be fixed by anybody nor anything. So buckle up and decide to give it a go — the nice way! On another level, this skill always leaves a lasting impression.

When used constructively this is your way to build your image, get remembered and pursue professional growth. As long as it comes from within, you will be successful. Make it your own. Find or simply be aware of what it is that makes it your own. Define ways that come naturally to you because those will be easiest to implement on the spot or on demand.

And the verdict is...

Let's state the obvious benefit first: you will get the results you want, people will praise working with you and tend to cooperate with you even during difficult times. This skill will always provide you with an option to start over (in particular after using this very phrase: 'Hang on, this is going nowhere, let's start over!'). You will never be stuck again!

And the fact is that it spreads around you like sunshine and will make you the catalyst of positive vibes. Numerous sociological and productivity studies state time and again that positive office vibes make teams better and more productive. It's a win-win-win-win (you-team-company-your exec being pleased with results). The core element of being personal will lift the overall quality of your relationships. All that will make you a whole lot more relaxed and confident. By the way, the confidence will be a byproduct of getting things done easier and faster. And there is nothing that can make us happier than going through our to-do lists like a smooth operator.

Of course it will also have a profound and untouchable effect on the relationship with your exec. If you tend to be in a good mood a lot and be a pleasant individual, it makes you a good company. It will be easier for them to open up, blow off steam or just chat away as a change of pace. We know they are human too behind closed doors and we human beings tend to relax in the presence of positively charged people. You being able to create that comfort zone for him will be invaluable. That is one of the hidden powers and core qualities of Assistants. When people are relaxed they recharge faster and more effectively. That will make your exec excel almost instantaneously. Don't forget about this tiny 'positivity' detail — it can make all the difference.

Also, your exec will be checking up on you in action to be confident that you are in control and that you can handle the responsibilities well. They may not tell you, but be assured: they do watch your every move in certain situations. We are their representation to the outside world so they need to make sure that it is still up to standards and requirements once in a while. And it better be in a nice, professional and ethical manner!

Just to add one more point: others see us as a gateway to the exec. No matter how much execs proclaim to have an 'open-door' policy, they always stay beyond the reach of most team members. They will always be seen as 'The Boss'! People will act in a cautious way around your exec. Of course it differs for the members in his direct report lines, but keep in mind that you are the most likely person others will talk to when they want to get a message to your exec. So be especially nice in those situations. Make them feel at ease and if possible maybe even introduce them to your exec if he has a spare moment. They will always remember you for this — it happens to me all the time!

The verdict:

**Your capacity to incorporate this skill into
your daily doings will make you the 'enabler'.
It will make you and your exec excel!**

Take-away notes

 ACT

✓ Being Nice has many forms. Choose the ones that fit your personality
✓ Use being Nice to change the vibe of loaded situations for the better in a snap
✓ To be truly Nice usually means being personal
✓ Find a couple of role models that you truly admire for being sincerely Nice

BE

✓ If you are not sincerely Nice, people will know and it might work against you
✓ Be aware of people taking advantage of you by being Nice
✓ If you are not very 'emotional', remember to use good
manners to be perceived as Nice
✓ Use this skill to resolve conflicts with a gentle touch. Being Nice is contagious

THINK

✓ Remember to be Nice, even in an unguarded moment
✓ Have a few preset Nice communication elements
that you can use on the go or on demand
✓ Focus on ways to act that come naturally (aka making them your own)
✓ Remember, being Nice is a powerful image-building block

Chapter 10. Tenacious State of Mind

Results you will achieve:

- ✓ Accomplish the 'impossible'
- ✓ Use your triggers to snap into the mindset of being super productive
- ✓ Become a go-to Assistant and get recognition
- ✓ Use this mindset as your value-defining tool
- ✓ Get things done by enabling cooperation
- ✓ Acquire new skills of finding resourceful and smart workarounds

Being *Tenacious* is one of the most obvious and infamous core values of Assisting Professionals. It's the basis of all the PA stories out there. The rumors about the crazy things we achieve, and the fact that 'impossible' is just a nickname for things PAs manage every day.

I love the flow we get into on some days, when nothing seems to hold us back! You are so sharp you can cut through any crisis like it's warm butter. No, it does not come easily. It's a very specific and very strong mindset that needs to be controlled, tweaked, quickly adjusted or rapidly killed after you are done with the task at hand. It's the times when your tone of voice changes. When you understand everything in seconds. It's when you have the solution even before the issue has been properly stated. It's the posture of calmness and confident attitude. You get heard in any busy meeting and people will actually listen to you. It's the way things are carefully formulated in your head and the way they get out into the open with astonishing effectiveness. This is an amazingly powerful state of mind. But it's also a tricky one — staying too long in that 'fetch, kill and attack' mode can make you come across as rude or inconsiderate after a while. Don't blame others for judging the book by its cover in those moments. Other people rarely understand why getting a fire department to open up a closed dry cleaning shop at 4am is so important it might seem life threatening. Or why we are being firm about the way lunch is served in the boardroom, checking that every sandwich is carefully folded and even going through the ingredients for any little black pepper grains that might have slipped in. Or why we are irrationally snappy while staying on the line with an airline agent for four hours straight, just not to miss out on an empty seat on the way back to Europe, on any flight and to anywhere out of the US, because the airspace is about to be closed for a few days...

Sometimes there are no limits to what we can achieve! And the only reason things get done is because we simply don't know how to give up on something before we have tried everything humanly possible. We live for this! That is why we put up with a lot of other mundane stuff while being on the lookout for something 'crazy' to do.

And let me state here that 'crazy' also describes printing, labeling and coding 693 legal documents, getting them signed by four execs in the time frame of one hour and then scanning them, archiving them and dividing doubles before sending the rest by a special delivery service. The poor guy had to walk up and down to our office on the 5th floor six times to get all the boxes in the right order, and labeled with four different receiving addresses. That is definitely the most insane, but oh so satisfying, duty of a PA during a huge M&A process. I don't know about you, but I got all warm and fuzzy inside when my exec explained what was needed of me earlier that day! Do you see why some call us crazy? Oh boy — I was flying on the wings of empty cartridges, ink stains and paper cuts for a solid week!

It's the way that we tend to sink our teeth into some process so deeply that without the skill to snap out of that mindset on demand, the pressure to perform would be unbearable. I came to understand that it's a version of 'fight or flight' mode that we Assistants have adapted to serve our circumstances. The ad hoc element is very important — that is the trigger that unleashes the effective beast.

Another trigger for us is getting the answer 'no'. The more we hear that word, the more persistent we get in finding a 'yes'. And boy oh boy, how a 'maybe' can catapult and skyrocket our confidence. The moment we see a micro way out, a tiny flash of light at the end of that gloomy tunnel of 'nos'— then we get the momentum where nothing can stop us from actually becoming the superheroes of 'impossible made doable'. To the outsider's eye, it might look like a fussy stamp on a document in a weird language, resembling an ancient hieroglyph. But to you, at that moment, it represents everything you stand for! It's your value-defining moment. It makes you proud to be called an Assistant and it is the moment where you know you are needed. (Yes, now I see why others sometimes perceive us as weird!)

The quality of 'not stopping easily' and being so resourceful that there is not even a word for it, that is our way of making a difference. Even one task performed in the 'I'm gonna make this happen no matter what' mindset will set you apart on the professional chart. You will become the go-to PA and we all know how that will affect you. And again, I believe it has to come from within (because let's face it, nobody in their right mind will run around a city for six hours to find the right density fabric samples that they used to produce four years ago). It's our willingness to get ahead, even if we have to do something small but very important and usually difficult.

It's all in the system

For this skill to be useful, you need to make it your own (as with all others) or at least know what that tenacious way of execution means to you. When you know how to operate, you can switch into it easier while understanding its power and effectiveness. It will make it faster for you to get the impossible done. It's also good to know how to switch back to normal, because this state drains your energy, patience and good mood. Too much is surely not good for too long.

Furthermore, it would be great if you could package the whole shebang into one 'Tenacious Action' system: the trigger mechanism, the autopilot 'high-volume' multitasking ability, the high-sensitivity sensory capacity and a way to slow down again and to cool off the engines. Putting it into a system that can be triggered on demand will make you perform miracles. I know this might sound weird and unclear right now. Just hang on until chapter 14 and I will reveal a very cool way of managing your energy and being in control of your wellbeing. You will love it! For now, let me assure you, there is a system of switches in your head that can transform your state of mind and your intentions in a snap. Master that and you will be 'happy go lucky' in every aspect of your life!

Remember, the way you act in this state of mind has to fit your ways, your manners and the expectations of your exec, but within certain limits of sanity. Because it's way too easy to appear like a headless chicken running in circles. Sure, we go a bit further if possible to impress our execs. But good is sometimes really good enough. Even more so, making the 'impossible' even remotely look like something they expect might be already good enough. We are not one-trick ponies and there will most definitely be other times when your super powers will be needed again. Maybe even sooner than you hope for! Save some energy for a really rainy day — we all know that most Assisting Professionals are surf masters of problem waves. Remember the universal law saying that life is a sequence of seven problems: for every six little ones, there is one big crisis and they will keep on coming. So let's get you a bulletproof, durable and, if at all possible, a flattering wetsuit!

Ready, set, oh yes — before you go...

Before we move on to how this skill can actually be your spirit-boosting potion I want to consider a very special timeframe. A moment of clarity before things start to unravel into a hurricane of looking for answers, hitting dead ends, being creative on roundabouts and trying to cut corners on your way to the deadline. When you notice that you are being sent into the midst of something difficult and potentially impossible — take a second to focus. Here are two things to consider to get yourself ready for what's coming:

Get your focus right

Clarity is crucial in any situation but here it is a matter of life and death. Here's my 'pre-action' checklist:

✓ *What's the objective*? It's crazy how many times I have been chasing ghosts because my exec told me to get something that has a different name/issue/characteristic than he originally envisioned.

✓ *What's your route*? You almost certainly won't find what you are looking for at the first stop, so make a list of options of where and from whom to look for the solution.

✓ *Understand why you, or your exec, think it's impossible*. This might sound weird, but sometimes it's not that difficult. And yes, in the beginning you can forecast that you will be running around all day to do it, while in reality you will manage the task in exactly five minutes.

✓ *What are the obvious substitutes*? This has saved me a lot of time on a few occasions. When my exec asked me for something and I knew with 98% certainty that I wouldn't be able to get it or do it on time, or in the requested fashion, I came up with variations of the outcome which I thought would fit the purpose. He immediately agreed to the new solution, which took me about 15 minutes to arrange.

✓ *Do I need to be* Effective *or* Efficient*?* I will explain the main distinction in the chapter on the *Effective* soft skill later on. For now, know this impacts your actions big time.

Realize that you need at least two other soft skills here, *Willing* and *Nice*

✓ *Willing:*

I actually think that this skill is the driving force behind getting through really impossible tasks! Usually people are willing to give it a try. Do me a quick favor: try to drop your pen on the ground. Did you do it?! No, because you cannot try something! You either do it or you don't! When I heard this explanation from Nisandeh Neta, business coach and trainer, it hit me like a cold shower in the middle of a desert. Here is what this understanding does to your mindset: if you operate with the intention of 'trying', you are already accepting that failure is an option. That is why PAs achieve the impossible, because it's impossible to others! In that sense, it's not that big of a deal for us. But it is cool to state our accomplishments as numbering it 'doing the impossible'! We'll get to that in a second...

So, how do you set your mind to getting things done? Do exactly that — get on with it! It helps me to be aware of the fact that there is always a way, I just don't know about it yet. That is what's so powerful about this mindset: seeing the options. By the way, you can practice it in any area of your life. You are not the wisest and the most experienced person alive, there is always something that you don't know. And if you are *Willing* to accept that, it will open you up to new ways, information and possibilities almost instantaneously. It is conducive to a new way of thinking. You will notice new patterns and make new connections. A very cool process!

✓ *Nice:*

This one is obvious and easy. If you are nice and considerate to others, you will achieve more. Just remember that these actions need to be real and authentic, otherwise it will work against you. Oh, and a variation of this skill is a form of openness — that is the key element here.

I mean, if you just say to someone that you are in a pickle, you don't know how to proceed and that you really would appreciate anything they can do for you, that will open up *their* minds to creative thinking as well.

And, this way you touch a profound side in all of us, as we all tend to want to please others on some level. That is how impossible things get done — two minds are greater than one!

Start your engines

As I previously mentioned, the results of this skill are a great motivator. They clearly show that you walk your talk and that you are worth the money. This is exactly why the stories of the crazy things PAs do get out there — because we are proud of them!

Even if it's ridiculous — it just means that we have survived! Now, I don't actually encourage you to get all of that out there. As a matter of fact, I think most things you do should stay private and confidential. There is always a fine line of integrity: to yourself, to your exec and to your company. There are some cases where PAs telling their story in public actually diminished our images as Assistants overall. Unfortunately, it happens regularly so be careful not to spoil it for everyone else. If you keep up with PA communities on social media then you know what I mean. If not, Google it...

The safest and best way to benefit from your achievements is to make a victory list. Keep it close because some things on there might be confidential. But use it regularly! It will cheer you up and keep you going at dull or difficult times.

Here is a very useful fact about positive vs negative thinking. There is a certain ratio, or call it an equation, that balances our moods, and it's a scary one to be honest. The official ratio is 1 to 5, but some optimistic experts like to work with a 1 to 3 equation. It simply means that for one bad or negative experience/thought we psychologically need five positive ones to balance the effects. And that only means bringing your state of mind or mood back to a neutral zone! So if you want to be in a good mood, you need to go way above five to get into that happy state. In other words, your achievement list should have at least five cool and uplifting things on it and preferably more — go for as many as you can! And just like with your secret boost card containing the reasons why you love your job and your profession (which we talked about in chapter 7), you can use this list as a motivational tool. So don't forget it's there.

The quality of your achievement will also get you some (much needed) recognition. It's a well-known fact that a lot of things are expected from us. Even impossible accomplishments are not always noticed by others, let alone labeled as such. Fortunately, usually you do see that your exec is content with you and the things you achieve. Maybe not in the most obvious ways, but you know him well so you should be able to tell when you have checked that box. I like to call this a 'silent underground booster', because even if the 'thank you' is expressed in just a few words, his tone of voice will reveal the gratitude and the vibe forward will change for the better!

Wrong turn, move on

It's true, sometimes things don't go the way you want them to. Even after being a tenacious warrior, not sleeping much on your quest to solve mysteries, losing a few pounds of sweat, tears and skipped lunches along the way. I admit it, sometimes I don't get things done. And it hurts! A few times I was so close I could taste it, doing the Macarena in my head and then things fell apart literally the last minute before deadline. It's a hard pill to swallow! Luckily I only had one really significant failed attempt in my PA career, something impossible that stayed that way. Did it affect me? Absolutely! Did it affect my relationship with my exec? I'm afraid it did a little. Did it make me work even harder to maintain my credibility? You bet!

To get through this there is only one thing you can do: accept defeat, be open about what went wrong (to yourself and your exec), don't blame yourself or anyone else, learn your lesson and move on. Yes, you will have to work a little or much harder (depending on the magnitude of the slaughter) after such a misfortune. Especially if it happens early on in a new position (as it usually does by the way, new surroundings are never beneficial to impossible tasks). In some cases, when you have a great track record of success your exec can cut yourself some slack, but never count on it. People are very unpredictable when things go wrong! Some words of wisdom that I always keep in my mind: you have only two certainties in life — that you will die some day and that people will never be as you expect them to be (in a good and bad sense)!

Be aware of times when those smackdowns happen frequently. I mean, things do go wrong continuously, that's the name of the game. What you need to watch out for is when you are the main reason things don't go to plan. This is tricky, because it's not in our nature to admit when we are at fault. But it is the wise thing to do. Let's be honest, you might not say it out in the open, but you always know deep down when it's you who is causing those bad things to happen. The bad news is that it's a vicious circle. Once you're there, it is not easy to snap out of it. The main reasons are that A: we promise to make up for it, B: we make even bigger promises to top the screw up and C: we are in an exhausted or unmotivated mood by the time it all goes down. That makes it more likely for you not to be able to walk your talk. Such situations breed breakdowns.

The only way to escape this madness is to do the exact opposite: A: admit your error, control the damage and move on. Be at ease with it, otherwise it will freeze you up for things to come. B: Don't try to overachieve right away to make up for past failures. Sometimes it's better to stop and leave things behind. Focus on the future, prepare better and overdeliver on the next assignment. C: Get your head together, take a break, regroup and do so very consciously!

Another thing is to know when to stop chasing the impossible. Admitting that something is not doable requires certain qualities. One such quality is maturity. This is a skill senior Assistants are very good at: being able to stop with confidence and with a grounded belief that it's the best thing to do. It's not about proving yourself. It's about being able to see the situation as a whole and having the ability to predict the outcome.

It's like a game of chess. To an unskilled spectator it can look like you are giving in way too early. But the experienced player, who has already played out the next five moves in his head, knows when it's done, finished and hopeless. So it actually saves time, effort and a lot of hardship. The closer you get to realizing that it won't work out while still trying desperately, the more demoralizing it will be. You are making it harder and needlessly depressing for yourself.

Learn to stop when you can predict with some confidence that it won't work. Use your senses, try to think of an appropriate alternative if possible, or just let it go. The earlier in the process you analyze the chances of failure, the more time you'll have to find ways around it.

I see how some of it might seem contradictory. On one hand it's good to be persistent, as that is one of the most admired and vital skills of successful people. On the other hand, you need to know when to stop. It's the quality of a true professional, no matter the profession. Additionally being aware of your limitations and boundaries is crucial and courageous. Yes, some boundaries can be stretched a little. And of course anything in clash with the law is out of the question. It's the personal boundaries that are most flexible here. Know yours, and get to know and respect those of others.

It's a known fact that PAs, especially in the early stages of our careers, tend to stretch more than what is generally accepted by others. It's part of the job and sometimes it's what makes it special and gets us incredible results. The issue here is that people get used to it. Our execs will expect us to perform like that all the time, and might push us even further. It's up to you to decide when enough is enough.

Personally, I moved my boundaries too far so often that I sometimes caught myself doing things that were actually ridiculous. And the crazy thing is that I only realized it when I was pushed even further. For some weird reason we don't see our boundaries move if they are moved slowly. Here is how it works...

Hocus pocus

I was at a PA conference lately where one of the speakers, a Dutch neuroscientist called Erik Schreder, did a little experiment with us. He proved to us that when a big and obvious change happens very slowly, our brain doesn't notice the transition! At some point, our brain does not connect the dots and we don't register it at all. The experiment involved a photo of a garden and in less than 30 seconds the whole center changed into a concrete platform with a huge statue on it — and you don't see it happening when played at a certain slow speed! You don't see the result, no matter how long you stare at it. I felt like a right fool! It sounds ridiculous, but there were a few hundred Assisting

Professionals in the room and he showed it to us three times — nobody saw it. And no, it was not about us as a particular audience because he apparently knew the outcome before he made us his guinea pigs. It's how our brains work! It's science, physiologically impossible!

Now, this scientist wanted to enlighten and empower us to use this method to incorporate change for the better into our jobs and companies. Change is difficult and people generally don't like it nor want it. This 'slow motion change' is a great way of achieving anything — just do so very gradually! Also be aware that this 'slow motion change' principle works the other way around with the same effective result. You can end up in unwanted situations that you did not expect or prepare for. You'll catch yourself doing things you actually don't want to do — all the time! The way you work will suddenly veer off from the direction of your goals, or suddenly you find that your surroundings are turning out to be depressing, poisonous and hostile.

This might sound like overkill. But unfortunately, quite a few companies don't pay enough attention to team building and ignore team disputes. Many unfortunate situations arise when working in teams of equal Assistants, some are even described as beehives or snake pits. Those situations did not develop overnight and they won't be turned back around overnight either. We need to be aware of it and set new directions that are well planned and most of all — happen gradually.

Back to our boundaries. Knowing about this 'slow motion change' principle, it's good to focus on yourself once in a while and compare you, your thoughts and your actions as a whole to some specific time in the past where you can pinpoint a similar experience and your previous you. There are naturally three types of situations where life pushes you to do that by default: a victorious moment, a moment of defeat or despair and ends/beginnings.

Being aware of your boundaries is important in all of them, but absolutely crucial in the last two. Note that victorious moments might just as well be the product of you stretching or crossing your boundaries. Logically, feeling downright exhausted in some situations means that you have passed way beyond your limits. And during ends/beginnings, you are very clear on where your boundaries are. This time you are focused on communicating them to others and quite determined to guard them while acting boldly and knowing how far you can go. In any case, decide your values for yourself and stick to them. Yes, boundaries are determined by our values. That is exactly what we'll see in the upcoming chapter about me time and implementation of the W.A.N.T.E.D. technology in your life.

For me, those moments of clarity come kind of naturally every time I switch jobs or, as lately, switch clients. Closure urges me to think back about how it all started. Most of the time it helps me to acknowledge my growth (both personally and professionally), revisit my victories, refresh the lessons learned and just be very content with people I've met as I usually gain a few good friends and warm contacts from each and every involvement.

Last resources

Before we summarize all the good things this *Tenacious* soft skill will bring you, I have a few more tools I want to share. What to do when you think you have tried everything, nothing works and you are ready to throw in the towel?

I already mentioned being resourceful, but what does it actually mean? Let me repeat a very simple but extremely effective way of being resourceful. This is a system I learned from Brian Tracy. And what Brian says is that you need to get into the habit of always asking yourself the following question: *what else* is the problem or the solution?

Sounds simple right — and here is why it works like magic. It's based on a principle of being wrongly aware of problems and solutions with only *one* definition. Because it's never that simple! Once you have answered the question above, you have to note down the answers and then clear your head to think of other options. You have to do that at least three times over. I'll admit, coming up with the second option is fairly easy, but after that it gets tough. Especially for action-oriented PAs like me who want to give the first two a fair go right away. You have to force yourself to keep on answering that question until your mind won't give you any more feedback. There is a certain magic happening when you get to number four or five. Your mind gets very calm, clear and super-duper creative.

The scientific trick is that your mind is an *answering machine*! It has nowhere to go but to answer the question and when the obvious options are mentioned it is forced to go beyond normal everyday practical thinking into that creative 'anything is possible' mode. That is truly where the magic happens! Give it a go. And it's especially powerful if you do it in a team.

Another cool thing to remember is that to think creatively and resourcefully is all about thinking 'non-logically'. Nisandeh Neta teaches that it is only after unlearning your current thoughts, habits and beliefs that the path to growth and new possibilities will be revealed. I love to use that piece of wisdom when struggling with a dead-end I can't seem to figure out how to get past. What was it that I took for granted? What was the logical outcome I expected and didn't get?

Our minds tend to take well-known paths and for very good evolutionary reasons. But sometimes we need to slay the dragon of our ancient lizard brains to get something done in the twenty-first century. Here is cool thing I do when I think about alternative roundabouts: what if there was a perfect universe where my will could command the elements — how would I want the result to happen? The answer is usually a straight line to my goal. But our minds nowadays 'know' it's not possible. And that is exactly what you want to eliminate right now. Sometimes the solution is simple and right there in front of you. We just disregard it because it sounds too good to be true. Guess what, sometimes it is so good that it is true! As Confucius said: 'Life is easy, it's us who tend to make it difficult!'

Next thing on the list: always expect misfortune. It doesn't mean that your overall mood shouldn't be positive and you should sit and wait until Armageddon comes over for a cup of macchiato. This expectation simply prevents you from falling apart when things don't go the way you plan. Believe me, being/thinking/radiating a positive attitude and thoughts is an amazingly effective tool in life! Please, use it as often as you can. At the same time, knowing about the law of 'seven problem waves' makes it more manageable to encounter and deal with them since you know they will come anyway. It won't snap you out of your good mood and that's the contradicting truth. Expect difficulties to stay positive!

Let me quickly give you some other reminders. It's (usually) not personal and not your fault per definition. Things happen and let's face it — sometimes the things we are asked to do/get/fix are downright impossible and ridiculous. In some cases you need to put your foot down and find fitting ways of saying 'It's not going to happen!'

Another quickie: you don't have to do it on your own. I mentioned it before but still I catch myself trying to get things done on my own in times of crisis— just because it seems faster and easier.

Sometimes it is, but occasionally I think it could have helped me a lot to ask for some assistance. Asking for help and support is actually a skill of mature Assisting Professionals. So my hopes are still high that it's in my future!

And of course, don't forget to celebrate your achievements when your tenacious efforts crown your masterpiece plan with success. Even if it's a small celebration all by yourself, in the company of the biggest dark chocolate Magnum you can find, kicking off your high heels for a second — yes, the simple pleasures! And if it doesn't work out – learn to let it go, pat yourself on the back for invested efforts and move on peacefully.

Always take a conscious moment after such a race to cool down and get yourself into that serene place after the cascading waterfall. Create a cooling down ritual for yourself, let everything calm down, regroup to proceed with the steady flow in a new direction.

Down there below the water is clear, bubble free and all smooth with a steely edge, stealth and composure that makes it look so powerful and sleek. You have to love water metaphors, they have a very transformative power, won't you agree?

And the verdict is...

Being tenacious will bring your character a whole spectrum of new skills. It will reveal new ways and manners of doing things. It will show you how creative you can be. Your communication skills will be put to the test. You will find out that even a slight variation in your tone could bring you the results you seek. You will learn ways of communication that don't work at all or are only applicable to certain people. Situations where being persistent is a prerequisite to succeed will definitely lift your interpersonal skills. Those will gain you plenty of new contacts. They will show you the value of your existing relationships and can also revive old and forgotten ones. It can make them stronger, more detailed and deeper, or quite the opposite. We all know people that tell us we may always call them for help, but when it is actually needed they are nowhere to be found. I hate it when that happens!

Furthermore, this skill will teach you a lot about yourself. You will learn what makes you fly and what holds you back. How do you act in stressful situation where nothing seems to have the outcome you want? Getting a 'no' often reveals our true colors! What does a 'no' show you about yourself and others? How do victories feel and how do they affect your mind? How much and how fast do you learn on the go? Can you make an accurate assumption about when to move on despite every sign of defeat or when to stop although there are numerous ways left to give it a go? This is a skill that tests our wisdom, stealth and decision making. I would almost say that this skill is crucial for any professional to master. Most importantly, this skill has an unknown power when comfortably supported by the rest of the W.A.N.T.E.D. super team. Make it your own!

The effects on your exec and mostly your relationship with him are again pretty obvious. First of all it shows that you care like nothing else. Or that you are very afraid of the consequences of incompetence. But even that too shows that you value your job and this position so much that you run a little further and faster. In case of failure, topics of respect and trust are on tricky ground. Logically, it will boost them when you succeed. In situations where you won't achieve the requested outcome — well, the impact will depend on your track record.

Sometimes, even if you fail, your exec will see your efforts and appreciate them. Whether that will happen out in the open will depend on the topic of your defeat. Just don't make this occasion hold you back from going after something impossible again. Don't let that defeat break your spirit. Remember the law of the 'seven problem waves' — you will get a second chance soon enough. (Actually, let's rename this universal law to: 'seven challenge waves'. Mindsetting in action!)

And don't forget to mention to your exec that next time around you will do A, B and C differently and show that you have learned the lessons if there are any.

Most of all, no matter what the outcome is, I personally love that feeling of going for it! It gives me a deep sense of fulfillment. No matter how small it might seem. That motivation of being persistent is a great skill to train on small things. The stronger it will become over time the more effectively you will be able to use it for other and bigger goals. Professionally or personally, being tenacious is one of the greatest skills of the most successful people on the planet. So just go for it!

The verdict:

**By being tenacious you will achieve results
that will make you and your exec
excel on so many levels!**

Take-away notes

 ACT

✓ This mindset will enable you to make a difference and position
your professional value
✓ Define the checkpoints and triggers of your own 'Tenacious Action' system
✓ Before diving into action – take a moment to analyze the situation
while you still have your patience and your cool
✓ Create your own victory list, but remember to keep it private and confidential
✓ When things go wrong: do admit it, make up for it if possible and move on

 BE

✓ Be prepared to switch on this mindset regularly, there will
always be problems and challenges
✓ Be proud of your victories, no matter how small they may seem to others
✓ Don't be too hard on yourself if you do
make mistakes, it will not benefit anyone
✓ Have a ritual to cool down, regroup and refocus your
spirits after challenging times
✓ Prepare for and accept problems to stay positive

 THINK

✓ Realize that this state of effectiveness is what makes our job so amazing
✓ Remember to snap out of this mindset after the job is done
✓ Know when to stop chasing the impossible
✓ Focus on future overdelivery when things don't go your way now
✓ Know your boundaries, check up on them regularly and guard them well

'

Chapter 11. Effective State of Mind

Results you will achieve:

✓ *Position yourself as an expert go-getter PA*
✓ *Build yourself a shiny track record that will win you goodwill*
✓ *Take the role of 'leading from behind'*
✓ *Create your own version of a 'love sandwich' confrontation method*
✓ *Become a master at difficult conversations*
✓ *Switch 'mindset' roles to get things done*
✓ *Create your own well-balanced circuit of productivity*

Meet *Effective* — the most valued core quality of being an Assisting Professional! Just like being *Available* this core skill is the reason our profession exists. We get things done, it's what we do. This skill also has a twin brother which is usually mentioned in the same go — efficient. This is an ultimate combo, a match made in business heaven.

If I had to choose one, that would surely be the *Effective* sibling and for a very good reason. Sometimes the available road to Rome is not always the shortest one. But that doesn't matter, because what matters most is the end result. If my exec wants something badly and it's truly of life and death importance (to him) then it doesn't matter how many resources I use to get it. Being efficient is a very useful skill and I definitely empower you to be good at it, especially in terms of time. Time is and will ever be our biggest frenemy, our scarcest resource and we need to use it wisely. So for now, let's focus on being *Effective*, becoming a super achiever, building your image and positioning yourself as the go-getter. Once the basics have been absorbed you can perfect this skill to any level of excellence you desire, starting with doing so more efficiently.

The bad news about this skill is that it is expected of us to begin with. It's so funny to see the difference between how Assistants are welcomed in a company vs any other employee. A while ago I was working regularly as an interim PA and visited a few companies. When I started in a new place, the first week looked like this: here is everything we have — the bad, the very bad and the ugly. Let's meet next week and you can tell me what you have done, fixed, planned, organized and structured. What the heck?! The load of outstanding issues was a result of months or even years of ignored archiving, unfinished projects and behind-schedule tasks. But hé, an experienced PA with a shiny resume should be able to fix it all by Monday, right?

On the other hand, when I assist in the hiring process of any other team member they are given a few months to adapt, are held by the hand the whole way through the company's processes etc. Now don't get me wrong — I love that responsibility and the trust in my abilities. I do my outmost to position myself in a way where these things do happen to me, so I'm not complaining. But you have to admit that it is a funny comparison...

Pros and cons

The good thing about this skill is that it's the most practical and measurable skill of the W.A.N.T.E.D. family. This gives you the power to control your success rate. It's also very motivating to strive for and it's ego-boosting to talk about. So set yourself a goal to create a track record to be proud of. And I'm not talking about outrageous accomplishments. The extraordinary thing about being effective is that the strength of it lies in consistency over a prolonged period of time.

The longer you are performing to the expected levels the more powerful your image is. It's all about being able to perform constantly, providing order, structure and the peace of mind of things going in the right direction. It's about you being consistent, to the extent of being able to do it on autopilot.

This flow of effective delivery is the key to creating trust. It makes you dependable in the long run and proves you are the professional that deserves the title. Remember, with Assistants the expectance levels are the highest in the beginning and after a period of consistent performance the urgency of putting you to the test eases up and the only thing you have to keep on doing is maintaining the flow. After this reverse climax trial period there is a new expectation waiting for you to be conquered: take the lead and get in charge. That is where the true meaning of 'leading from behind' comes from.

All execs are result driven and you being right there nurturing their craving of seeing things happen as expected is really supportive of their good mood. I've often heard phrases like 'at least something is going right!' after reporting back on something small being taken care of.

Usually it's after I told him that the reports are done, the contracts delivered, the boardroom is ready for the important meeting, reservations are confirmed or that the last-minute flights are booked. To be very honest with you, if I sense that things are tense and not going the way my exec wants them to I tend to use this 'small-task completion' tactic to break through the negativity. It works even better if you collect a few things that are going well and then sum them up for added impact. Give it a try! Breaking negative thinking patterns is a very powerful skill.

Another good thing about this skill being so visible is the fact that it can be learned and tweaked just as any other hard skill. Revisit the chapter on physical skills to get a refresh on how you need to be on top of your skillset, whether it's physical or mental. For the purpose of your *Effective* mindset let's see what you can do to make it support the practical application.

Your way or no way

The key mindset setting while being *Effective* is the helicopter view. A bit farfetched you might think, so let me explain the mechanics. It's not the same helicopter view managers are talking about. It's about knowing that you have a system, a list or any other structure for anything that might come along. Most experienced Assistants know this principle as the 'Assistant's bible'.

As I mentioned before, it's a book with all the information, websites, lists and templates you might ever need. It can be handwritten, typed out, digital or just a binder as a central place for any bits and pieces you collect over time. Yes, it is mostly a practical guide of references. You do need a specific vantage point while compiling it. Rethink any situation, when you might need what information and create a system to get it most effectively. Sometimes I call it the 'Emergency Guide'. And this guide will have every detail that will save you a huge amount of time and effort while working on urgent matters. It will speed up the implementation of any action. Most importantly, you need to keep it updated. You don't want to lose time discovering the information is outdated and you just lost precious 15 minutes. You will need every second to finish the board presentation update in time and incorporate last-minute changes.

Another mindset setting is all about believing that you can do it *before* you start doing something! It's the reassurance of the wanted result being a definite fact even before you start that makes it way faster and easier to finish a task. This is a method that is used in sports a lot. Every sportsman visualizes himself achieving the wanted result before he starts the game or whatever he is doing. For us Assistants, it's the consistent delivery and completion to the expected levels in the past that empowers us to be sure of our effectiveness the next time around. It's the knowledge that our system works, that our approach has proven to work time and again. It's our past experience that makes the next task just a little something to complete before lunch.

Some call this the miracle of repetition, some call it a routine. Let's make it sexy and call it your excellence! I get a secret kick out of doing something for others that they see as huge and difficult while I know I'll be done with it in ten minutes or less. And the great thing about this state of 'been there, done that, got the t-shirt' is that it makes new stuff seem less scary and impossible. It's not about the task per se — it's about how you go about it! It's the ease of your mind saying: 'I can do it, pass it on and let's go to the next thing!' So, see it as done and you will be done with it in no time. A self-fulfilling prophecy that works. Let's call it the 'forward completion' method.

Here is another cool trick. I read a book lately by a brilliant female entrepreneur, Annemarie van Gaal, and she recommends that you write a 'pre-mortem' for every big and scary project you are about to take up. The theory goes like this. Think forward to the moment you decide to give up, throw in the towel and declare this a huge failure. Then, start summing up everything that didn't work, every element that was against you and every possible roadblock that was just too big and impossible to move, any external or internal situation that might have come to bug you and anything that discouraged you from actually achieving your goal. There you have an actual list of things to get rid of now: deal with them before they actually happen and think of a plan B, C or even D to have on hand when all that stuff turns up in real time! How brilliant is this strategy?!

It's a bit controversial in terms of the previous point of thinking positively and seeing something as complete and done. But you badly need this emergency planning on big projects. Let's remember the teachings of Brian Tracy who says that you need to be aware of problems and solutions that have only one definition. You have to ask yourself at least three times over and over again to be sure you have covered every possible angle to every situation: what else might go wrong? What else can I do to make it better? Etc., etc. Don't stop until you have at least three to seven answers to the same question. It trains your brain to be and get creative. It will save you time in the end — I guarantee it! It will deliver you results — I guarantee it! And believe me, it's a skill that you can develop.

Additionally, other W.A.N.T.E.D. skills empower the skill of being *Effective*. Needless to say, being *Tenacious* will create a good track record of past successes to build up that reassurance of you being *Effective* in the future. And the next skill of being *Dedicated* will push you even further into being *Effective* in new areas of your job. It's one big apple pie that tastes best with every ingredient fairly represented.

Being the messenger

There are two specific areas where Assisting Professionals are expected to be extremely good. The first one is delivering bad news and the other one, closely related, is having difficult conversations.

Both occurrences originate in the fact that we are somehow in-between the team and the management. We are gatekeepers and we have the task of representing the needs and wants of our execs to both the rest of the organization and the external world. It's not always solely up to us, but we see every communication and are often asked to review or execute the message delivery.

Let's start with bad news delivery and the oh-so-familiar 'love sandwich' method. I won't give you a long lecture on this one. It's a well-known sequence of starting off with the positive, then discussing the issue and always closing with something uplifting and positive again. There are a few variations on this method, like starting with repeating a mutual goal or interest, then discussing what went wrong and not to the agreed expectations (the focus needs to be on the negative impact of the situation here rather than on the actual misfortunes) and then closing with a solution and declaration of trust.

While I'm not saying it doesn't work, I do have a personal 'but' to this method. First of all, when the bleep hits the fan the other side knows and expects a difficult and emotionally draining conversation. So starting off all positive won't have any effect at all on the rest of the conversation. I've had my share of those so I can tell you it doesn't. Furthermore, many people know about this 'love sandwich' so they kind of expect you to do the thing, which again makes your approach less effective. Well, at least it's the way I experience it when people start applying this method with me. My mind shuts off for a second waiting for the real stuff to come.

The second issue I have with this method is the cheery and happy closing. It doesn't work that way because usually you don't really mean what you say in the end. Let's face it, shit happened and you're upset, pissed off and frustrated. If you ask me: acknowledge it, share it and leave it at that! Truth be told, only time and future developments will tell how happy and satisfied both of you will be in the end. I say close neutrally if there is no further contact needed or required. Close with an agreement to do a proper follow-up if future cooperation is still important. But still, do so neutrally and stay real. A happy ending in those situations is not logical or natural, so don't push it.

What also helps here is to be personal. If you are dealing with someone who you talk to and work with regularly then really expressing what that situation is doing to you will result in a real turnaround. It somehow triggers goodwill to come out of it together with mutual effort and benefits. It works every time I use it and I highly recommend it! And it works well because for some freaky reason, the other party usually comes out with an extra 'free' effort to smoothen out the situation. The rest is up to your guidance. Note: there is a zero-manipulation policy here! You need to stay real and honest, that's the only reason it works!

And action!

Here is how I came to deal with these bad news deliveries. Of course there are some variations depending on whether it's delivery only or if you have a target to get things to go your way forward. I think I read about it in one of the books written by Napoleon Hill and no matter how scary it is, it's the only way I act now.

Start with the issue! Shoot the bad news first! But again, try to bring it across as neutrally as possible, in straights facts. Then it's out there. There is no more guessing from the receiving party of where the conversation might lead. You're now ready to deal with the feedback and reaction from the receiving party, and continue to implement your own intentions of telling the news. So, after clarifying the issue, be ready to receive uninterrupted feedback. If the bad news is personal then be ready to get a very defensive and critical response. Don't be surprised by it. Then it's your move of explaining the reasoning (if any provided), the occurrences that impacted the decision and the gravity of the impact on future developments. Stay close to the facts, but mention emotions if you feel like that is an important part of the current decision.

As for closing, I already mentioned that it depends on your future intentions. In case no future contact or cooperation is foreseen try to leave the conversation with a short summary. If there are any feedback facts that you think might have any impact on the decision after all then agree to come back to it at a later stage. Otherwise close neutrally. It's important to be polite and professional, but there is no need for any overly positive displays of emotion. In my experience nobody takes them seriously after getting bad news!

In case future contact or cooperation is needed and important proceed with an open invitation as to how the receiving party sees this going ahead. Even if you already know what needs to be done give them the stage first and share your options second (here is your opportunity to agree on something and switch to a positive vibe). If your options are the ones your exec needs to see happen then simply state it like that and brainstorm any possible solutions. Then agree on specific actions and discuss the next point of contact. Again, avoid an overly positive ending as you simply don't know how things will go from this point on. Be fairly optimistic, with a sprinkle of motivation, and express your wish to see this handled well.

I had a situation once where I had to deliver bad news four times before the requested result was achieved. I did send them flowers in the end for solving the issue; you need to be considerate and small things like that often help future cooperation. What also often softens the blow in extreme situations is giving an option for them to contact your exec directly for any clearance. They rarely take you up on this and if they do your exec won't mind it.

Now, it's important to follow up on the agreed actions in a neutral, non-offensive or defensive manner. And yes, unfortunately sometimes going ballistic does help in getting what you want. But it's never the way a professional acts. How some people do their jobs nowadays bugs me.

Things rarely go well the first time around. And what bugs me most is the ignorance of the receiving party. I'm not perfect, sometimes I need to walk away from things empty-handed, but it only motivates me to get a suitable replacement.

Every situation is different, try things out and see what works for you. The last thing I want to leave you with is this: deal with these situations consciously and practically. Feelings will get hurt sometimes and there is nothing you can do about it. Express your regret where you see fit. It helps me a lot to see every situation as personal first while keeping the facts straight. That changes your tone of voice and softens your attitude and believe me, the other party will sense it and become a little more understanding and willing to cooperate.

Difficult conversations

Now let's move on to the more general topic of having to deal with difficult conversations. First of all, you have to read the book *Difficult Conversations*, which is the product of an extensive and pioneering Negotiation Project led by Harvard Business School. I have mentioned it before and I will probably do so again and again. It's an absolute must for any Assisting Professional, no — correction — any human being! It's a huge topic and I won't get into every nitty-gritty detail, just read the book and make it your own. Here is a short summary of things to remember:

- ✓ Every conversation is created by three realms: 1. what actually happened aka the facts, 2. the feelings involved and 3. identity impact. You need to understand and operate effectively in all three realms!

- ✓ Difficult conversations are created by assumptions and conflicting perceptions.

- ✓ It's never about the facts or what is true. It's about what's important to the parties involved.

✓ Avoid a battle of messages. Try to understand the reasoning behind the perceptions. Never assume others' intentions!

✓ Never ASSUME = when you assume you make an ASS of U and ME.

✓ Avoid blame! It will just weigh on hurt feelings even more. Instead try to figure out why you didn't see it coming and figure out how to avoid it from now on.

✓ It's always personal and it's always about feelings. Address the feelings involved first! Understand the impact on the identities involved and share yours.

✓ Every conclusion is personal and has a very real and valid inner reason. Everybody is *always* right (a tricky concept to grasp), you just need to understand why (from their perspective)!

✓ Even if its business, it's still *always* personal. It's about personal perception and understanding.

✓ Interpretations are dangerous as you *never* have the same information as others. This makes your perception always *different* from that of others by default. Always know there is a very important piece of information that you don't know about!

✓ Curiosity in the other's *story behind the story* is usually the key to conflict solving. It's not about whose point of view is right, it's about the fact that they are different. Urge a mutual understanding of each other's stories.

✓ When you've reached an understanding of each other's stories, only then you can move on to problem solving.

Again, it's an amazing book and you just have to read it! It will change your way of dealing with difficult conversations forever, whether they are professional or private. It will make your life so much easier and way more *Effective*! It's a soft skill you need to master to the absolute level of excellence!

And then there is this: be willing to compromise! It's a mindset that will open up a whole new spectrum of possibilities and cooperation that might never seem possible at the first glance. Have an intention to go for a win-win and you will never lose! That is a true skill of a great Assistant and you simply need to want it to be your own.

Kiss and make up

By now you can imagine that one of the elements that will define your level of effectiveness is the way you deal with situations where things don't go according to plan. Here is what I found to work when finding myself in a pickle with a brisk order from my exec to fix it! Clear your head for a second and imagine yourself in the role of mediator. The goal of a mediator is to find out what actually happened beyond the layers of mixed/hurt/aggressive feelings, find some common ground, and come up with solutions that work for all. I'll admit that it is difficult if you are closely involved with the party you represent. Here is where your mindset will have to do the trick and make the role switch work.

Before we move on, I want to quickly share a few ways of achieving a radical mindset switch. It is actually so easy you won't believe it to work, but please don't disregard the simplicity. It works like magic. I will start with a tricky one because you need to practice this one for quite some time to master it. In a moment of serenity of your thoughts you need to state to yourself that from now on you are switching to…. (fill in the blank role). The tricky part is finding that serenity and being able to stop your current thought process. It will take you a while the first few times, but with practice comes perfect. At some point you will just close your eyes, focus on the new role and you're done.

The other tricky part is that you have to train yourself to be persistent in staying in the new mindset without switching back to the previous one. By the way, this whole 'mindset roles' thing is hugely important and I will cover a few more essentials later on. For now, just know that a certain mindset means a specific set of values, qualities, thinking processes and actions that differs from any other role you play in life (for example, a role of an administrator is different to the role of being a caregiver). So by choosing to take on a specific 'mindset role' you actually need to define the appearance of every role upfront. That's why this needs to come with practice. Defining different 'mindset roles' is a skill and you need to master it to be successful in life. We will come back to switching mindset roles later on.

Now, back to switching to the role of a mediator. Let's say you managed to do that and now this is what you have to pay attention to. First, understand the different vantage points and their reasoning by asking questions. The more you ask, the more you'll get.

Remember not to stop at the first answer, go at least three levels further before you continue. The psychological result of getting people to talk is automatically creating room for negotiation, understanding, variation and compromise.

There is a certain automatic goodwill when you see that you really have been heard. Then try to evaluate the facts and clarify the events. Be careful not to end up in excuses or in-depth exploration of details that are too specific to this occurrence. You just need to understand the flow and causalities to know what to correct in the future. Then define and agree on new flows, procedures and agreements.

This mediation can only be executed after the event (definitely not in the heat of the moment), but don't wait too long. And don't forget to show your appreciation for any cooperation and be grateful if the other party goes to great lengths to make it up, even if it's their fault or negligence to begin with. Use your common sense when it comes to rewarding behavior. It's a nice quality and I always appreciate the gesture if it happens to me! Goodwill — it's a valuable but untouchable substance that forms the core of any successful relationship. Being sincerely *Nice* is the only way I have found to contribute to goodwill *Effectively*.

The writing on the wall

Getting things done and being a consistent overachiever is great. But it's also a state that can make you blind to some elements around you that might throw you off your throne. Speed: we love it, we live and breathe it, we want it, we miss it, and we fear it. Having systems in place that work is cool, but when things are moving way faster than usual any system tends to overheat. We need to be cautious at times where we experience an acceleration around us. Have conscious time outs to regroup. That makes us even more effective because these are the moments where we analyze our systems and tweak them to fit to new situations or new people.

I already mentioned the twin brother of *Effective*, *Efficient*, and I want to get him back in the picture again. Sometimes efficiency is the main goal. And yes, being efficient definitely supports being effective — but not the other way around! Think about it: if you have little time to do something you first of all find ways to cut corners on quality. And that is the main reason why I prefer being effective over being efficient. And yes, sometimes being efficient is what your exec wants so you need to be exactly that. To get you out of possible trouble inform him upfront when you foresee that the quality will suffer due to a time/budget deficiency. Sometimes that will be just fine. Just make sure that everybody is on the same page. In such a scenario you'll be *Effective* but with a different result. Knowing whether you need to be *Effective* or *Efficient* upfront is important. Clarity is king!

And remotely linked to the previous point I want to mention workload. If you have a period of overload then reconsider your levels of excellence. Sometimes good is good enough and nobody will even notice the difference from your usual delivery as they won't have anything to compare it with. Know that you have an option to vary the delivery standards. Be aware of what is really needed and what are the extras that you think could make things special. Try to have a measurement system to know the delivery level in a split second. It can save you a huge amount of time and effort. It might even result in having more time and energy to get other stuff done, making you more *Effective*!

In case people are used to your level of high-end delivery you can also say you're trying out some new methods so the result might vary a bit and see how it will be received. It's one big circuit of productivity we need to create, guard and nurture.

Money is in the list

Before we close this skill I want to revisit your list of achievements. As we talked about before it's your source of motivation and an ego-boosting tool you definitely need to have. I want to add one more reason to have that list somewhere at hand: it's a great source of innovation! It's a tactic I read about on a forum a while ago and I occasionally apply it with amazing outcomes.

It's meant to stimulate your thought process in case you're stuck and it goes like this: have a separate section of your own or others' stories of surprising and creative solutions. Sometimes it's a funny story you read. Sometimes it's an inspirational act of courage and example of out-of-the-box thinking. Sometimes it's a tragedy-turns-miracle or really just anything else that sticks with you after hearing or reading about it. You won't believe how powerful those examples are.

Even if they're not related to your issue whatsoever, it's the thinking pathway that will inspire you! It can cultivate a solution that you would never ever have thought of otherwise. And the funny thing about those stories is that the resulting action is usually very small but it gets you exactly where you want to be.

I even had a situation once where just telling one of those crazy miracle stories to the person next to me inspired him to come up with a solution to our mutual problem.

Maybe it's the vibe, maybe it's a supernatural force or maybe just a coincidence. I don't know — but it works. In case of emergency or desperation you can always give it a go!

And the verdict is...

Let's conclude with all the good stuff that this skill of being *Effective* brings you. This skill makes you an expert in what you do and how you do it. You grow by learning from precedents and tweaking your systems to get more productive in the future.

In a weird way, this productivity flow also tests the quality of your network while looking for better ways to get things done. Experiencing problems in this context is a great way to clean up your network and make choices of whom to keep and whom to ditch. No hard feelings, sometimes things don't work out and don't fit anymore.

Then there is the matter of communication again. The more *Effective* you are the better you'll become at communicating. Actually it might be better to mention those in different order. You see, communication is partly a hard skill and partly a soft skill. There are tons of techniques to improve your communication, but even the best technique might not work well if you ignore the personal touch. Don't forget you are always talking to a person, even if you're writing an email.

Get comfy with a variety of communication styles and don't forget that even in established relationships communication styles tend to change over time. To keep the effectiveness you need to evaluate your communication skills once in a while. I know that is easier said than done. But don't worry, life is a funny thing! You will notice deficiencies in your communication when bleep starts to happen. Don't be surprised by it, just know what to do when it happens.

The impact of you being effective in your relationship with your exec is pretty out there so I'll keep it short. He will trust you more, he'll appreciate you more and he'll have peace of mind while delegating. Actually, you being effective will make him more effective by default. No question about it!

The verdict:

**By being *Effective* you will be empowered by the results
and your exec will excel by being in control
while presented with results!**

Take-away notes

 ACT

✓ Manage expectations: be careful what you promise and what you promote
about your abilities. A lot is expected of you, you better deliver!
✓ Use this mindset as a controllable tool to build trust
✓ Have your 'PA Bible' and don't forget to update it regularly
✓ Use the role of mediator to get things done with a win-win outcome
✓ Experience confidence backed up by your past
track record and accomplishments

 BE

✓ Be a mood changer by using the 'small-task completion' tactic
✓ Become a master of difficult conversations
✓ Be willing to compromise to achieve your goals
✓ Be good at switching mindsets of your desired roles
✓ Be considerate and nice to create goodwill in your relationships

 THINK

✓ Remember, consistency is the key to a shiny track record
✓ Use a 'forward-completion' mindset to get things going faster
✓ Focus on the facts while delivering bad news, but be
considerate of the feelings involved
✓ Always know there is an important piece of
information that you don't know about
✓ Decide upfront whether you need to be Effective or Efficient

Chapter 12. Dedicated State of Mind

Results you will achieve:

✓ *Win respect and acknowledgment by showing your dedication*

✓ *Immerse yourself in the satisfaction, pride and fun of your job*

✓ *Be the anchor and the connector for your exec's office and teams*

✓ *Create amazing relationships by matching integrity values*

✓ *Find out what connects you to your workplace and use it to boost your spirits*

This is the most misunderstood quality for the simple reason that dedication is asked and assumed to be an automated skill. Almost every resume contains this skill as a prerequisite and for a good reason; it gives the employer security that the employee will do a good and honest job.

Most people confuse being dedicated with being responsible. There are overlaps, but there are also very clear distinctions. First of all, you can measure being responsible through results, you can only measure being *Dedicated* through the way the actions are provided and that is intangible. You cannot describe being *Dedicated* because every person shows it, or is at least capable of showing it, in a different way. In other words, being *Dedicated* comes from within and usually doesn't ask to be compensated. Being responsible always asks for a payment in one way or another. And here lies the dirty secret of being truly *Dedicated*: it's not a duty and the only one who can summon that quality is *you*. Your exec cannot make you be more *Dedicated*. He can create the arena for it to be likely to happen, but that's about it. It's the way you are that can give birth to dedication! It shows that you care about what you do. It shows you value something intangible and that same something gives you inner satisfaction that really has no price tag or title. That is, in my opinion, the most valuable and most underestimated skill of being that needed Assistant.

Being in that *Dedicated* mindset makes your job so much more satisfying, no matter the circumstances. Not only does it unify all previous W.A.N.T.E.D. skills, it also unifies you and your exec and your duties in a very profound way. That connection makes you superb at what you do, because it influences the *how* by having a strong *why*! This is a very particular personality skill that enables you to be more personal. It underlines your devotion and your goodwill. This is the right and sure way to make anything your own — by dedicating yourself to it.

101 essentials

The key concept of being *Dedicated* lies in the how. That makes it a direct byproduct of this very tricky term: integrity. I have defined a few different types of integrity to make it easier to understand and implement in my daily life: personal integrity, objective integrity and expected integrity aka loyalty.

Let's start with **personal integrity** because that one is most clear and dear to us. This one has two job descriptions. The first one is the well-known *righteous consciousness*. It's the voice and the standard within us that tells if what we're doing is in peace and accordance with our values, morals and virtues. And you better keep it a happy camper, because once upset it will bug you from here to eternity. Most annoyingly, it will not stop until you do something about it. We all know what I'm talking about so let's talk about the other power of this double shift.

The second one is your *teacher/broker/partner in crime*. You can actually negotiate with this one until you find a middle ground for the act in question. In other words, it's the part of you that keeps promises, honors commitments and delivers on agreements and goals. And yes, you can negotiate a little here on quality and time frames. The only part which is non-negotiable is the actual action and delivery.

Personal integrity is the building block of you as a person. Be true to it, listen to it, ask advice and comply with it. There is always a difficult startup process when you begin to actively engage with your personal integrity. Usually it's a very unconscious part of us that only matters when bleep hits the fan. The only way to actually get to know your personal integrity in all its glory is to consciously work with it. I love this companion. It really does make you a proud person, in business and in private — but only if you are a great executer of its set standards. This makes you an amazing human being to be around. Others just feel it when you are true to yourself.

It's not always easy, as we Assistants often sacrifice ourselves for our jobs and even tend to lose our identity to fit the prerequisites. So once you decide to pledge faithfulness to your personal integrity, it usually changes you from within in ways you cannot imagine. And after a soul-searching journey of finding and defining your inner values, you rise up from the ashes of the old you, and people notice it. This is the only way to become truly proud and confident, by devoting serious effort and fearlessly fighting for what's important to you. Once there, you will attract likeminded people, events and jobs by default. Magic in progress...

Moving on to **objective integrity**. This is the most simple one to incorporate and the most important in case you need to make a fast decision. It's all about protocols and overall agreements. It's when you actually don't need to ponder for too long. Just by knowing the 'rules' you can go ahead and resolve a situation or make an educated choice. You simply have to know your company's blueprint, guidelines, protocols and code of conduct. It will make your life so much easier. Whenever you circle around specific locations and institutions get to know their 'rules'. We already do that in our day-to-day lives anyways because it's the only way to organize things. Also, use this principle whenever something new happens and there seems to be an absence of structure — make one! We are good at structuring, use this super power. Yes, in the beginning people might rebel. People don't like change or structures that are foreign and alien to them. But at some point they see the benefits, there is no question about the direction, there is clarity and order. Remember the 'relatively predicted fixed points of reference' from Adam Toffler. A structure has the power to ground people.

By the way, creating a sense of clarity is the first and most forgotten tool to make any situation less messy or uncomfortable. As soon as everything unspoken is said, clearly put on paper and understood by all involved, there is a clear way out and all options are open for a solution to be found. When there is no set code of conduct try to clarify your understanding by asking for every detail that describes the situation by everybody involved and put it in writing. Then try to find a pattern of misconceptions and a few commonalities. Now you have to set your findings against the specific desired outcomes of all involved and you have a great starting point for a peaceful resolution. The solutions and variations will become very obvious at this point. People tend to over- and underexaggerate in times of stress. Simply focusing on the facts might be a solution in itself. Have your preset 'resolution plan' template ready in case you need to resolve a messy mystery.

And now let's surgically examine the trickiest integrity of the siblings. The third one is about the ***expected integrity*** that we are usually not aware of. And the reason I want to dive deeper into this one is because it is the reason why integrity is so valued and so virtuous. Let's face it, if you want to be labeled as someone with integrity you need to prove it in action first. And that is why it's important to know the expectations of the person judging you upfront.

For the sake of clarity here is a very simple example. If your exec values a timely fashion above all then you better be early on every occasion. Now, let's say that you instead think that overdelivering on results is the key ingredient of pleasing your exec. Being sent on a mission, you found a way to get something important done even better than he expects but that would take an extra few hours after deadline to accomplish. You might find yourself in a pickle when your exec won't be so happy with you after you proudly present your accomplishment. You see, the tricky part of expected integrity is that usually people judge us by their own set of standards of integrity. And only when those match your own will others applaud you and tell the world that you are a person of integrity. It's a practical example which may differ from soft-skill integrity expectations, but you get the point, right?

Of course big bold acts of integrity are always met with admiration. But examine those and you will see that most of them are based on standards that are largely accepted as pillars of integrity in general. To translate this theory to our job, here is one big lesson. Get to know the integrity standards of people you work with on a regular basis and you will have a magic secret weapon for amazing relationships and results. You can categorize these as 'like attracts like'. You can play this game fairly easily because it's all about virtues, there is no manipulation by design. It's all based on choosing to act in a way that suits both parties' best interests.

It goes without saying that if you don't see any fit between your set of standards and the person you work with, don't bend too far to please them. It's the combination of all three integrities that makes each very important. The one cannot act without the consent of the other. You just need to be aware of different natures and sources. You can act boldly, but only after understanding the compatibility of all!

It might seem like a lot of work, but we all have this great tool that is (almost) never wrong and works at the speed of light — your gut feeling. Listen to it and rely on it. From experience, I can tell you that having that internal conflict of integrity standards can be an ever growing pain. In the end I could not succumb to the standards of a particular person as they were too much in contradiction with my own personal integrity and I had no choice but to leave.

Yes, it was uncomfortable, because there was no apparent reason for my departure. Obviously I could not talk about it or mention it in any way, shape or form. But it was tearing me apart inside and in the end, the sibling closest to your inner core usually wins. Don't be afraid to leave the battlefield. Your internal wellbeing is very important if you want to be that superb professional. Every jar has its own lid, you'll find yours.

Secret ingredient

For this skill to be present and strong there needs to be one more thing in the mix: something that connects with you! That is the secret to being *Dedicated*. Something in your workplace needs to speak to you on a very profound level. It needs to spark your enthusiasm, your understanding or curiosity. It needs to connect to something that you believe in, cherish, admire or aspire to. It's a deep admiration of the skillset of your exec or maybe the product of your company. Maybe it's the way people work together or how people are supported and motivated. Maybe it's the cause your organization fights for or represents. You get the point — it's the intangible resonance of something around you with something within you. One point of connection is enough for you to become very *Dedicated*.

Looking back at every place I've worked there was always something amazing that kept me going like a Duracell Bunny. Sometimes it's the genius people. Sometimes it was the industry I so wanted to be a part of. Sometimes a combination of the community we served and the ideals of the leaders. On some occasions it was simply my duties. Or even an amazing location that really triggered a spark of wanting to get the maximum out of it. Whatever it is, be aware of it and cherish it.

At times when you lack energy or persistence remind yourself of that connecting factor. Take time to experience the divinity of the attraction: that will surely boost your spirits. OK, OK, don't get me wrong — there is nothing airy-fairy about it. It's just that when you talk about the intangible it has a tendency of running away with your imagination. In the hard cold light of day it's the trigger that makes you want to be exactly where you are. You just need to be present in that moment and feel you 'belong' there. Enjoy the momentum and use it to get ahead!

The cool thing about this connection is that it makes you want to get involved in the processes on a multilevel, which will make you a great go-to person. It will also make you more observant. You will see the themes behind the conversation. You will sense the mixed feelings during meetings so you can jump in proposing a coffee break at the right moment. It will make you work an hour longer after everybody has left the office and not feel depressed about it. The company's results will feel like your own and make you proud and cheery. You will ask the right questions with the right amount of interest. You'll be able to make links between two less than logical topics creating something new and helpful. You will have a great relationship with the teams around you. You will make it easier to get something done because you'll know how to 'play it'.

The extra mile

This skill will enable you to go the extra mile even when you don't really feel like it. You'll know it matters so you will go for it. And that will show. The honesty of your actions and involvement will shine through. Let's face it, we admire people with dedication. But think about it — why?

I ask this question a lot because (not to blow my own horn) people frequently say that I'm oh so dedicated. But it wasn't really something I did on purpose. So I often wondered what makes people say it. Because I was working late evenings and weekends? That's not dedication, that's an extreme sense of responsibility that easily deprives you of having a private life. And that's surely not something to admire.

Is it because I usually know a lot about how things work? Or who to go to if I need something done ASAP? Or is it because I always tend to squeeze another meeting in although there is barely room to breathe? Not really. I do all that because I have to get a lot of things done. I talk to many people. I can always figure out a way to give someone five minutes of alone time with my exec if asked nicely and appropriately. Is it because I tend to get things done at the right time and in the right fashion? No, not that either. It's my addiction to perfectionism, which, again, is not always a good thing. So, if that wasn't it, what was it?

Only when I started my own company and had to write an 'About me' page did I discover that every job I had prior to that moment had something amazing in it for me that made me blossom from within. It's this freshness of wanting to get up and jump around without an obvious reason. That is what made me dedicated and people noticed it.

It's the intangible made visible! And I truly think that most Assisting Professionals know what I'm talking about. We cannot really describe it, because when said out loud it sometimes sounds stupid. You will see that people don't get it. You will see faces staring back at you still waiting for something to come that would make more sense. Funny, I see so many faces in front of me right now that it makes perfect sense why I love my job and this crazy profession! It's a weird sense of pride that moves me. Now, let's quickly move on before you discover you're reading a book written by a lunatic.

Mix and match

I already mentioned it but it's quite important so let me spend some more time on it. As showcased above, being *Dedicated* is not a standalone skill. Actually, it cannot stand alone because even if you are passionately connected to the sacred element in your job you will still need other skills to make it happen. Dedication makes the rest of the execution easier and more fun, but it has no voice of its own.

Actions speak louder than words! This saying reflects the essence of the point I'm trying to make. It's the last skill in this W.A.N.T.E.D. collection and for a good reason. It's the missing link. It's the reason and the fertile foundation for other skills to come naturally. Just remember to use a variety of tools, mixing all the skills together in a fine and personalized mix.

What makes this skill practical is its amazing power of giving you a *focus*. In times when my mind is running in circles, a reminder why I love my job makes me snap out of it. In a split second I'm sharp again and ready to dig in. It's very cool how things change when we make ourselves think about *why* we actually do stuff. We are such creatures of habit, even our habits have habits. So be strong and break a habit once in a while, just to know that you can. Push yourself to make a new habit, just to know that you can. This is by the way a great bridge to the upcoming chapters where we'll do some soul-searching, but in a concrete and constructive way. It will be all about templates, lists and one-liners used by personal development and business gurus that are stuck with me forever.

How to make dedication work in your favor? Let's first give this animal a name — how about, interconnection! It's a strong skill of Assisting Professionals anyway, so why not use it to make ourselves bigger, better and stronger! Try to interconnect stuff you like with stuff you really avoid doing. You will be amazed how many mundane tasks can be made fun.

Here is such a dull task that a lot of us are very familiar with: try to think of a vague connection between your passion for the industry you work in while going through the monthly piles of receipts and expenditures. When I used to work for three super-busy execs who all travelled across Europe three times a week you can imagine the daunting pile of receipts I had to deal with, in different languages and currencies. While trying to decipher them, filtering the extra tips, guessing what they were actually for, trying to match the expenses to projects or categories dictated by the accounts department, I then had to — here comes the kicker — staple them onto an A4 sheet next to each other in the right order of dates. Afterwards, as I also assisted accounts, I needed to enter all of it into the admin system. It usually took me a full day a week to do only that. So here is a challenge, try to make that fun and something you actually look forward doing!

Now, do you want to hear my version of fun receipt time? For this job I really had to rely on my 'dedication connection': the awesome industry! The inspiring thing about that job was definitely the live entertainment industry and the amazingly cool stuff we had to deal with on a regular basis. Therefore the link was very easy to make:

I imagined it was me who had this amazing life of traveling around. Of course it included an awesome wardrobe filled with the latest fashions, visiting beautiful hotels for exciting projects, eating in fancy restaurants with extraordinary people, hearing crazy stories every time I took a cab etc. I saw all that happening in a Hollywood-like movie setting (in the meantime conquering the pile of colorful receipts).

And it was even more fun trying to think of an unusual explanation for something I found on the receipt that was a bit out of order and logic. I mean — if you buy a sandwich with a questionable name, wash it down with a bottle of weird water costing four times the amount of the sandwich (some people dare) at 3am in the middle of a city that never sleeps, followed by a shopping spree featuring a camera, mouthwash, a book on crime, a ticket to a museum and a new tie - it does make me wonder. Believe me, I had some fun doing that!

And so, dedication mixed with creativity is the remedy for making your job a lot easier and more fun. And I'm not even talking about seeing things coming from far away because you just know how your exec acts in certain situations. The times that I made bets with myself, obviously winning each and every time and having a good reason to go out for a treat are countless!

Body of proof

Now, I hear you're thinking: what all that has to do with real dedication? I bet this might be the first time you've heard such a serious topic as dedication linked to fun stuff and wild fantasies. Well, here is my plea...

First of all, the very fact you are trying to make boring and mind-numbing tasks fun means you really love your job and yourself. Second, the fact that you know exactly where your exec has been, things he needed on his trip and places he has visited will make you very effective when it comes to follow-up planning. You will be prepared with an extra supply of what he might need and you will know exactly which restaurant he means when he asks to book that funny little place he accidently found in the middle of the night while walking back from the office back in January. It will make you prepared and look very involved and dedicated.

Overall, being *Dedicated* will prove you are a true professional. Especially for us Assistants, who are not bound to one single industry, it will make you look suitable for any job if you show that you can make it work wherever you are. Remember, it has to trigger you on some level. The 'dedication connection' needs to be present and vivid. And if your personal integrity is strong you will truly be boosted in any place you end up working. Because really, every place has its magic, you just need to look for it as sometimes it is a bit more hidden. Assisting Professionals are true chameleons. We have the ability to blend in everywhere quickly and seamlessly. That is a strong selling point for a good Assistant. And another tip: don't forget that *you* can be that interconnecting factor. It's a very inspiring place.

Green, yellow, red…

Like every skill this one has its own pitfalls. The obvious one is losing yourself and any entitlement to a private life next to your office existence. It happens to me every time, I can't get over it. It's a skill I haven't mastered yet. I'm getting better at it though and being a mother kind of demands it. But still — it's difficult to keep both worlds in good proportions.

That's why I'm so happy I discovered that being or living in balance is an urban myth! It's physically impossible if you are a passionate Assisting Professional. The stress of being in balance is not worth it in my experience. To make life great and suited to you as you see fit I have discovered a great way of being in a state of equanimity. I will explain it more extensively in the following chapters. So if you are anything like me, don't despair! There is a way to make it work without a Zen-like state of life that you only read about in magazines. It's very fulfilling, and the cool thing about it (spoiler alert): it's a movement and you are in total control. Oh my god, we love that word!

That was the red light. The yellow is bit more personal. It can be anything where you catch yourself wanting to reverse time so you can go back and act differently. Here is my confession and hopefully it will make it easier for you to locate where your own downfalls might be. There are two things I tend to do when I'm overly dedicated to my job and my profession. The first one is overdoing it and the second one is getting too nosy.

They are slightly connected because if you act like that in the beginning of your employment people tend to interpret your questioning, high activity and obviously eager presence as suspicious. After a while people get to know me and realize that it's because I'm really interested in the things I ask 1001 questions about and they will talk freely. But there were a few occasions where it got me in trouble.

Overdoing has everything to do with my tendency for perfectionism. Most of the time this also occurred in the beginning of a job, when people were just not used to a certain level of service. That created uncomfortable situations because occasionally I was doing things which were not really needed at that time. The funny fact is that by the time I was leaving, those initial unnecessary overdeliveries became the new standard. But in the beginning it was awkward, also because it obviously took me quite some time to deliver and make it look nice. I'm more conscious about that element now, but I still get remarks along the lines of: why are you trying so hard, it's fine as it is, let it go, I'm not used to it so drop it etc. I guess it's a maturity skill, so it's all in my bright future, I hope!

Remember that being *Dedicated* is something that you cannot actually say about yourself. The true labeling has to come from others. The same goes for when you want to locate your own areas of danger: pay attention to what others say about your efforts. Yes, it's not always nice and can be difficult to hear, but it's very rewarding, giving you tools to get better or adjust your ways.

And the verdict is...

In closing, I would be delighted to repeat myself. This skill makes all the previous skills come together to make you look like a real pro. It gives you the ability to have a helicopter view. It will make your job easier, faster and more fun no matter what anyone drops into your lap. This skill will make your journey interesting. You will be involved in your surroundings on a very profound level which is actually a very safe place. You will see and notice more stuff and you'll use that to your advantage.

All the interconnections considered together will give you sure tools for being and feeling in control. Results will provide you with a deep sense of fulfillment. It will surely make you needed and as close to being indispensable for your exec as practically possible. You will love what you do more consciously and not only in good times. You will understand that there is a deeper connection to your values and virtues. Your exec will have peace of mind, a sense of security and trust in both of you as a solid team. And he will certainly be proud of you as his trusted Assistant. Whether he shows it or not — you know it's there!

The verdict:

**By being labeled *Dedicated* you will make all the difference
to the way your exec relies on you and your qualities.
That will make your team strong, sincere, and valued.
It will excelerate both your and his performance!**

Take-away notes

 ACT

✓ Create predictable structures/procedures in your work territory
to provide your teams with a secure and safe working environment
✓ Know and study the expectations of your
workplace, especially those of your exec
✓ Consciously perform your job with a deep sense of pride
✓ Be creative in finding fun elements in your job

 BE

✓ Be clear on what your personal integrity values are
✓ Be protective of your personal wellbeing
✓ Be aware of the elements that connect you to your
workplace and cherish them
✓ By being connected to your workplace you will
become the connector for others
✓ Experience deep pride of yourself and your job

 THINK

✓ To level up your integrity focus on the why of the how
✓ Remember to evaluate all three integrities combined to
find your match in your ideal job
✓ Knowing your 'dedication connection' will give you the ability to think on
a multilevel about various processes, information flows, relationship
benefits and beneficial cross-over outcomes
✓ Remember: this skill connects all the other W.A.N.T.E.D. skills and
makes your job fun and satisfying

Chapter 13. '3What' Method: Action Plan

Accept responsibility for your life.
Know that it is you who will get you where you want to go, no one else.

Now you are familiar with and educated about the six W.A.N.T.E.D. mindsets and you have a lot of examples, explanation and tools. But you might still wonder how to apply any of the above and if you even need it. I'm sure that every Assistant has all those skills already in them because those are the universal qualities of an Assisting Professional. Here is the thing, you can always improve. Even if you have been in this profession for a long time. Maybe things got rusty. Maybe it's less needed at times or maybe you are really comfy with where you are right now. Whatever your situation, I'm totally fine with it. Although, there is always a level-up!

This book is written to guide and inspire PAs to strengthen their passion and do their magic in a more conscious way. We are never too old or too skilled to grow. The growth won't be the same at every level, the core values will only get stronger and better. Be a lifetime student! That is the most glorious skill of any human being and the core secret of any successful person. I'm sure you'll find something to tweak. I'm sure this book will give you a moment to reflect about your job. There might be stuff that really sparked some resistance or curiosity. Our profession is never dull and life will always give us things to solve that are new to us in some ways. I hope this book will be a reminder for you to pay attention to the untouchable. Your soft skills are the actual reason for your greatness. And soft skills are all about *you*!

If there is nothing new in this book for you up to this moment I would like to congratulate you. I hope you will make time to think about *you* once in a while: be nice to yourself, spoil yourself, take care of yourself, invest in and stay affectionate to your own needs, aspirations, hopes and dreams!

For those who are still there with me and curious — let's go for it! I have cool ways of working on yourself, top experts tips and tricks on ways to do things more effectively and more models, methods and scientific stuff about our big beautiful brain. Keep on reading, you will love what's to come! One point of thought — this part will primarily be about personal development strategies and wisdom, with a pinch of airy-fairy mindfulness (it's what our brain needs to function to its best after all) and most of it won't come from me. I'm merely a scrambler of things I have read about and heard about in the last decade.

> *No map would do you good if you don't know where you are.*
> *No shiny destination would make you happy*
> *if you don't know its location.*

I've been on a quest for growth and development for a long time now. I just couldn't understand and didn't want to believe that hard skills lay at the heart of amazing people. You can sense their inner power, their mental togetherness and the wisdom that has nothing to do with practicalities. It comes from within, it's born in their minds, patched together with inner values and transformed into one big magnitude of character which moves through the years of experience and cultivates willingness to grow.

I have quite a few role models and people I look up to. Do you? They can be big names but also people all around you — you meet and work with such people all the time. We just don't recognize their inner strength, powerful attitude and wise approach from a distance. And due to our fast-paced culture, unrealistic deadlines, stress and information overload, we don't know how to stand still anymore. There is so much negativity around us we don't even seem to notice it. News channels report mostly on tragedies and problems. Even sitcoms (some of which I dearly love) are all about something bad happening and it being made funny. We need to get some distance, look inside and see what's really going on!

The following chapters are all about digging into your own mindset, rebuilding and refurbishing it if needed and making yourself feel and look stronger, happier, relaxed and in control of your life. Yes, you do have control over your life — just not in the way you expect. We commonly perceive control over details as full control. I call it maintaining after-actions. What I mean by control is getting a grip on the big things in your life and leading them in the desired direction. No more blame, no more playing the victim. Define what you want in life and plan for it to become reality. It's all in your mind, thoughts in combination with coordinated actions will make it all happen.

I have collected many things over the years. Various theories and methods helped me get going, including shortcuts and a bit of psychological trickery. Yes, it's possible. You just need a system for it! I hope you are excited and eager to get to know yourself on a more profound level. I'm not a shrink, but we'll do some soul-searching together.

You will see that your success lies in your mind. It's born there like everything else around you right this very moment. Your mind will make you the person you want to be, you just need a few tools to get there. You are the 'personal' behind the Assistant. You make this profession wanted and needed. It's you who makes the difference behind the scenes and we all know it. So let's polish you up, give you some attention and get you into shape so you will feel comfortable with yourself. You'll be prepared and ready to grow. And most of all, you'll be proud of yourself and know all about being a powerful and self-assured Assisting Professional.

The '3What' Method

There are three stages to every plan of execution. I called this plan a '3What' method. Virtually every program out there has its own name for the same thing, so it's nothing new but very logical:

What's now?

Evaluating where you stand, what brought you here and the circumstances that define this moment. This is where you gather facts, assess the situation, define the momentum, collect the good and the ugly, identify any emotions present and put it all together to paint a picture. Most importantly we need to accept the situation today as the reality that you have created through your own certain actions, thinking in certain ways and expecting certain results.

What's new?

Goal-setting time. Did you know that the majority of us set the wrong goals and aspire to unachievable definitions? No wonder we don't get what we desire and get disappointed by the results, leading to an unwillingness to set new goals. What's the point? Most of us set goals because you have to or because society around you dictates it. But did you really ever set a goal that made you jump out of bed in the morning all prepped, knowing what to do, for how long and what part of the end goal the completion of the next task represents? I collected bits and pieces from the world's greatest goal-setting experts to share with you. It's not all of it, but enough to get you going for the purpose of cultivating a stellar 'PA state of mind'.

What's next?

Implementation is hard work. Working on yourself is intense, confrontational and difficult because it's intangible. You can measure the progress by the amount of aha-moments and wonderful insights, but that is just the beginning. After getting the 'aha' you actually need to do something with it. Luckily, brain science gives us a lot of tools and clues on how to work with this important grey matter. Did you know

228

that we still know relatively little about our brain? In fact, it's the least known part of our body to this day. It controls everything, but we don't really know how and why. Most neuroscientists admit that although we know more and more thanks to modern technology (there is even a machine that can deactivate parts of our brain now), we still are just at the beginning of brain and mind discoveries.

By the way, I use brain and mind as synonyms, but of course they are not. You can divide them into physical and mental elements or anything else if you prefer. The point is that they both correlate deeply and profoundly with each other. I'm not an expert on this, just a very curious PA looking for ways on how to use and improve what's in my head to excel and help others do so. Spoiler alert — you will see that everything is defined and controlled by your thoughts, whether you like it or not!

In the upcoming chapters we'll explore every '3What' question in depth and I will sum up theories, tools, templates and quick wins for you to try out. Find something that works for you and remember that everything is difficult at first. Everything in this book is proven to work by experts, multiple studies, research and world-class brainiacs. And some of it is so easy and fast — you'll love it.

One warning here — the '3What' plan is a stellar compilation of traditional, heavy, psychological, airy-fairy, business and ancient ways of personal development. Just pick things that you think sound good and give it a go!

Exit your comfort zone = resistance list

As I mentioned to you at the beginning of this book, it's good to collect things you have a very strong reaction to. Usually it's the resistance to something new, outrageous, unknown, bizarre or just weird. It's a sign that you came across something that your mind does not have a fitting context for and the first thing it does is disregard its purpose. It's our primal instinct of survival and protection! You have to understand one crucial thing here — the key to successful personal development lies in new knowledge, new ways and unknown methods. It's everything you have not done yet, not executed, not tried or thought of before. So it's very logical for our habitual personalities to keep all of that as far away as possible. You have enough in your head, new stuff will have to wait, right?

You see, people don't like to change. Change brings a component of insecurity and nobody wants that. But what if instead of asking 'What if it doesn't work?' you ask yourself 'What if it does work?'. Just pause for a second and see what this little alteration does for your mood. It's uplifting, it changes the whole perspective and ingredients of your mindset — and it is just one little word switch.

This is the power of thoughts in a snapshot. People can change, but only if they want to! You can change somebody, if you lead them to believe it's the best thing for them and ignite the willingness to take the needed steps towards the goal. But it's ultimately not you who change them, they take the action to do so. And here is the whole power of change: it's this holy combination of thoughts and coordinated actions. I will explain it in more in detail in a bit, but for now this is important to understand. This is why we need to work with our points of resistance first.

Your resistance list is your fast track out of your comfort zone and you know what they say: success lives on the far side of your comfort zone. It's like a filter system that shows you where your attention needs to go. The stronger the emotion that goes with a point of resistance, the more there is for you to deal with, but the gain is also bigger!

This is really hardcore psychology here. It's the theory of resonance: it doesn't matter how, but if you react to it, there must be a connection! And for you to grow, you need to at least be aware of those connections.

In case you are still not convinced that you need to work on your resistance first, digest this fact: rebels are actually most heavily controlled by what they resist despite what they think and how they act. Everything about them, usually even unconsciously, is focused on the thing they are against. Their whole existence is focused on proving something wrong or trying to ignore it. Go figure!

Get your gear

Before we dive in the practicalities of the '3What' method let me shortly summarize the obvious situations where you deliberately want to go through the steps to tune yourself, empower your spirit and heighten your qualities.

First aid kit

These are situations when you feel stuck in your job, or any life situation for that matter. It's also a good band aid to use right after a major happening, usually the one that is bad. This can be any situation where there are lots of emotions involved, heated arguments, surprising turns of events that you did not foresee but rock the boat big time. This usually happens because we tend to get caught up in life. And if you additionally experience stress or the sense of being overwhelmed, we miss signals around us indicating we are going off course. We don't even see the red lights flashing in front of us and the result meets us right in the middle of the crowded junction. It's also good to practice '3What' when you consider quitting — take the time to review things first. Not to make you change your mind per se, but to make a careful decision on how to proceed and which direction to take.

Change alert

When your job adds more execs, responsibilities, new team members with persuasive reputations or anything like restructuring, take overs or new chains of command come into play is a good time to crack it up a notch and boost your perspective, overview and reference standards. This goes for any transition from old to new where some elements remain the same. You're not totally out of your comfort zone, but there are definitely some alterations and tweaking needed.

Point blank

This is where you are absolutely out of your comfort zone like when starting a new job with new rules in a new industry: new everything. PAs are rarely Assistants by desire. I found that most PAs kind of rolled into being an Assistant from all walks of life. So wherever your life takes you next, make sure your mindset is attuned and prepared. Hard skills can be learned and measured but your willingness, soft skills and mindset need upfront conscious definition, thought creation and repetition. Similar handlings, but the approach is oh so different!

Bigger, faster, stronger

And then there are people like me, who never stand still and realize they need to grow if they want to stay at the top of their abilities and accomplish even more. The A-game is not a matter of standing still! It's running a marathon and you need to keep up. You need to have a strong desire for a moment of awareness, to balance your life's checkbook, to set the right goals and to find smarter ways to operate. There is a fire burning in you and you want to feel alive, challenged and rewarded: this is where you need to master the process of reflection!

The next stop is...

Wherever you are on your path of being a professional Assistant you know it's ever changing! Our profession will always change because people change, the economy changes, technology changes: everything is on the move and it's expected of us to be on top of everything. We need to go along with the waves of constant change and preferably be ahead of them. Our responsibilities are not set in stone. Nowadays for example, there are more sessions and courses on management skills for Assistants than ever. We get the responsibility for leading the leaders from behind and we actually get the room to do so and recognition for doing so.

There is only one thing that stays the same in this whole game — your core W.A.N.T.E.D. qualities! They are not specifically applicable to any time, industry, economy or even character. If you master your W.A.N.T.E.D. soft skills you will be a trooper anywhere you end up and you'll stand tall behind any leader. This is why implementing the W.A.N.T.E.D. skills to the max will make you a needed Assistant, anywhere, anytime!

This soft skills core always stays close to you and it is the one that actually makes you authentic (which is the most valued quality given the latest studies). All you need to do is regularly review the '3Whats' and make a new game plan, each time with a specific course of implementation clearly defined. You will be laser-focused, motivated, engaged and adaptive to the needs of your exec, no matter what life brings. You stay true to your aspirations and that will show in your execution. That will ultimately manifest in diehard results, and that is what makes you an indispensable Assistant.

These steps made a huge difference to me and I'm sure you can find something that will benefit and elevate you! You just have to be willing to change your mindset!

Don't get confused between my personality and my attitude.
My personality is who I am. My attitude depends on who you are.

Chapter 14. What's Now? – Evaluation

If you know where you are, something shifts.
The perception, vision and retrospect of the past vs now vs future.
It requires a degree of surrender and it enables you to move.

By now you should have a list of things you might want to try out, tweak a little or (if you're anything like me) you have already Googled training material and started reading 'smart' books. Here is the tricky thing about just diving in headfirst into development programs and theories — if the topic you're trying to conquer is not connected to your 'pain point' right this moment, then you will not grasp the full meaning of the teachings!

I can explain this phenomenon with a simple example. The daily quotes! We see tons of those in emails, forums, blogs, Facebook feeds, LinkedIn groups etc. You read them, some you like, some don't make any sense and sound silly and some just hit you like a heat-seeking missile! The latter one is usually actually seeking a heated warzone inside you and it lands exactly where it hurts the most! That 'pain point' is your zone of inner conflict that you're dealing with right that moment. It's astonishing how well you get the wisdom or silliness of a quote if the timing is right. I had a few of those moments — being saved by a quote that changed my perspective in a split second and helped me to move on. The same goes for training and development courses... So pay attention to your reactions to your current 'pain points'. They will guide you towards the content needed to enable you to deal with them appropriately.

Brain radar

This 'pain point' principle explains why some attendants love a training session and why some don't see any point to it. On a neuroscience level it can be explained by your RAS brain. The Reticular Activating System is the way and the why your brain controls your attention. The RAS filters all incoming information, directly deciding whether you have to pay attention or let something go and skip to the next information flow. The cool thing about your RAS brain is that you do have a certain control over it.

Here is how: you need to tell it what to look for! Tata! It works like a radar. If you have clearly defined goals in your head then your RAS will constantly be on the lookout for anything that might get you closer to your desired outcomes. Whether it's a relationship, a new job, a new house, those spectacular shoes, a name, a service provider, anything! It just needs a purpose.

We all know those situations where if you're thinking about buying a new car you see that car everywhere. It's your RAS brain in full action directing your attention to the desired topic. It filters out the things that are important to you. Things that you think about the most or worry about. By some weird mechanics it provides you with solutions and guides you to the next step. That's exactly why I keep telling you to only focus on things that stick with you while reading this book. It's the natural selection process of your own mind. A magical process! Without RAS, you will have to invest way more effort in finding your ways. And thank god for those filters, or we'd be distracted big time by every little thing in our proximity.

We Assistants are smart creatures so let's use our RAS brain to our advantage. How does RAS know what's important when you don't use it consciously? Everything you think about on a regular basis is simply labeled as important. That's why we need to watch our thinking! This is exactly the reason why they say that you become what you think about. Hold this thought, we'll come back to it in a short while.

What this means at this stage is that we need to know and define our goals and objectives first. To do that we need to know where we stand right now. I have collected seven ways for you to get a clear picture of where you stand so you can efficiently decide where you want to go.

There is only one big rule at this stage of the '3What' plan: it is more about the determination than evaluation of the current position. Just paint, don't color! It's essential to stay non-judgmental here. There is no right or wrong — it just is! When we get to the third step (planning forward) you'll have your chance to see whether you need to do more or stay comfortably where you are. For now, be a non-judgmental witness to your situation.

The main reason for this approach is to avoid guilt management to take over causing you to freeze up, become unhappy or unmotivated to set your goals at the next step. Refrain from judging and this amazingly powerful hidden skill will help you not only in terms of personal development, but most definitely in business situations too.

Here we go — defining where you are! You're on the road of evaluation now and these are your possible exits:

Exit 1 — Big picture

I want to start with one of the most frustrating things I personally struggled with: the balance myth. Note that I used the past tense because when I had an insight that I was chasing a ghost I found a strange peace of mind and figured out a way to make it work. See, balance is a state of momentum! It's impossible for us humans to be balanced all the time and at every momentum snap shot. But the world dictates that we have to be balanced in order to be happy.

I found chasing that balance very stressful and frustrating and it required a lot of effort. My job got in the way constantly. It was almost like the universe was proving a point to me: I was no good at it, no matter how hard I tried. Balance is a photo moment of being in the middle of heavy burdens and the insecurity of getting off balance in the next moment is not motivating. And by the way, when do you know that you are in balance? What's the formula?

I went on a quest to find something that could work for me in combination with being a super-duper devoted PA to my extremely busy execs, keeping my 24/7 support role up to speed.

And by setting that goal, my RAS brain guided me through several training programs where I selected things along the way that worked for me. I combined all of them into a system that looked like it would be workable and it even became kind of exciting.

Being a control freak PA I created a position where I could be in control of my wellbeing whereabouts and there was no rigid framework for myself.

This means you can't really go wrong, but you are motivated to stay in the game! I call this system an 'Empowered Professional Triangle'. The main principle is: don't butcher yourself by not being in balance — play the game of controlling your efforts within the frame that you decide on.

There is nothing airy-fairy to it and it's based on a business model of quadrants. Did you know about our mental predisposition towards quadrants?

Most training and development programs work with some kind of quadrants and I will introduce to you some of them later in this chapter.

The reason for us to accept anything that is divided into quadrants as 'useful' is because the quadrant principle is based on a fundamental stability shape. Square shapes are in balance, represent equality, overview, recognition of a solid base and clarity in positioning. So whenever you want to present anything for our minds to accept as reasonable and trustworthy, pour it into a square-shape model and people will unconsciously tend to agree with it.

Meet the **Empowered Professional Triangle** system!

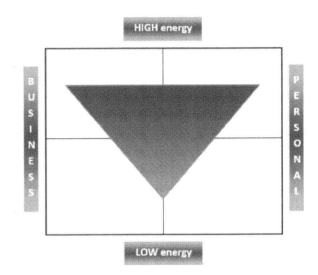

First of all, this system is only meant to make you aware of your patterns and your (mindset) state whereabouts. Knowing where you are (approximately as that is not a precise science) will enable you to make changes if needed. Also, this is based on very wise words I received from my father once while asking for advice on how to deal with pressure at work. He constantly works under extreme pressure being in politics, side by side with demanding government officials. Here is what he told me that has never left my mind's eye: 'See your life as 100%, but there is only this 100%. It's up to you how you divide these 100% into parts and sectors of your attention.'

In translation: if you decide to set a bigger piece aside for your personal life, your business side will have to give and vice versa. It sounds simple, but it's difficult to comply with in our society where we want every sector to be 100% each. Just think about it, this 'only 100%' principle is exactly how life works! And it's OK to give a little in some areas once in a while to focus on others. The cool thing stays: you control how you divide your time and energy and how you partition your 100%! Yes, you have the power to change everything right the next second by deciding

239

what's best for you now and acting on it. Keep this in mind and you'll understand the huge advantage of the 'must' element below.

The theory of the triangle is quite simple:

The horizontal business/personal measurement is your focus direction (are you all over your work or are you paying attention to your private life?). The vertical intensity measurement is your energy supply barometer. The inner space of the triangle is where you want to be at all times! You have to reside in the triangle to be balanced! Here are a few rules to follow: three don'ts, one must and a huge may.

Don't

- ✓ Obviously, don't stretch to the extremes and don't stay there for too long. You may change the form of the triangle but don't stretch it to the far ends.
- ✓ Don't cross over to the opposite side too fast, your mental and physical systems can't handle the contradictions in a short period of time. Make a plan and change gradually.
- ✓ Don't define your triangle towards the downside of the quadrant and don't forget to revisit the favorable shape once in a while.

Must

There is only one must and that is that you have to move around! Here is the reason why I love this system: it's OK to be in the out corners of the triangle, as long as you get into the habit of moving back in any other direction when you're too close to the border or realize that you have been stuck for a while in one spot. It's up to you in which direction you move, as long as you are moving. It's like the circus artist that balances on a tightrope, he never stops, he constantly makes mini movements from left to right, finding his balance in the middle – by moving! This comes from the ancient wisdom of Tao. That is life, it's the flow!

Another unfortunate truth is that your personal life will always be affected by your business life, they are placed as opposites for a reason (and it's not my invention). It helps to get the best of both worlds if you see yourself as a pendulum, swinging back and forth within the framework which is set by both your ambition and your limits. Remember to learn from Icarus: aim for the sky but keep your limits in mind (or you'll be burned by the sun aka the 'burn out').

May

You have total freedom and control over the shape of the triangle! Make it fit your purpose or your goals and aspirations. Change it or adjust it whenever you want, just don't forget the don'ts and you'll be fine. Make it longer if you have a stressful job that is often very tiring. Make it closer to the business side if you're very career oriented and don't have a lot of family ties that ask for attention. Move it closer to personal side if you are the mother of a toddler. Make it smaller if you don't want to permit yourself too much playtime and discipline yourself. Make it bigger if you are positive about your power of self-control and your ability to get yourself back to the other side when approaching the limit.

The centered big triangle is in my opinion the optimal shape, maybe even a bit closer to the upper side. To be honest, our profession will always have stressful moments so permit yourself to be low on energy once in a while. Only on the low do we realize we need to slow down and take some time off. Also, being tired after a big project or event is a very satisfying feeling. It's just a mindset of how you look at the situations you are in. The main thing is: don't be too hard on yourself! Play around the center and indulge yourself to go to the extreme corners if needed.

Make your triangle in your head or even better on paper and have it somewhere in sight if possible to remind you about the urgency of 'centering and moving around'. It looks simple, but it has a huge effect on my life. It made me relaxed and I feel so much more in control of my life. And it's definitely not as strict as being balanced. You know why this system is so effective? If I ask you to pinpoint your 'wellbeing' location right now, you will flawlessly point your finger to the right spot. That is the power of simplicity and visual representation. You instantly know where you are. So judge whether you are in or out of the power zone and what your next move should be. Play the game!

There are only three quick questions you need to ask yourself while working on your 'swinging' balance:

✓ Where am I in the triangle?
✓ Am I too close to the border?
✓ How long am I here?

By answering those you will instinctively know your current position and any action you need to take to adjust the situation if needed. At some point, you will do it automatically. It's a cool place to be, in total control of your wellbeing!

Exit 2 — W.O.R.M.

Let us continue to the next mode of analysis. This discovery is actually a direct result of my RAS brain in action. On my quest to fine-tune my qualities I got into a position where I was well aware that some things needed to change and most of them where connected to my soft skills and mindset. I was relatively new to that principle, so I was constantly looking for theories and methods on how to reset your mindset. And things just popped up as I went through my days...

One of those 'coincidences' occurred while tidying up the private library of my exec back then. Out of the hundreds of books which I was packing into boxes one little old book caught my eye. The title was so compelling and struck such a cord with my own inner battles (my pain points) that I could not keep my eyes off of it. The book is called *Working on Yourself Doesn't Work*. I asked to borrow it for a few weeks (I had a crazy schedule so reading a book was really a luxury and I had to 'invent' spare time to get on with it), but I was so intrigued by the title that I read it that same evening from cover to cover.

What a revelation! Life is simple, you just have to know about that principle! There are a lot of useful facts, most of them based on the long and spiritual journey of the couple that wrote it. I don't mind the airy-fairy stuff if it helps me to grow easily and faster than I ever imagined. I will share with you a few elements from this book, but I strongly suggest you read it to get the whole picture. It will simplify your life for the better. The book is about instantaneous personal transformations and it's written by Ariel and Shya Kane.

The wisdom that is fitting in this section of the '3What' plan is the W.O.R.M. principle.

Did you know that we have close to 200,000 thoughts a day?! And the crazy thing is that 98% of them we also had the day before and the day before that! Our mind replays the same content but has the creativity to present it as brand new each day time and again, and we all fall for it. That is what W.O.R.M. is. It's actually a computer programming term (Written Once Read Many).

To translate this into your daily life looks like this: once-made decisions or defined emotions are remembered as 'the truth' in our minds. This is of course very useful evolution wise, but it can also be a hugely limiting habit. Going through life, it's activated automatically and unconsciously when you are placed in a situation similar to the one when W.O.R.M. was formed. We think it's new! We think we are making a new decision and we act without questioning. It's a totally unconscious strategic move. And so it becomes just another repetition in the endless chain of events. We forget that we are listening to the same recording time and again. And the sneaky thing is that it's updated over time so the origin is disguised and we don't 'see' the historical facts of the original formation.

Just a quick side note here regarding limiting beliefs. It's a huge psychological area and it's believed to be the source of all evil in situations where people are feeling stuck or truly unhappy and blaming the world and circumstances around them for their misfortune. Here is a very clear metaphor to understand why limiting beliefs have such a big impact on us: imagine you are planting a potted tree in the fertile grounds of a rich forest where it will have all the required elements to grow and flourish to its great potential, but you forget to remove the pot...

Our limiting beliefs are exactly like that forgotten pot. We all have those limiting pots around some elements of our thinking process. It's good to discover and define them and put those on the list to dig up first. Again, no judgment here! Those limits and beliefs are there for a reason, they were useful in the past so we embraced them and recruited them to be our soldiers. But things change, we grow up, we get smarter and wiser (yes, we do!) and most of those pots lose their function of giving you the safety and comfort which was so needed when you were still just a seed of potential! (I just love visual metaphors, don't you?)

Back to W.O.R.M. This next shocking truth will hopefully urge you to take those wormy substances seriously: your current reasonable decisions are mandated by W.O.R.M.s, which means that a younger, less sophisticated version of yourself is deciding on your life now!

So it's time to get dirty — dig up rusty pots and look for outdated products of W.O.R.M.s!

Now, this seems a bit too scary so let's set the record straight right away. We need W.O.R.M.s for survival purposes. Most of them are good, but not all of them and maybe not right now! That's the right angle to work from. How to recognize a W.O.R.M.? In the book, Ariel and Shya give some simple and unmistakable tools to work with. Here is my favorite. It's the feeling of deep satisfaction after making a heartfelt choice of how to deal with a situation that makes it *authentic* (in other words, *not* a W.O.R.M.).

They give a great example: it's like buying an outfit that you like and just moving on with your life (which means a W.O.R.M.y automatic action) vs buying an outfit and liking yourself in it so much that you walk out of the shop wearing it, stopping at every shop window to check out your awesome reflection. That is what the authentic feeling looks like!

A feeling of déjà vu is a great sign of an automatic action just as when you feel a strong need to defend yourself after doing something. An authentic action does *not* cry for defense or explanation.

To jump to the last step of the '3What' implementation plan — here is the bad news... Per definition, as the term dictates, we can't get rid of W.O.R.M.s for good. There is only one way to bypass them, and that is by being aware of them and choosing to act differently, supported by your logic and beliefs.

Observe neutrally -> Notice objectively - > Disengage actively!

Acceptance empowers us to act responsively rather than reactively. And don't be harsh on yourself for past decisions and events. Brian Tracy teaches us not to worry about something you cannot change, and you cannot change your past! Instead, save yourself the trouble of going through this process of dissolving old W.O.R.M.s during the tough times our lives usually present us with. Give yourself the opportunity to battle those W.O.R.M.s in a controlled environment when you choose to do it. So pick a time and a place you feel comfortable with. Make sure you get into a positive and relaxed state of mind first before you deal with W.O.R.M.s and you can be sure of your victory.

To close this topic I want to mention a positive inner working of the W.O.R.M. By knowing all of the above you just created a new W.O.R.M. of making conscious choices and being aware of old (possibly limiting) habits. See how simple and automatically it goes — our mind is a beautiful but a complex matter.

Exit 3 — Mindfulness

Let's stay in the airy-fairy corner for this one. And I'll be really quick about it, because it's just a supportive tool for the bigger purpose of defining where you stand.

Personally, I always disregarded the act of mindfulness while being on the run and very busy (how ironic, I know). For the purpose of research I made myself switch to a curious state of mind, which is a brilliant move in case you're preconditioned to disagree with a topic, and get into the theory, books and even some practice of mindfulness.

Surprisingly, except for a few really diehard spiritual sections, it's a very practical and nonfictional method of getting centered and grounded (I did make it easy for myself though and found a book that also stated a lot of neuroscientific proof to support the act of mindfulness, *The Mindfulness Code* by Donald Altman). It's a great state to escape to when you plan to think about something totally different from your current situation. I have embedded a habit of going mindful when I need some clear thinking time. It's way more practical than meditation so I can apply it on demand and on the run.

The reason I bring up this topic here is because of the simple truth that your mind can only think clearly after about 20 minutes of calm, focus and solitude (aka meditation). It's like a bucket of muddy water. Let it be for a while and the mud will descend to present the clear water. Now, I know about all the benefits of taking these 20 minutes off, but I don't have the time to do so in urgent situations (yes, yes, I see the controversy). And then came the mindfulness, promising me to get me to that clear state of mind within just a few moments. Meet my newly discovered secret system: become friends with your big toe!

Let me explain myself before you declare me a lunatic (hum, did I mention that before?). In mindfulness training they teach you to get away from your head and thoughts and dive in to your body. And they actually mean a physical focus on your body parts. It's the simplest and easiest way of being mindful. You have to think about the sensation in every body part at a time: the temperature, the state of comfort, the blood flow etc. And most of the techniques start at your feet and then move up. You see the reason to my madness? Knowing the force of habit I became best friends with my big toe. So in case I need to ground myself I think intensely about every element of its wellbeing! (And him usually sitting very squeezed in my high-heel pumps makes it very important to consider his unfortunate state.)

Whenever you reach that state of mindfulness you can start thinking about a certain topic with an extraordinary focus and clearness, be it a problem, a situation or a diagnosis, like we're doing in this chapter. See mindfulness as a method to get in a clear thinking state. Coincidentally it entails a non-judgmental state of mind which is perfect for this purpose. This is my newly found ritual to get grounded and quickly return to my center (by the way, saying your own name out loud works like magic too). What's yours?

While being in your mindful state, run a quick check on your internalized values, the values of your personal integrity and see if some parts of your life are not yet congruent with the state you envision. Take note of discomforts and points that are lacking, and we will find ways to work on them in the following chapters.

Let's move on to categorizing — something that we PAs love to do!

Exit 4 — Quadrants

As I said before, there are countless quadrant systems out there. It's up to you which one you use to categorize and learn the inner workings of yourself and people around you. Use one of them or all of them. They all have something that works, choose the ones that work for you and use your RAS brain as preselection tool. I'm not going to go into every detail but here is a short summary of options which work well for me:

Communication styles

DISC Quadrant — Dominance, Influence, Steadiness, Compliance. There are a few versions of those quadrants and it's really good to know them. There are some free tests online that may be helpful. Fill them out for yourself but also for the people around you and you will have a great tool to know how to get your message across fast and effectively. I like www.communication-styles.com. They work with an extended quadrant, give immediate primary characteristics and explain how to use them. We Assistants know like no others that communication is important. Communication issues are the main reason behind misunderstandings and unnecessary trouble, especially when you work in teams.

Intelligence quadrants aka brain preference quadrants

I really like these because they give you a quick road to how others think. That has a crucial impact on communication methods and gives you an advantage. You will be less surprised by others' decision-making processes so you can be proactive. There are two main strands: the inner quadrants (how you think and act within yourself, reflecting and impacting inner dialogue) and outer quadrants (what other people see of you and how you come across, impacting external dialogue). You should know both your own and your exec's ruling quadrants: strengths, weaknesses, practicalities, shortcuts and growth/improvement areas.

Again, there is a huge spectrum, so here are my favorites:

✓ External Quadrants System — The Hermann Brain Dominance (ABCD Model): Logical Intelligence (IQ — facts), Creative/Conceptual Intelligence (CQ — future), Practical Intelligence (PQ — form), Emotional Intelligence (EQ — feelings).

Ned Hermann's discoveries created a true revolution back in the 70s. If you're up for some profound theories, his book *The Whole Brain Business Book* is a great source, including tests and practical recommendations.

✓ Internal Quadrant System — Big 4 and Advisory Board System by Erica Ariel Fox: Inspirational Dreamer — Intuition (CEO), Analytical Thinker — Reason (CFO), Practical Warrior — Willpower (COO), Emotional Lover — Emotion (HR).

Together with Erica's addition of your inner Advisory Board roles, her book *Winning From Within* is a must-read for any professional, especially for us Assisting Professionals. She emphasizes a cooperation of roles to make you successful. That goes against most quadrant systems, where you are normally bound to a corner and advised to live in it. The holistic nature of this concept is why I love Erica's system.

Both systems are great for evaluating your thinking process and people around you. It will make you way more effective and efficient in whatever you do. Also, you will be able to provide some guidance to get your exec to the ultimate leadership excellence by using and implementing every part of his thinking process in the practicalities of your daily business doings. A sure way to excel for yourself and your exec!

Exit 5 — Weakest link

The leading rule in any progression is defined by the constrain theory. It means that the constraining factor determines the speed of progression. In other words, the weakest link in your processes or your weakest skill defines how well you're doing and how fast you're going *in general*. That is an interesting perspective. This is huge! Another theory that goes well with this one is that 80% of your abilities lies *within you*, so you have control over it. To draw a very simple conclusion: we need to constantly assess our weakest links and target them to accelerate our success rate.

There are a few ways of putting this into practice: life area rating, performance gap definition and the frustration list.

Life area definition and rating

This one has many variations. About 20 years ago (yes, I started early) I read a book, *The One Minute Millionaire* by Mark Victor Hansen and Robert G. Allen, and in it was an assignment to write a perfect story about how every area of your life would ideally look like, such as finances, romantic relationships, social relationships, career, health, wellbeing, fun etc. You can flip this assignment into zooming into every area of your life and defining what's not working and compiling a weakest link list. Additionally, those areas are great to work with when defining partitions of your 100%, guiding your focus and efforts.

The best way of training your mind to do the heavy lifting is to apply the Law of Three. This is one of 100 laws that Brian Tracy is working with. I would absolutely recommend getting familiar with all of them as these laws are universal and they work, whether you believe in them or not (compare it with the law of gravity). They work like mechanical principles and physical laws. And once you know them you will automatically shift your behavior and your thinking. It's more related to the implementation part of the '3What' plan, but for now let me quickly repeat the Law of Three.

Again, the truth is usually very simple as is this one, no matter if you are looking for a problem or a solution, always come up with three options! So while looking for a weakest link you better come up with three options for every area. Don't worry, nobody is perfect and we certainly don't think of ourselves as perfect — we always demand more of ourselves.

By the way, there is another application of the Law of Three and it has to do with memory. Our brain has a disposition that lends itself to threes. Multiple studies show that no matter how long a list is, you always remember the first two and the last items on the list best. So if you ever want to remember something quickly, make pairs of threes! And another memory trick is to color-code the groups to make it even easier to remember (green three is personal, red three is urgent, yellow three is groceries, blue three is admin etc.).

Once you have defined the three weakest links per area choose one to work on first and make an implementation plan for it. Once you have mastered it, you move on to the next thing on the list. Nothing more, no overkill! One at a time, but forever moving.

Performance Gap definition

This is the crucial part of the *Winning From Within* method by Erica Ariel Fox, who teaches at Harvard Law School and was mentored by the founders of the renowned Negotiation Project. I suggest you read that book to fully understand the meaning of it. Here is a summary in one sentence: Performance gap is the difference in the real-time performance resulting in a different expected outcome by doing something else than what you have planned to do in a certain situation.

In other words, if you logically prepare yourself to do one thing but keep on doing something completely different in real time, you miss something and don't get what you want. It's quite logical! Usually, it comes down to understanding your inner drives (the why) and realizing that you miss a specific skill when push comes to shove to act on your intentions.

I'll admit it, it's a bit messy when taken out of context. That book is really an absolute must-read. Yes, you can define recurring situations where you are not getting the results that you plan for. Yes, you can guess what skills you miss and work on them. But what usually happens when we don't get our way is that we rather blame others (because it's easier) than admit that we miss a skill. That book takes a very warm approach to yourself in a non-judgmental and supportive way. It actually motivates you to grow in ways you would not think of otherwise. When you know your performance gap you can make a plan to work on it and close it over time.

Frustration list

I don't need to explain a lot here — we are usually very good at pointing out what's wrong with us. So make a list of things that bug you right this moment about your life in general. Then choose the one area that would bring you the biggest peace of mind if you got better at it and or if you deal with it right now.

Whatever approach you choose or maybe a combination of them, know that you need to be aware of your weakest link. And remember that they change over time, so do this analysis on a frequent basis. Quarterly is a good pace as you need 21 days to form a new habit and get it into your system on a cellular level. That means you can learn at least one new skill every month. And, sometimes, by learning one thing other things become easier. So don't panic if you have a huge weakest link list — you will probably only have to deal with 20% of it (according to Pareto's 80/20 principle).

By the way, Tony Robbins has an online test that is a compact combination of all of the above. He calls it the 'Wheel of Life Identity

Test'. It's a grading system of the seven areas of your life and your thinking process. Check it out, it might be exactly what you need if you don't want to perform full in-depth psychoanalysis on yourself.

Exit 6 — Role-playing

This is very down-to-earth psychology. Swiss psychologist Carl Jung, a student of Freud, defined 13 archetypes of human characters. Overall, Jung was very influential and, among others, developed the concepts of the collective unconscious, archetypes, extraversion and introversion, the complex and synchronicity principles.

Jung understood archetypes as universal, archaic patterns and images that derive from the collective unconscious, the psychic counterparts of instinct. They are inherited potentials which are actualized when they enter consciousness as images or manifest in behavior on interaction with the outside world. They are autonomous and hidden forms which are transformed once they enter human consciousness and are given particular expression by individuals and their cultures.

In other words, there are twelve sets of behavioral and mental definitions which define how and why we behave the way we do. They are universal and everybody on the planet falls into one or more archetypes. They are:

- ✓ Creator, Caregiver, Ruler (Stability and Control)
- ✓ Jester, Regular Gal/Guy, Lover (Belonging and Enjoyment)
- ✓ Hero, Outlaw, Magician (Risk and Mastery)
- ✓ Innocent, Explorer, Sage (Independence and Fulfillment)

There are many tests online. It's interesting and useful to see where you find yourself and what your exec's habitat is exactly. The definitions of those archetypes provide a lot of clues to patterns, downfalls and areas of opportunity. It can give you an instant answer to how to build a relationship with a new exec in an instant. And no, you cannot compare them to horoscopes. I know enough people who do not match the profile of their star sign.

These archetype descriptions are connected to your behavior which can be changed or embedded by certain acts and decisions and nurtured by persistent application. They work well in getting to know the fundamentals of a person, even if there are a few archetypes combined in one personality.

Again, it's just a push in the right direction. It's up to you to do the nitty-gritty work of getting to know people around you on a more profound level if you want to build lasting and durable relationships. This labeling is good to begin with, it will spare you some bumps along the road. Also, it's a good way to find weakest links, which are apparently universal!

This is one way of role definition. Let's call it psychological role-playing. The other one is called practical role-playing and is connected to the tasks you have to do in your daily life. I have already mentioned this earlier, I love this role-playing version because this is more manageable and has an obvious setting. The practical roles you can define include secretary, advisor, travel officer, housekeeper, partner, friend, mother, manager, colleague etc. The possibilities are countless. The roles can be fixed or they can change. You lose some or you gain a few over time. It's good to take some time and define the practical roles you play in life. This will give you some perspective. You'll also get an instant picture of your time management and your attention management preferences. In this way you can compare your reality with your ideal situation.

I usually prescribe this exercise to people that are very stressed. Whether it's a colleague PA, an entrepreneur I meet at training or my exec. It is a magic relief formula that gives you instant peace of mind. It's a sneaky way to get control of your life in a snap. Why? Because understanding your roles gives you power to shift. Decide to upgrade or downgrade your attention and efforts in some roles. That frees your head up from stress and tension by default. Give it a try!

The next step, after you know the roles you play, is to define a mindset for each one of them. This is actually a way to achieve exclusive focus when you perform that role. I can't really explain this one: the common reasoning is that a clearly defined mindset has magical ways of just working things out and being effective. The deeper theory is all about automated task selection and preferences which match your current mindset. And you can switch mindset by telling yourself: 'And now I'm going to play role X.' It's the same theory as with multi-tracking, I can't really explain it but it works.

The easiest way to start practicing this switch is with the 'relaxation and me time' mindset. Kick off by closing your eyes and saying 'And *now* I'm in my relaxation and me-time mindset!'.

Pause for a second and start to recite all the qualities and actions you identify with this mindset (quiet, peace, enjoyment, pleasure, sleeping in, couch potato, lounging, daydreaming, listening to music, grabbing a massage or time in the sauna, sports, going to your favorite restaurant, nature retreat, being by yourself, reading etc.). At some point all of that will take over and you will be inspired to act on some of those propositions. Et voilà! Once you experience this mindset switch as quick and effective you can practice with other mindsets. This will change your life for the better and make you *Effective* in everything you decide to do – guaranteed!

Jay Abraham, a world-class business consultancy guru, actually goes a step further and tells us to create templates for every mindset. I have translated it into and combined with a well-known 'if/then' construction. I will explain this when we talk about behavioral change since it's a very powerful thing to apply when you want to change your practical ways. In this context of mindsetting and roles it's all about predefining recurring situations (the 'ifs' aka the roles) and then connecting them to the preferred behavior or a thinking pattern (the logical practical expression of that mindset aka applying chosen mindset templates).

It's all very theoretical so here is a mindset template example from my life. As I mentioned before, I usually urge and advise my execs to tell me anything that comes up in their minds that should go on the to-do list or any ideas that we need to look into. Whether it's by text, WhatsApp, a quick call or an email — I want to have it! That is the role of a receptionist that gathers all incoming info flows. So the mindset template tells me that I need to check devices ABC regularly for those messages. Then I have to verify if any of those messages are urgent and ask for any other preferences (sometimes it's not as urgent as my exec originally tells me). Then I have to gather everything in one place, categorize and order per topic, execution method (to email, to call, to research) and by the right exec (I assist a few clients at the same time). What follows next is another mindset template, that of the secretary, who needs to deal with those actions. There is a separate action template to support it and the behavioral definition of how is clearly defined. But it's a different set of skills that needs to activated. When the time is there (my 30-minute blocks), I act on those roles separately which makes execution faster and provides a clear overview of things on my plate.

Another mindset template is the one for being a mother. The action template: I need to block out uninterrupted time for being with my daughter, I need to demonstrate calm and patience with her as she is starting to put together longer sentences and sometimes cannot find the right words or combinations straight away etc. Or the being a partner template: ask about his day, remember the projects he is working on, plan quality time and actually relax during those sacred moments...

The good thing about mindset templates (aka checklists) is that once familiar with them, you don't have to think too much and can just get on with it. You switch in a snap and the more of the same you do, the more focused you will be. The multi-tracking! It sounds like a lot of work, but you don't have to predefine all roles in that much detail. For this purpose, evaluation, just list your most recurring roles, divide the time spent in each role and think of the amount of time you would actually like to spend in it if the world was picture-perfect. You will get a clear picture of where you stand and what needs to be done.

It helps to predefine your mindset tactics (mindset templates and checklists) once in a while. The reason for this is to remind yourself why these roles are important to you and how you would ideally execute them to your utmost fulfillment. You will act on them with confidence and be there, present and alive, 100%. This is the way to a happy and mindful life. Make it your habit and comfortably rule the realm of unconscious competence!

Exit 7 — Buddy

This last one involves some real-life perspective — get a buddy or someone who can play the role of external confidant. Most of the time we are so caught up in our lives, the rat race and ongoing responsibilities that we have simply unlearned the ability to reflect. A buddy of some sort is a good way to return to now, get a little grounded and see things as they actually are. Things have only the meaning you give them. Often we label things wrong as we are too biased, have strong preferences or just follow the social expectations.

It's good to get a second opinion and preferably from a person who is very different from you. That person does, however, need to have a basic understanding of your life or your area of expertise.

Usually we find that support in a family member or a friend. You have to be able to talk freely; we all need that once in a while. Personally, I found it difficult to open up as our profession is kind of a loner positioned, especially with all the confidentiality and integrity issues. But I was pleasantly surprised and greatly supported by (relative) strangers once I reformulated my issues in uniform stories. Very fulfilling, I can tell you, and it actually taught me a great deal about thinking creatively and the ability to change vantage points.

Having a mastermind group, a local chapter or a circle (like LeanIn.org circles) is trending. It can be a group of likeminded people or just a group of people looking for a second opinion or outside support. Social media provides us with multiple options, choose something that fits your needs.

And hopefully our Global PA Academy society and our upcoming online PA mentoring platform could fill this role for most Assistants. I will tell you more about it at the end and I have a great proposition for you to join us free of charge and see for yourself how we can support each other to grow and excel together. Stay tuned...

Review

By now you should have a pretty clear picture of where you stand, what your challenges are and, being a proactive hands-on Assistant, you already started to plan the execution. I really want to ask you to hold your horses for just a little while longer. The trick is to first define and agree with your end destination. Drawing a map and making course corrections is way easier than stopping along the way not knowing where you should go. Next chapter is all about goal setting and I will share with you some great pointers on how to get your goals into a template and actually achieve them. The downer is the fact that achieving a certain mindset or soft skill is not an exact science. Usually, the only way to know that you're there is putting it into practice over and over again for someone else to notice. Live and learn — we'll get there!

Before we move on I have one last point for you to remember. It's logical to evaluate when you experience a change in your life or when you're stuck. What is really important along the way is for you to put together a collection of winning systems and practices. It doesn't matter if it worked only once and in a very specific situation — you never know when, how and in what circumstances you can use it again.

We tend to forget good things, strange but it's a fact! We might get lucky and the victorious way of acting will automatically become your new W.O.R.M. through the emotional intensity of fulfillment. But it's better to handle these treasures consciously and with care. Create your our inspiration guide with tactics and strategies. It's different from your achievement list, by the way.

The latter one is about the end results, the inspiration guide is about the methods. We discussed it in prior chapters. And I don't think it would be a long list either, but it can be a true lifesaver if you're really stuck or feeling down in a certain situation. What helped you snap out of it last time? What did you do then to change the course of events? We usually remember the moment of a turnaround. Think back to those moments, what triggered the change?

Most success stories are based on extraordinary applications of strange and uncommon strategies and tactics. And if you don't have a list like that then Google some extraordinary stories.

Some ways of getting to amazing results can inspire you to try something new or be a motivational resource. You never know from where the helping tips will come!

We are born naked, wet and hungry. Then things get worse...

Chapter 15. What's New? — Goal Setting

If you fail to plan, you plan to fail.

We all know that goal setting is important and actually, we all do it. The irony is that for something that positive and motivating it usually ends with big disappointments, false expectations and low self-esteem. It's an unfortunate fact that most set goals are not achieved. And to make matters worse, mindset goals are even more challenging to achieve because they cannot easily be measured. There is a constant battle with yourself and your mind has a lot of automated tricks that make it tough to turn around on demand.

The good news is that once you consciously decide to change, the transformation takes place almost instantaneously. More to it, once you experience the impact of your new mindset and the effectiveness of your new soft skills you will be addicted to getting better and transforming faster. The very cool thing about your mindset and soft skills is that the closer they are attuned to your core values and personal integrity the easier they will be mastered and the faster you will apply them with ease.

They feel good! The most amazing thing about the right mindset is that you become an immense magnet for all things alike and situations that would give those qualities magnitude. Those are the laws of life, the Law of Synchronicity and the Law of Correspondence. Brian Tracy gathered them all for you — have a look!

Why bother?

The second step in the '3What' plan is goal setting. Before we go on I need you to be positive that you will get where you want to go. Yes, it will take hard work, blood, sweat and tears — but you'll get there! Those battles make life interesting, right? I've read a lot of quotes about this battle of life and the gains, and the insights, and the outcomes — but they never really touched me. My RAS was not on for those tips and they never landed with me. But then I discovered Gary Ryan Blair, aka The Goals Guy.

For a very down-to-earth European PA living and breathing Dutch culture Gary's message is over-the-top American. But boy, that message landed! The way Gary views and talks about goals, or better yet challenges, is truly inspiring. In my quest of setting big New Year's resolutions (of which 96% fail according to research) I discovered Gary's 100 Days Challenge. It's an online coaching program launching worldwide at the beginning of the year and followed by approximately half a million people around the globe, who are chasing their goals together for 100 days.

I had big plans last year so I decided to join in. Actually, I was sold after reading his free manifesto — it all just made perfect sense to me. He clearly says it's going to be tough, you will have to change and you will have to endure lots of difficulties. Wow, that's a slap in the face followed by a gentle motivational push. A very weird but effective method. Anyway, the thing that got me fired up were these two quotes from The Goals Guy:

- ✓ Don't limit your challenges, challenge your limits
- ✓ It's not actually about achieving your goal, it's the journey and the person you'll become while achieving it!

I just loved it! It brought everything in me together. I knew and had experienced the fact that after achieving actual goals, the festive state of mind was fairly short-lived. Now I understand why: I was celebrating the wrong outcome! It's not the objective that is to be applauded (at least not exclusively), but the person I've become after a grueling journey! A person that is so much wiser and better equipped. This new and improved person could take on bigger challenges and do even greater things. Now that was something to be really proud of and celebrated. That is exactly what I passionately want for you to experience!

While most of this chapter will be about tips and guidelines on how to set goals that you will actually achieve, my advice would be to think of the outcome in a more intangible fashion. Who is the person who will get there? Who is the person who will stand at that finish line to go on and undertake even bigger things? That is the person and the compelling qualities you need to describe in the form of goals. The 'reverse' goal setting you might say.

We human beings are very practical, so we need actual tangible goal setting to keep us moving and get us going. In the bigger sense of this journey, physical and definable goals are your tools to get there, to the desired emotional state. To be proud of who you are, be passionate about what you do, be content and fulfilled with your situation and still have dreams, hopes and plans for more. It's that emotional state that will stay over time while achieving countless goals.

Pushing your limits to the next level by doing practical things in your pursuit of new goals to conquer. The physical outcomes and goal completion will continuously prove it to yourself — you still have it in you, you're *awesome*!

State of mind at the finish line

This is the main thought and a new vantage point for you to practice during the act of goal setting. It will (hopefully) motivate you. If all of that is way too abstract for you here is a simple example to demonstrate its core sense: while you pounder yourself in a gym with weights, running your butt off on treadmills and participating in countless group sessions it's not the fact that you lost excess weight that counts. It's how you feel about yourself looking in the mirror! You'll say, duh, of course. But let me tell you about a tricky experience where things are less obvious.

At one point I was in charge of a tough negotiation process simply because of a language barrier. It happened totally by coincidence and I found myself facing experienced opponents with way more skills and knowledge than me. In other words — I was thrown in to swim with the sharks. I fiercely defended my break-even numbers (as strongly expressed by my exec). I was being forced to give in and occasionally humiliated. I cried in the bathroom because others just don't take a young blondie with high heels seriously. I stayed awake in foreign hotels thinking about a possible strategy. In the end I was able to close the deal with a win-win proposition. That outcome was absolutely to everyone's surprise I must admit, including my own!

That is a personal growth path that you can only celebrate by acknowledging your journey and seeing the person you've become at the end. It was not about the deal itself (I don't even remember the specifics of it today). And it was not even the fact that I had set a goal for myself to become a good negotiator (I never strived to be in that position). My goal at that time was to prove the value of our product and proposal with confidence and dignity on behalf of my exec. I was his delegate and I had to prove myself (because what I really wanted was to get a shot at another project). That tough negotiation was a tool for my growth that I didn't plan for, didn't foresee to happen and didn't expect to bring the result (of learning to negotiate) with my initial goal of doing something seemingly unrelated.

That's exactly why we're setting goals first, before diving into the practicalities of implementation. The path to completion can be very different from how you want it to be right now. Even so, you could probably never imagine the physical form it can possibly have. Let's just set a goal to get to Rome. Which road will lead you there will be chosen by your RAS brain and the laws of life!

In this sense, just a quick side note. I'm not a big fan of traditional project management that dictates that you predefine every step in detail, budget and precision. Those details require a lot of work and will probably be largely obsolete after just the first weeks into the project. Set big intermediate review moments, set estimates and plan only until the first outcome will be visible and quantifiable. I have experienced lots of U-turns early on in the projects. And it's such a shame to see all that hard work and planning go down the drain.

Agreed rough estimates (usually not too optimistic so it's always a win in the end, which motivates all to go on) and short time frames until the next review — that's how I have conducted most of the projects I run for my execs and with a 99.5% success rate (yes, I'm not perfect). It's way less stressful, less time-consuming and urges you to be more proactive and connected to the ongoing developments.

Remember — make things doable and easy for yourself to keep on going. The flow matters most and your mindset is your 'underused' tool to get it going! Think of how a river finds its way to the ocean. It bends to find an easier pathway. No matter how many detours it takes, it always ends up in the ocean.

Rules of engagement

Let's start the actual goal setting. Here are the rules of great goal setting masters. Firstly, it's not a coincidence that I mentioned evaluating each area of your life in the previous chapter. It's common practice to set goals the same way, so you can see it as a template. Here are some guidelines that you need to stick to while settings goals:

> *Fantasy is a dream without a goal,*
> *Dream is a goal without a plan,*
> *Goal is a plan with a deadline*

Write goals down on paper!

Research shows time and again that the probability of you achieving your goals increases by almost 50% if you write them down. Mind you — only 3% of the population have actual written goals. Only 1% actually achieves them on a regular basis. To do that you need to review your goals regularly. Coincidently (not!) — only 3% of the world's population is labeled successful. It's your decision to join them!

'3P' concept

Write your goals in a Positive sense, in the Present tense and in Personal 'I' statements. Example: I master the art of positive thinking. Note: our subconscious mind does not understand nor registers the concept of 'not'. So don't use it in your goal setting or you'll achieve the opposite. Example: I'm not punishing myself for stupid mistakes. Instead: I forgive myself, I'm kind to myself.

'3D' method

Make sure your goals are three-dimensionally compliant (emotion, time bound, specific win):

They have to be connected to a bigger emotion, they have a sense of urgency, and they need to have a specific element of contribution to yourself as a person (here on the subject of soft skills).

Deadlines

No goal will motivate you to get into action if there is no sense of urgency. As Brian Tracy says: most of people send their goals to the island called 'Someday'. Better yet, send your worries there instead on a one-way ticket, with no passport and an expired visa! Note: deadlines are meant to be moved. Never give up on your goals, move the deadlines! Keep asking yourself: what's more important, the deadline or the goal?

S.M.A.R.T. system

Specific, Measurable, Attainable, Relevant, Time-limited. I would tweak a few of those into a more explicit method:

✓ Specific and Measurable + add Simple/Childproof:
Make it childproof and ask yourself: does a six-year old child understand the goal and can explain it to another six-year old? Could a six-year old child tell you how far along you are and when you've reached the finish line? The definition needs to be that simple.

✓ Attainable + add Doable:
The renowned Izek Ajzen (who is an acknowledged planned behavior and behavioral change psychologist) said that the key to behavioral change lies in the precision of a 'behavioral definition'. That implies the rule: if you can *show* it to someone else, you can learn to do it! Every time you set a goal ask yourself: can I demonstrate it to someone else? It's very important to understand what this implies. It will change your world, literally. Example:

Can you *show* me how to be healthy? No! You *can* show me how to eat two ounces of veggies every day, drink eight glasses of water and perform physical exercises for 30 minutes.

Can you *display* 'be careful' to a child? No! You *can* tell them to walk slowly while holding a glass or how to hold on to the ropes with a firm grip on a swing.

Can you *show* me rich? No! But you *can* show me a bank statement with a specific amount, invite me to a 'mortgage-free' mansion and pick me up in a private jet.

✓ Relevant + add... to your current moment in life:
A lot of people are chasing their childhood dreams that have no urgency or fulfillment value anymore. But you are used to saying it's your dream so you just keep on going without any attached emotion or willingness.

✓ Time-limited + add... in foreseeable future:
Again, you do need deadlines, just make sure they are not too far away in the future or they will not be seen as urgent. To do that you need to break your big goals into smaller pieces with the first deadline approaching at least in the next quarter, or even better by the end of this month.

✓ Practice the Law of Three: set three goals for every area of your life.

Fast tracks

Once you have your goals there are several things you can do to set yourself on a fast track to the finish line.

Rewrite

If you rewrite your goals regularly (preferably daily as that is a habit of the most successful people in the world) you will get there faster. It's the inner workings of the Law of Attraction combined with the eagerness and focus of your RAS brain. Remember: things that appear in your mind frequently are labeled as important for your RAS brain to consider. So those recurring thoughts better be your shiny and awesome goals!

Visualize

See yourself as if you already achieved it! Your state has to be festive, happy, content, proud aka very emotional. Just imagine you could do magic and everything would go according to plan: smooth journey, favorable circumstances, luck and the needed resources at your disposal. By the way, you know what they say about luck: luck is when preparation meets opportunity! A great guide on how to effectively visualize your goals and get them into your system is a book by Nisandeh Neta, *Elements of Success*. It is highly recommended as a practical guide to achieving any goals you might have.

As your soft skills are not easily translated into clear pictures it can be helpful to see yourself play a role in a movie with just the qualities that you want to acquire. The ease of the implementation, the finesse of the handling, the direct impact it has on circumstances and people, and the gracefulness of your actions.

You are a hero in that script! Or maybe find inspiring stories from your role models, that is always a great way to develop something you desire as you have a perfect practical example right in front of you.

Personal vs business

Make two lists, personal and business applications. The same soft skill can be applied quite differently in those areas. Also, learning to apply that skill might be easier in one setting than the other (if informed upfront, your friend will be much more forgiving than your exec if you plan to master 'giving constructive feedback'). Once mastered in one area, you can translate the skill to the other spectrum. Remember the 'Empowered Professional Triangle'? Those two worlds are the opposites of each other, that's why your goals need to be separated but not exclusive, as both of them complete a bigger picture!

Time-frame planning

Usually we are told to divide goals for the short term, mid term and long term. To me this doesn't make sense! It's like planning to take road C before having traveled road A and without having found road B yet. I certainly do plan in time frames, but I work with only one timeframe (future) and then work backwards. It works for me and it works for people I help plan their life. I call it 'Plan forward to today' (*Back To The Future* kind of concept):

✓ Choose a goal from your list and set a deadline. I'm willing to guarantee that this goal will end up in a long-term range.
✓ Break it down into two (as that is the only measurement that we can instinctively pinpoint with relative precision) and set that 50% deadline in the time frame. You will probably find it in the mid-term section.
✓ Then, define the first three actions towards your mid-term goal and put the first action on you to-do list for today or at least this week.
✓ Only after you complete these first three actions can you move forward to define your next three actions towards your mid-term goal. When you get to your mid-term goal celebrate, as you are halfway there. Experience the energizing effect of the Act of Completion! This will motivate you to get going, in pairs of three actions at a time, to achieve your end goal. This is a very human-friendly and procrastination-eliminating way of working towards your goals!

I have a template for this process which ends up in a daily doable Focus List with only six actions. It works well for me and my clients. You can make your own to fit your needs.

Of course you need to prioritize your actions: your business actions usually are the priority. But if you will never take the small steps towards the bigger goals as you have 46 other urgent things to do, you will never reach that end goal. Sometimes it will bite you so often and so hard that you will make a priority out of it. That's why working towards goals derived from your frustration list works great with me because of the urgency. I know it might not the best way to go. But at least I'm working on something!

We Assistants are great planners. So chop your goals, big or small, into smaller doable *one-action* items and you will be amazed at your speed of completion and success. And here your W.A.N.T.E.D. skills will help you from within, no doubt about it.

Not to-do list

This is such a funny thing! We all know what not to do, but it's not collected on any list. You will see, once you write things you don't want/need/have to do you will imprint it on your mind like a writing on the wall and you will actually do less of it as by magic. Write things down that are very time-consuming and low in added value. It's OK to update your Facebook status once in a while, but doing it daily is an absolute waste of our precious time.

On the topic of soft skills, make a list of frequent behavior that you don't like, recurring thoughts that poison your mood and limiting beliefs that you want to work on. This can be a very fast-flowing chart so keep it updated and within reach at all times. To make it even more effective: write an opposite version of those items next to them so your brain will be activated to spot the intruder and replace it with a suitable candidate. Remember, it's impossible to remove the W.O.R.M.s, so be prepared to create new ones in the heat of the moment — they stick better with emotion and direct action, remembering the result. The fact that you can only think one thought at a time will do the 'transformation' trick here.

Growth mindset

Carol Dweck outlined a principle of growth mindset vs fixed mindset. A very interesting theory! In short, growth mindset enables progression and seeds opportunism. A fixed mindset tells you that you are OK with what you have and where you are. It defines your limitations as a set frame you cannot and don't want to get out of. A fixed mindset sees only the obvious sequential steps to growth, whereas a growth mindset knows the principle of a quantum leap and seeks for ways to get there. Simply put, there are two things you need to do in order to get to the growth mindset:

- ✓ Decide you want to grow or get something/somewhere. In other words, you want more!
- ✓ Think of everything you want to achieve as in: not yet! It implies that success is only a matter of time.

Focus

I've mentioned setting priorities in combination with time planning. Here is an additional rule: do only one thing at a time! You have set three goals per area of your life (and you can have as many of areas as you please), but start by choosing one thing to tackle. If you are just starting to work with goals and action plans, then choose the easiest and most fun-looking item. Get it done, experience the Act of Completion, get charged up feeling happy and confident and move on to the next. If you are an experienced goal planner then go for the weakest link that would be the toughest to conquer.

Especially in regard to soft skills and mindset it's almost certain that achieving one item on your list will have an impact on the rest. It's usually because soft skills are never standalone and they are born, work and develop together. So if you're sure you have reached the next level of mastery within one section, check if that will cross any similar goals of your list. You will be pleasantly surprised at how fast you'll go through your list. Not only will you be motivated to get on with the next thing, you will understand the process of personal development and you will find shortcuts within your own character to get things done better and faster. The downside is that you will also see that there is much more to learn — and it doesn't matter how senior you are. There is always room for growth and it's the secret habit of all successful people on the planet. It's not the specific habits that differ from person to person — it's the habit of working on yourself!

Support

Before you start with your implementation create a support team around you. You can share your goals so they will know why you're changing (and be more flexible and forgiving). They will know why you call them upset in the middle of the night (as emotional stuff pops up when you let your guard down at night).

They will tell you how far you've got and keep you on track if you slip back into your old habits. You're very welcome to join our exclusive Global PA Academy social media groups or any other online circles. It's good to have a group of likeminded people to support you on this journey of personal growth. We know and understand each other's battles. Assistants are a special breed after all! Find more information in the back of this book and more on the PA community in a later chapter.

In closing

I can go on forever on the topic of goal setting. It's a very extensive area, there are a lot of experts, training sessions, courses, websites, coaches etc. The things I mentioned above work for me. Choose the ones that correspond with you and your ways or find completely new things that you want to try. We all know about the importance of having goals. Now we need to act on them fearlessly, stay inspired and track our progression. Just don't forget to set mindset and soft skills goals too.

Vision without action is a daydream.
Action without vision is a nightmare — Japanese proverb.

Chapter 16. What's Next? — Implementation

Good things come to people who wait,
but better things come to those who go and get them.

You know where you are, you know where you want to go — now it's time for action. The thing about Assistants is that we usually skip the first two steps and dive into action immediately. I love the process of taking action and I'm pretty good at keeping on going. That said, I think this chapter borders on irrelevant as it's our second nature to do things. I even think you have already done some things on your way to your goals and challenges as we speak.

Furthermore, working with your mindset and soft skills doesn't really require an action plan. The awareness of areas to improve or ways to think differently is already embedded in your brain — that's the beauty and downfall of it all. The beauty lies in the simplicity. The downfall is that if it's not your habit or your W.O.R.M. yet you will probably forget to act on it. To tackle that last statement I will share with you a few methods and theories on the implementation process itself, but not the practical description of it.

What follows now are some powerful things that helped me in my development. It's the longest chapter in the book as I wanted to share with you as many extraordinary tools as I could think of so you have an extended menu to choose from. These are definitely not the only guidelines and I am sure there are many more I haven't even found yet. I had to start somewhere and as I went along I stumbled upon things that helped me in that particular moment. On that journey I learned to see myself from angles I didn't even know existed.

Here is a painful example. While becoming an entrepreneur I turned out to be pretty afraid of the competition, even when they were not around. Just the thought of others like me stressed me out. Don't get me wrong — I am confident about the service I'm providing and my dedication to my exec, so it was not a worry about quality or even my fees. Why didn't I experience this being an employee? The employment market is way tougher and even more objective when it comes to hiring an Assistant. The first judgment you undergo is without any personal presentation — your delegate is your dry and static resume. Being an entrepreneur I got clients mostly by referral which is a way more positive and subjective manner of getting to know me.

What's even more paradoxical is the way I got to know my competition. Here is a positively charged situation that led to a confrontation that freaked me out. At one point I had to look for extra Assistants for my clients as I could not handle the amount of requests on my own (no, I'm not bragging, I'm just painting a picture). Instead of rejecting those new clients I tried to find suitable Assistants like me to fulfill their requests. That is how I found out that there are a lot of freelance PAs out there and it scared the bleep out of me, for no obvious reason.

My RAS brain was my feared enemy in that situation because suddenly I saw freelance PAs all around me, closer than I ever noticed before. I even used to be involved in recruitment and had to go through huge piles of PA applications, choosing the right candidates for interviews for my client's management team. And as that wasn't enough, there was a constant flow of Assistants trying to get the PA position I was currently holding. So I had to excuse my exec for not needing a new PA on many occasions, something I did for a long time but that didn't bother me until that moment. It was crazy and it drove me nuts!

To learn this lesson I needed to dig into my mindset, my beliefs and convictions to find out the big why and how to overcome it. The situation was clear, the goal was clear but the implementation... There is no textbook procedure for that. Believe me, I Googled it! There are practical tips on how to deal with competition on the outside, but how to deal with the emotions that it triggered on the inside?

To make an already long story short: the things below all contributed to my mindset victories, like the one above. See if something clicks with you. Otherwise go on the lookout for ways that fit your goals. There are tons and tons of information out there.

The basics

The first thing I came across at the right time and that sat well with me was the theory, or better said the definition, of transformation vs change. In that quirky book *Working on Yourself Doesn't Work* it's the first thing they start with.

And it's the most powerful thing that you need to be aware of if you want to change your inner workings. The core wisdom lies in the fact that one is a momentum and the other one is a process.

The actual shift lies in a momentum of transformation. A new something that clicks with you with a certain degree of confidence and therefore influences your mindset into getting you where you want to be. But it would not be a lasting effect if it was not repeated to become ongoing and habitual. The change is something we see only over time as a result of that new habit.

Transformation is a state of being — there is no work involved. It's something you cannot *do*, you *are* transformed. You do reach the actual station of change by proactively doing things in favor of your intention. And there is a certain and specific order in the flow of implementing something new to be able to change effectively:

✓ Engage consciously and privately (as it's very personal) with a new concept — the topic of your transformation. This is a creative process and you have total control over it.
✓ Have a proactive awareness moment and a deliberate decision moment to transform into something new.

✓ As a result of the reactive cause/effect law, you define new ways of acting automatically by setting the first steps to get familiar with the new territory.

✓ Repeatedly decide to act according to and consistently with your new direction. This is when you need to deal with problems differently and come up with 'never seen before' solutions, manipulating your stubborn old mindset into keeping on going until your goal is reached in a newfound fashion. The fact of your transformation is still a fact, you just need to find a logical translation of it in your daily life. I love this quote. It gives me the right motivation every time I think about quitting: *'Sometimes you face difficulties not because you're doing something wrong, but because you're doing something right!'*

✓ Once you get the new way of thinking or doing in your system and it's a habit, you will surely want to expand your expertise to get the most benefits out of this newly acquired ability.

You can clearly see why all of us are not perfect. It's because any change requires a certain ongoing conscious awareness and a huge amount of determination. Only the tough get going when it's difficult and tempting to safely return to your comfort zone. It's the W.A.N.T.E.D. qualities of *Willing* and *Tenacious* that are ruling this principle, collecting the prize of being *Effective* in the end!

Now that you know the underlying basics of change, here are many tips and tricks to get you through every step, getting you motivated and fired up on your winning streak. When you know what you're dealing with, like the nature of your thoughts, your habits and your brain functions, you will know how to apply and fast track things to suit your ways.

The untouchables: thoughts and awareness

It all begins and ends in your mind.
What you give power to has power over you.

As the theory of challenges dictates, it's not about the goals itself at the end of the race but the person you become when you arrive there. It's clear that every challenge requires a personal change. It always starts from within. It starts with your mindset, your thoughts and your drive. Here is a controversial truth: your mindset is intangible and that is exactly what makes the tangible reality!

There is a huge theory on why and how our thoughts have the power of creation. It's a cool fact that is supported by the science of quantum physics (which means it's proven by physical experiments). I'm not going to explore it here though.

Deepak Chopra is the king on this subject and he explains the whole concept clearly with great insight. What I do want to mention is the actual process prior to the creation of thoughts and the effect of thoughts on your reality. This flow originates from the teachings of Buddhism, one of the oldest sources of wisdom known to men.

It all starts with *intention*. It's the ultimate drive behind everything happening inside you and therefore the pre-stage to any thought. Intentions are driven by your emotions and intuition. To be airy-fairy for a second: some call them the whisperings of your spirit. The fact stays that intentions have the power to set a whole set in motion, creating a butterfly effect that ends up in what we call habits. It is also a fact that most intentions unconsciously manifest themselves. However, Benjamin Libet, a researcher of human awareness and author of *Mind Time*, found that it's possible to veto every intention, even the unconscious ones. The only problem is that you have a time frame of a third of a second to do so. So the more mindful you will be the more able you'll become to control your intentions and cultivate sequential behavior.

Now back to Buddhist teachings. Controlling your intentions is one of the most important core abilities you possess and it's one of the first things Buddhism teaches you to do. It's a long and intensive mental journey and I'm definitely not asking you to undertake it. It's good to know the reasons behind any process. By the weird ways of mental preference, the understanding of inner workings enables us to act decisively and have faith in its effectiveness. To keep it simple for us mere Assisting Professionals in down-to-earth business life, here is the flow that derives from intentions. If you know about it, you might learn to (and even want to) interfere with your initial intentions and guide them more effectively:

> *Intention breeds a thought.*
> *A thought gives birth to a word.*
> *That word will manifest itself in an act.*
> *The act has the ability to develop a habit.*
> *Habits are building blocks of a character.*

The more you are aware of why you do the things you do, the more control you have. And your brain is very supportive in this process, because you can only think *one* thing at a time. Become a frequent observer of your intentions. If you have something unsupportive in your mind simply think the opposite and repeat it over and over again — until the original intention is gone and your substitute rules your mind game. The Law of Substitution!

To support your change in planned ways, make a 'Substitution List' of new beliefs and great motivating thoughts (have a copy on your phone) and reread them when it gets crowded in your head. You will see the miracle of change in action!

Controlled substances

That was it for spiritual beginnings. Now let's revisit practical habit creation and routines. I love this part, because I have the full authority here. If it doesn't work, then I'm the one to blame. By the way, it's not a bad habit to take responsibility for things if they don't work out. I like to think of it as response-ability! That takes the negativity out of the act that follows. It takes away the blame element and triggers you to focus on the way you respond to the situation. Also, asking yourself all the tough questions is a powerful weapon of all successful people.

This act of responsibility is good in combination with an inner drive to back up the change you envision. This leads us to the principle of 'pull vs push'. It's smart to make the benefits of your goals *pull* you into action instead of pushing. You want to be motivated — not annoyed! It's all about the difference in the strength of your motivation, the vibe of your

276

emotions, the speed of implementation and the willingness to get to the next step in the plan. It's the ease vs friction, it's gentleness of movement vs strictness of regulations, it's the 'yeah' vs 'pffff'.

Practically, you need to go towards 'pull' actions as often as possible. But not any action — the action that leads to a new habit based on your new intentions derived from your new goals. So we're back to habits and I can assure you that everything from this point on is controllable! I have talked about habit creation already so let's revisit the highlights:

- ✓ Everything is hard the first time.
- ✓ Make a list to remind you of your new endeavors (check the workbook lists at the end of this book).
- ✓ Create 'if-then' scenarios with an extra step in between to connect an old habit with a new one (If I need to do A, then I will do B first before doing C like I used to).
- ✓ We need to repeat a new action for 21 days for it to become a habit.
- ✓ Work on one habit at a time.
- ✓ Choose a certain time frame or a day when you start new things (which will become a habit on its own).
- ✓ Regularly evaluate current habits and analyze which ones are or have become unsupportive.
- ✓ Only focus on things you can change (you cannot change your past).
- ✓ In tough times remember to see the shiny end result: when you're facing the sun, the shadow is behind you!

In the making

Here is a different take on habits. Every now and then I bump into webinars and short videos from Tony Robbins. That is one of the big personal development gurus who is still on my list and I haven't participated in any of his live training sessions yet (note the *yet*!). But every time I come in contact with his content I always find something that sticks with me. Tony is also a great believer in the power of our RAS brain — what a coincidence! One of the things I picked up that fits here is this — see your habit creations as rituals! It's just a simple play of words, but it makes a huge difference. Instead of bickering with new habits, I now have cool and beautiful rituals to perform. Also, know this about the power of the rituals: your current rituals brought you to where you are today! So be careful and thorough while making new rituals as they will take you on a certain journey. You better be the captain setting the course!

The cool thing about rituals is that they are more effective than your willpower. To act on your willpower you need to be pushed and vice versa. That requires a lot of effort and it is time bound. A ritual is based on your vision of an improved you, so it will create a pull that is easy to follow. Rituals expend your identity and they stay for a lifetime! I don't see any reason not to become BFF with the concept of rituals.

Being a practical PA, I actually tweaked this concept to fit my intentions of growth as followed. You can create a ritual template that fits your way of implementation. The only thing you need to do afterwards is to fill in the blanks with any new targeted habit.

Let me give you an example of my 'ritual' template:

- ✓ I'm a firm believer that on every topic out there, there is an expert and surely a book about it. I love reading 'smart' books so when I make a choice to inhabit a new ability I get a book about it.
- ✓ Then I think of one strong and current habit that I'm aware of that I could combine with the new action.
- ✓ As an inspiring 'pull' technique I stimulate a positive intention by defining a word that will represent every aspect of a new habit. In many situations that word for me is 'dragon fruit' (I have my own emotional reasons!). Once I think 'dragon fruit' it gives me the right vibe and I connect that vibe/emotion to a new habit. In NLP you call it the emotional anchoring. A very cool and effective concept!
- ✓ Keep a SYSS list: a list where you Share Your Shit and Success along your journey. It can be a bullet point list or a kind of diary. It's a great reflection method: once written it creates a surprising distance, gives you a clear perspective and usually motivation to move on.
- ✓ As it's difficult to know when you have mastered a new ability here is a trick that you have to try. When starting, think of a situation that you definitely cannot handle properly right now. Then use this

situation as a test at a later stage to apply your new strength. Of course you have to define and describe the end result application of that ability in full color and as much detail as possible. Only then can you compare the outcome with the 'perfect picture' scenario you have visualized at the beginning. Works like a charm!

Brain duty

Now let's see how the actual grey matter of our brain can assist you on your path of growth, habit creation and self-mastery. I have mentioned a lot of scientific studies already but there are still a few that I think you should know about. Let's call it overdelivery!

Thought training

Dr. Richard Davidson, director of the affective neuroscience lab at the University of Wisconsin, carried out research on how positive thoughts impact our brain (not the untouchable mind, but the physical grey matter). And you should know that they tested this theory on the trusted monks of the Dalai Lama. Their religion is based on positivity, love and compassion and they are masters in controlling their thought process to the very core of the nature of their intentions. They might be the happiest creatures alive — but they were not born that way. It's the result of systematic repeated training of their thoughts that got them there.

Davison's work defined triggers in our brain that stimulate happiness, fulfillment and welfare. He proved that you can learn to be happy and that living in that state of mind stimulates the coordinated ways of behavior that will benefit you and people around you. How cool is that!

You can train your brain (specifically the left prefrontal cortex) to activate those areas by experiencing a state of calmness, relaxation, optimism and happiness. Coincidently, those are byproducts of mindfulness and meditation. There are various ways to turn on those peaceful switches from within you (read books like *Happiness* by Matthieu Ricard, for example).

Dictating ego

It's your purpose in life to be yourself! Our brain gives us the possibility to make a distinction to create an ego and form an identity. This process is not as self-evident as it seems and it's what makes us humans so special. The thing you need to know about the process in your brain regarding the concept of your ego is the function of the left side vs your right side brain.

- ✓ Left side (the logic) is equipped with powers to actually create a template for your ego, the 'I', write personality stories and maintain a self-image that we identify with. It's the part that screams 'me first' and is definitely the dominating part of our brain. The downside of this superpower is that it has a tendency to get stuck in rigid analytical thinking patterns.
- ✓ Right side (emotion, intuition and empathy) has the cognition role and is the one that makes sure the system as a whole gets updated, and therefore permits change and flexibility.

To creative a healthy balance between those two polar systems we need to welcome cognitive flexibility but still stay grounded enough to walk our distinct paths. There are a few things in this theory that we can take with us on our quest to growth and development.

Let's look at the logic side first. Our brain is preprogramed to be receptive to storytelling. It's very true that we all have our own story but it doesn't have to be a true reflection of who we really are. Very psychological stuff, but here is a parable of how it can work against you:

A baby eagle falls out of his nest situated high above a farm and finds himself in a poultry house. The chickens see the stranger as a being in need and adopt him as one of their own. Time goes by and the eagle becomes this magnificent creature. At times he does suspect there is something different about him, but he cannot pinpoint the unique element. All this time he stays close to the ground, running around with the chickens. He even tries to cluck like them but is unsuccessful. He must be less fortunate is his conclusion. One beautiful clear day he sees eagles soaring high in the sky, gracefully gliding and looking absolutely majestic. But the story in his head tells him he is one of the chickens, so he never tries to spread his wings...

The fact is we are all eagles destined to fly and it has nothing to do with our egos! We created our ego over time. We are influenced by our society, the family we grew up in, our experiences and overall convictions and beliefs that may or may not be particularly yours. Being true to your nature, to your unique mold of your character, is something entirely different.

Yes, it might be a lifelong search but don't confuse it with the meaning of life. I just want to introduce you to your eagle, your potential. And it's there within you. No matter what happens to you, no matter what stuff you have to deal with. Nothing can take it away from *you* and nothing can change the fact that you are one. So try to be aware of the stories you tell yourself, especially limiting ones. Ask yourself: how come I believe that to be true about myself? This question activates your whole brain and will enable you to grow!

The second brain element in our favor is the power of your emotional 'change' side of the brain. Although this side doesn't rule your brain, it has the power to initiate and enable change. Now, I believe that being an Assistant requires us to be flexible anyway, it is part of the resume requirements for Assistants. And so I know we use this part of our brain in a more or less equal capacity compared to our logical brain. This gives us an advantage since we have the expertise. We just need to turn the spotlight on ourselves to make it work for us, as simple as that.

To make sure you challenge and please both sides of your beautiful brain you can think of a new ego story that will be supremely attractive. You make it a factual one, based on practicalities, but also a fulfilling one by adding the emotional ROI of being true to yourself.

Creative brainiac

It is generally believed by society that a genius mind is first and foremost a creative one. This is the reason the world is changing and we prosper. Being creative is often called genius and the word by itself puts the person in question on a pedestal. Assisting Professionals know the power of creativity. For some of us it's even a preeminent survival strategy. Most of us have integrated creative processes into our code of conduct. How else would you coordinate four full international agendas from three different time zones for a 15-minute chat? Or get your hands on a nationwide sold-out product? Or even something as simple as getting the reports printed while every printer in the building seems to be out of order or out of cartridges?

Now, some people say that they are just not creative. In real terms, it means they cannot access the right part of their brain to make it happen. It's a skill and all skills are learnable! The secret lies in *letting go* — letting go of the analytical thinking.

Have you ever experienced a stressful period (a stupid question, I know) and after pondering away without result you deliberately let the issue go and declare yourself checked out? Suddenly — there it is! The redeeming answer to your problem!

Another example that is familiar to everybody is that if you are stuck with something we usually decide to take a break from heavy thinking and go grab a shot of much needed caffeine or something unhealthy to snack on. And in the middle of your second sip or your third bite, while enjoying the intoxicating effects of consumption, you're hit by the perfect solution to your problem.

What happens behind the scenes is that the right brain takes over when the left brain is exhausted and we become super-duper creative. It's not a question of having that creative thinking or not — it's a matter of permitting yourself to let your brain work in ways that are unfamiliar to you (or better said, unfamiliar to your analytical brain). You see, being creative means your brain makes a whole lot of interconnections which are totally new to your well-known ways and daily practical patterns. And the only thing that you can do to make it happen is to let your logic go for a second. How in god's name can you do that when your exec is magically appearing at your desk every 7,3 minutes and your phone is ringing off the hook? The impossible answer is the aid of (background) music, in particular jazz music and classical baroque-period symphonies. They stimulate your right side brain like Red Bull on XTC.

There is also a brain director on your internal payroll, situated comfortably in the corner office of your frontal cortex (the area just behind your forehead). His name is 'working memory' (who is extremely trainable by the way) and he has the ability to keep both sides in harmony, asking both of them to show strengths when needed. But you need to let go of control for him to do so. For us control freaks to achieve this seemingly impossible task, you need a moment of relaxation. That's why I urge you to chop your big break into five-minute mini breaks and to take them throughout the day. That will make your brain work like Swiss clockwork. Even Einstein said that our intuitive spirit is the Holy Grail and our rational spirit is its loyal servant. But we live in a society where the servant is honored while the generating source is forgotten...

The last cool thing I want to share with you about our brain is the definition of super intelligent people. I'm talking about absolute savants who can learn to speak Islandic fluently in a week's time. The thing you need to know about your brain is that it's designed to think in concepts (the left brain superfood). But, science found out that the capacity to learn quickly and to an excellent degree lies in letting go of those very concepts. Our logical assumptions block our dormant but existing capabilities.

By letting go of conceptual thinking you give way to divergent neuro interconnections, which lead to creativity, extraordinary invention capacity and results. Moreover, there is a 'ski hat' (TMS-cap) developed at the University of Sydney that can turn off your conceptual thinking by magnetic pulses! Unfortunately, it's only used for scientific purposes. Otherwise I would have found a way to get my hands on one of those!

In conclusion, if you want to prevail or come up with a creative solution — give your brain the order to solve something... and just go for a walk, listen to music or do something completely unrelated. At some point your lightbulb will shine bright!

Practical trickery

OK, I'm done with the science stuff. It's not even the fact that we have to use all that wisdom. The moment we understand the way our brain works, that knowledge will work in our favor by default. Our brain is as simple as it is complicated! Now let me share some last practicalities that helped me in my endeavors to change and support my personal development.

Let me repeat the first trickery — I love shortcuts! The focus of this trickery is basically making your mind believe something that it's not — yet! 'Fake it till you make it' is the biggest 'in plain sight' secret to change. Generally, this act is not really appreciated by the public, but it's the most used and applied method to growth and expansion by successful people. Of course you should always stay close to your personal integrity, this is not meant to be a matter of deception. It's merely the illusion of an expert state of mind. The more you apply the belief of our excellence the more you will own it. It's a proven fact too!

In the background, this new 'fake' belief gives your whole being solid permission to act in such a manner and challenges your every capacity to prove it is up to the task. It works unconsciously, but the outcome is external and visible. Do you not want your inner you to work overtime to agree with the image of your new belief? That is the magic of controlled change.

As a matter of fact, it's been proven time and again that by forcing a smile you actually become a little happier. Just do a real-time experiment right now: force a smile, hold it for a '1 Mississippi, 2 Mississippi, 3 Mississippi' and see how it will slowly move your mood into a happy place.

The great Aristotle once said: 'If you desire a quality you don't have — do it anyway and it will become you.' Who am I to argue...

The same technique applies to many other areas of business and interpersonal connections. There is the well-known 'mirroring' method. Here you imitate and take on every movement, gesture, speech pattern or attitude of your opponent to create and build rapport, a greater connection and mutual understanding.

Note: 'mirroring' is different to imitation. While imitation is a conscious and overt effort to copy another person, mirroring is often covert and goes unnoticed in the situation. It works, but demands quite an effort and expertise on your part. Although we human beings do most of it automatically, it's only easy when you genuinely like that other person. When that other person is a stranger and you badly want to create a bond then this is a great way to get connected.

Then there are all those profiles that you gather describing people around you. Anything from their star sign, their communication style, their mental preference etc. All of those profiles usually have guidelines on how to deal with people that fit those profiles.

Sometimes, when you are desperate or too tired to tune in on their personalities, you can try to apply those guidelines. Some of them will work, some won't. In the same way you can apply those guidelines to yourself and see what works!

And don't forget that it's all about *attention management* nowadays. It's how good you are at switching and focusing on one single target, the quality of your attention by shutting out all disturbing factors, switching on your *Willingness* to pay quality attention to the issue or the task at hand. Most of all, it's your ability to react in a controlled and sensible way.

Continued attention to a problem attracts it into your experience.
To remove it from your experience,
you must remove your attention from it. Abraham Hicks
(Aka don't think too much about something you don't want to be true or stay with you for too long.)

Rules of the game

To close this chapter I want to share with you a major breakthrough I had not too long ago on my journey to self-mastery. As I told you earlier, I found out that I cannot handle competition too well. I'm getting better at it, but it's still a battle I need to fight with conscious attention and well-prepared tactics.

The breakthrough understanding of the bigger picture of my issue happened during business training. At some point a presumed competitor (which later turned out not to be one whatsoever) caught my eye and I started fuming! This had never happened to me before, so I was thrown by my own emotions. And it wasn't specifically targeting the person behind the occupation, but the qualities I thought were on the table. Luckily, the person seated next to me came to my rescue (after openly admitting considering moving to another spot in the room just seconds before talking to me). I can get a bit heated when overly emotional — we're all humans after all. He offered me his advice and I'm forever grateful that he found the courage to calm me down!

This wise man said only three things and they instantly became lifelong anchors: *Eyes on the ball. Mind on the game. Don't mind the players.*

Now, the true power of these words is more visible if you think of a tennis game.

✓ You have to keep your focus on the ball itself. Its trajectory has the determining power in the game.

In translation to our profession: it's the capacity and appearance of the duties that you perform that are visible and noticeable by your superiors. The *how* of the outcome will determine whether your superiors will be pleased and satisfied. So make sure the deliverables are up to standard: you do have control over this part.

✓ Keep the bigger picture of the game in mind. It's how you play the overall game, how well you play by the rules of the game, how you distribute your energy levels, how you calculate the flow which is constantly affected by your and your opponents' participation. And don't forget the external elements like the weather, surface, crowd etc.

In translation to our profession: it's your overall performance that matters, but you need to know the rules of the office first. You need to know the team and direct reports of your exec. You need to know him and get familiar with his ways. You need to know the company's direction, goals and strategies. All that is important to be in the game so you can notice the changes, new winds, old pains, lurking dangers and disguised opportunities.

✓ The second you focus your attention on your opponent, you lose the game! You have to know your opponent, but that is only needed to draft the game in your head beforehand (I love the book *The Art of War* for this purpose). During the game you need to focus on how *you* play the ball, maintain your physical wellbeing and find that sweet spot so you can bring your A-game.

In translation to our profession: others will always be there. It's your job to be the best you can be — right now. If your exec is happy with you by his side, he will not have any reason to shop around. So don't give him one! Also, the click between an Assistant and her exec is crucial. Some execs know that there are others out there who might actually be better in some areas. But if he is very comfy, relaxed, trusting and satisfied with your support, he will not look further.

I was accused of being very eager to steal someone else's job as an EA to a higher exec once. The funny fact was that that was not true at all and that same exec had even asked me already to move up the ladder (I graciously declined by the way)! I was very happy with where I was and with my current exec. I did have a great understanding with that higher exec but primarily because my own exec was a direct report of his. That compels me to maintain a good relationship anyways. That accusation turned out to come from that EA's own insecurity regarding her position. And as it turned out, she was let go not too long after that very incident. Go figure... Her focus was on me, not on her own delivery.

Very recently, I made the biggest quantum leap in my 'dealing with competition' challenge. Now I can honestly say that I don't believe in competition anymore! Instead, I believe one is simply a better fit than another. The criteria of the fit are dictated by the values and needs of both parties. That fit is primarily defined by the well-known personal click (a predisposition to a brand is a clear example). The tricky part is that there is a need to present the probability of that click in a very 'marketing driven' but a non-pushy way. It's not easy, but it's simple! The next book in this *Next Generation Assistants* series will be all about personal branding and positioning, so we'll cover all the theories and tools there. For now, here are two daring one-liners that will make perfect sense when you are strongly positioned and confident in yourself:

If you strongly believe in (personal) competition,
then you are probably a commodity
We are all different, so there is no competition by default

That's it gals and guys! There is still a lot out there that is absolutely interesting and motivating. I'm still on the quest and I hope you will join me. In the upcoming chapters we'll explore the importance of giving yourself some much-needed attention and the power of a community of likeminded people. I'm also very excited to introduce you to my great endeavors and I hope you will be excited too!

Your attitude, not your aptitude, will determine your altitude. Zig Ziglar

Chapter 17. All Eyes on Me

I need to catch my breath, so I'll go stand outside for a while.
If someone asks I'm outstanding!

Step down, take a break, slow down a bit and have a me-time moment... The quote above reflects the result of doing all that: it will make you outstanding, vibrant, energized and boosted. We all know we need that time off, even if it's just a quick moment away from the chaos and we're hiding in the bathroom. We are also guilty of not taking enough time off for, or lack focus and energy when we are with, our loved ones. This issue is very much alive and urgent. I don't have to explain why it's an issue and I don't need to explain why it's important to take time off. Let's skip that part and move on to how. How you can manage to find time to refill your batteries. How you can do that quickly if you're really tight on time and how to make every second count.

Most of the things I will mention make perfect sense — we just don't act on them because we deny their simplicity. And I'm certainly one of the perpetrators, big time! It took me some time to realize that if I'm not there with at least 75% of my energy supplies, my motivation goes down, accuracy suffers, results are less driven by excellence and I look at the clock way too often. Brian Tracy has a very quick analysis when it comes to determining if you are rested enough: whenever you wake up in the morning and the first thing you do is look forward to the moment you go to sleep later that day, you are not rested enough. Ouch, guilty!

And the scary part of that statement is how true it is for most of us. Even after a vacation I have noticed that my storage is quickly emptied. Most of our drive comes from our passion for the job we do. That's a great generator to get that inner boost. But it is not enough! Assisting Professionals need to be enabled to wind down consciously. To soak up every precious second of peace and relaxation, induced by things that give them pleasure, fill up their senses and get their engines running on max again tomorrow at the office.

Research shows that it is possible to achieve all that in a short period of time. The ideal short time frame is 20 minutes, the preferred longer relaxation period is three weeks and the minimum supercharge moment can be downscaled to five minutes at a time. But you need to be skilled, disciplined and go through a certain routine to get those results that fast. Just google five-minute meditation or awareness techniques and you will find a huge number of options and explanations.

But even all that won't help you if you don't know how to switch your mindset!

Switching to a different mindset instantaneously (have a look at the previous chapters for the *how*) enables you to act according to a different set of rules, qualities and convictions. When making that switch skillfully you can be a different person in the blink of an eye. Again, your mind is very easy to handle, you just need to practice it and you will prevail. Learn by heart the few magic words that give your mind a direct order to switch uniforms and to adopt a particular set of qualities and beliefs. 'Now I'm going to be...' and add the needed mindset or role to finish the command.

Remember: your mind has no other choice but to act on your words! It's a complying soldier with no brain or will of its own. Its only duty is to do what you say! If you concentrate on saying those words, preferably out loud, your mind will switch to the requested mindset and get you the required abilities to perform. It's really as simple as that.

If you think that it's too simple and doesn't work, *that* is a limiting belief! Try it, train it and enjoy the ability of self-mastery. Nothing works the first time, remember? It's not your habit yet but you need to master this one for sure. If you are a parent then it's easy to demonstrate — just be aware of how your attitude changes when you are around your kids. It's a whole set of different skills and abilities that are triggered in a second. The way you talk changes, the way you behave alters, you try to think in the same manner as your kids etc... On this topic of downtime you need to say 'Now, I'm going to thoroughly relax and focus on me and my needs for a while.' Just see what will happen and get ready to be pleasantly surprised.

The cool thing about a mindset switch is that we do it already, but we are not aware of it. It's not something new to learn altogether. We just need to make that command as per our desire and enjoy the benefits. I've heard lately that the concept 'multitasking' is dying out. The new guy in town is 'switch-tasking'. I love it, because that explains a lot and gives you tools to become the war general of your own mind, the task-switching force!

Flow

Here comes a whole list of things that you can do to make sure you train yourself to pay a bit more attention to yourself. Remember these Rules of the Game: you need to keep up your physical appearance, stamina, mental wellbeing and physical fitness to be able to deal with anything that you may encounter – business or personal.

To adopt the '3What' plan for your personal wellbeing, let's repeat the same three steps for the sake of clarity and habit creation but this time with a specific target in mind: you!

What's now?

Make a quick evaluation of your state of wellbeing right now. Go back to the 'Empowered Professional Triangle', examine the % of your personal quality time out of 100%, determine your level of energy, remind yourself of your last vacation (oh dear, it's been 8 months already?!) or just notice how tired and exhausted you are (or hopefully the opposite). We all have 911 symptoms that indicate that we are about to crash into something (preferably your bed).

Be aware of those and if you don't know what they are — ask people close to you. My husband knows mine too well and can recite them back to me like his ABCs.

We usually know pretty well if and when we need to take time off and spend more time on ourselves. Unfortunately, it doesn't mean we act on that knowledge.

What's new?

✓ *Create or update your 'Happy List'*
What makes you happy? Music, food, scenery, hobbies, activities etc. It has to be something that you know works and things that you can engage in ASAP for some quality refill, maintenance and upkeep.

✓ *Create or update your 'Emergency Jerrycan List'*
This is a list of quick wins that you can apply when desperately in need of an escape or a boost. Don't forget that most of the items here are small guilty pleasures!

✓ *Define your happy town*
Ask yourself: If I had all the resources in the world available to me, what would my happy place look like? This is more for your mental excitement and motivation. Also, fantasizing and daydreaming is proven to do magic for your overall life satisfaction and expectancy!

✓ *Bucket list*
Oh yes, this list works like magic. If you haven't seen the movie *Bucket List* with Morgan Freeman and Jack Nicholson, do! The great thing about having a bucket list is having something exciting to look forward to. So plan something new for yourself, which is very energizing and relaxing in itself!

✓ *Create a 'Recurring Want-To-Do List'*
This list contains all the things focused on fun and relaxing events that you plan to do in the near future. Like, monthly spa visits, girls' nights out, weekly movie or date nights, yoga classes, reading your

favorite books, sleeping in, trying an exotic diet, city hopping, volunteering etc.

Recurring character of the items is the key element here. (You do understand that you will actually have to plan those in the next step, right?)

All of the above defines your personal safe haven. A place where you can be yourself in your best form. Most of the things you will do in solitude and that is just fine. It's a 'me, myself and I' kind of gateway. It's important to have this place and know exactly what it looks like, feels like, and smells like (aka sensory anchoring). This is where you will refill your spirit and energy levels. Cherish this place, guard it, retreat when needed and know it's always there for you! Combine you favorite me-time escapes with a 'uniform change' act and you will be golden.

What's next?

Now it's time to implement! Did you know that one of the weird habits of successful people is that they plan at least half a year off, every year! They know that their state of wellbeing depends on their health, physical condition, mental freshness and overall refueled state. So let's follow their example, maybe not to that magnitude, but we need to start somewhere!

✓ *Plan, block out time and spread the word*

Plan your time off, even the shortest amount of time, way upfront. Inform people affected by the planned time off. Yes, it's scary! What if Armageddon happens and they need me?! In a worst case scenario, you will alter your plans. But at the beginning of this new habit you have to 'pretend' to be very decisive. If people know upfront you'll be gone, they act differently and get prepared for your absence. Once I got into this habit I was amazed how well the news was received and how others adjusted their expectations and planning. No, it will not always work, especially if you have never done it before. Practice makes perfect.

✓ *Short getaways*

While daily planning, notice times when it would be OK and acceptable for your exec to miss you for an hour, or even half a day. Personally, I never took a vacation longer than ten days. But I do often take half a day off and for a very sneaky reason. It feels like skipping class and has a really uplifting effect. Also, because I plan those days way upfront, I also plan a lot of personal stuff to accomplish. Like dentist appointments, certain shopping trips, finalizing personal projects etc. It's that 'sneaking out' feeling mixed with sense of completion that makes these afternoons a blessing in disguise. I feel privileged to go for a coffee in the middle of the afternoon while others have to work. You really are present in that moment and you enjoy it to the fullest. Also, you can actually set your work stuff aside way easier as you know you will be back the next morning. The weird thing is that if I take a full day off it doesn't feel the same. It's actually rather the opposite — there is a sense of rush and of time being limited.

I will share with you a list of quick wins for getting destressed a bit later on. It's a list I made while producing a series of online videos with tips and tricks on how to get organized for busy professionals and entrepreneurs who don't have an Assistant (in Europe it's not as common a thing as in the US). They are simple, scientifically tested and proven to work.

✓ *A daily relax ritual*

To survive busy days I would suggest creating a relax ritual. It's a collection of five-minute breaks that you know work well for you. You have to put them to action regularly, preferably daily and or at least with a certain consistency so you can turn them into your new supporting habits. If they turn into habits then replenishing your fuels will be preprogramed, making you vibrant and energetic no matter what. Know that solitude is the best and fastest way to get grounded and relaxed — so plan those five-minute breaks to be taken alone!

It's great to have a list of things that you really want to become your habits and by using the word 'must' makes it stick to your identity! Be careful not to create too many 'musts' as that is very stressful. Choose one at a time, make it a part of you first and only then move on to the next 'must' on your list.

I like to see supporting habits as my own PAs. Wouldn't you like to have a bunch of 'yous' to help you accomplish crazy amounts of work, remind you to slow down, take care of your needs and be very good to you? (Watch out if the answer is 'No freaking way!' — you might have to rethink the bigger picture.)

> *'Busy is a choice. Stress is a choice. Joy is a choice — choose well!'*

Do not disturb

It's a miracle: you're on your break, enjoying time away from the office!

Unfortunately, most PAs know that we can be interrupted by our execs in our off hours for the smallest things. Sometimes it's OK, sometimes it's not. I cannot judge your situation so I won't advice you to ignore a call, that 'high-priority' email or the recurring beeps of messages. I cannot ignore them so I'm not asking you to do so either. I like to be informed and it's good to stay in the loop, even if I'm on vacation on a faraway island. Here are some pointers and guidelines that will help you get your well-deserved time off in a fashion that is acceptable to you and tolerated by your exec.

Going off grid

'Going dark', as they call it in time management. Turn off everything that produces sound or has internet access. It's a very scary thought, so start off with ten minutes at a time. In the beginning the suspense will kill you, but try to be rational — everything can wait ten minutes. At some point you will forget your connection to the world is off, which will also be scary. But after a quick check you'll find out that nothing important has happened and you will ease up. If people know you are on your break they tend to respect it and not send any messages at all. Even so, sometimes it can be depressing to check your email or your phone and not find anything waiting for you (have they forgotten me already, am I that dispensable?). So, adopt the mindset of being on a break! Usually we need a few days to change the pace of life, and don't be too hard on yourself.

Going dark for a short time is great too, once you've found that peace of mind. What helps me is to make two deals with myself. Firstly, permit yourself to reconnect your wires at a certain time. Secondly, reward yourself for staying in the dark until then.

Communication plan

A great way of controlled 'down time' is to have an agreed communication plan while you're gone. That means that you'll promise everybody to check in twice a day at a certain time. It manages expectations and people won't bug you as much. Extend the time in-between to what you feel comfortable with. Setting up an 'out of office' message is a great way of letting others get familiar with your communication plan or naming a victim whom they can bug with all their questions.

Yes, it's good to have a 'flying keeper' to be your eyes and ears while you're gone. Someone you trust will be the best option. Agree on special occasions when your 'replacement' will contact you or give you an update. It will make it easier and more relaxing for you to stay in the dark while sunning yourself (or whatever your poison is).

A sign on the wall/desk

Lately I have been reading about this new phenomenon everywhere: a 'do not disturb' strategy. It has many variations but it all comes down to this: you have to educate your direct environment to know when not to bug you. It can be an actual sign, or an object that you place on your desk as a sign of your focus time. The trick is not to abuse it, and it really seems to work. It can be a short break away from your desk, a note that you will be back in ten or in a week. This is a great tool for guarding your five-minute breaks. Let's say that a pink stuffed elephant sitting proudly on the corner of your desk means 'this PA is 'out of order' until further notice'! For this to work your exec has to have a good sense of humor.

Commitment guards

When you are really bad at taking time off (like me) then it's good to have a buddy to get you back to reality when it's necessary. A family member, a close friend or a community group is a great place to start. People that care for you and the ones who you actually ask for help and support will do that with precision and unsalted opinions (oh boy, you might regret that later).

Anything is good in terms of a wakeup call, especially when it doesn't come with a big flashy 'politeness' bow. Sometimes we need a kick to wake up. The rule of thumb is:

> *If you lack the ability to do something,*
> *find someone else who will make you work hard for it!*

Quick wins

Next to all the above here are some more things I promised you that can get your state of mind from stressed to impressed, a whole 15 of them:

✓ *Breathe slowly* with your belly when you feel agitated or need a clarity and creativity boost. Breathe in counting to three and out counting to three. This will bring your mind into a state of brisk relaxation. The trick is really in belly breathing, since when you do that your inner organs press sensory nerves against your spine which results in the production of the hormone serotonin. That is the neurotransmitter that stabilizes our mood. Repeat three times and move on. That's all it takes to bring our blood pressure down, bring our brain waves back into alpha waves and get us back in the zone. On the other hand, chest breathing stimulates flight and fight responses in our system, resulting in the production of hormones like cortisol and adrenaline. And we all know that those are the stress hormones. So, 20 seconds of belly breathing and you're good to go to win the battle with that Excel file!

✓ Reserve some time for your *positive social life*. The positive character is important here. This is a very easy and fast way to snap out of your busy mind! But it's not always the fastest way to go, as it usually does require some logistics and time investment from your side. A huge side note here: use this tool wisely, because it is a proven fact that other people are the greatest time wasters in your life!

✓ *Laugh more* — laughter has been proven to release and decrease stress! And the strange thing is that when you are stressed your sense of humor changes and you laugh more easily. It's the universe trying to help us!

✓ Get yourself a 'feel-good' *savings account*! Financial reserves turn out to have a relaxing tendency. So when you are overwhelmed, deposit an extra amount into your savings.

✓ Look at the *color green* — that helps you to relax and gets you grounded. Whether it's nature, a poster, a green wall, a plant or a screensaver... anything works as long as it's green!

✓ Look *up at something bright* when you feel down or get stressed. It's the motion of looking upwards that counts most. If it happens to be bright then that doubles the positive impact on your mood. This action lowers stress levels instantly by 30%. So a white ceiling with a lamp can become your best remedy!

✓ Pay some attention to *your style*. When you feel comfy and good, we act faster and better! And for the ladies, I've already mentioned wearing heels. They tweak our posture in a certain way that does magic for our mood.

✓ Be careful with using *too many productivity-assistance* tools like apps, websites, groups, blogs etc. Remember, those are merely meant to assist your thinking and organizing processes, not replace them. The shocking truth here is that on their own, all those tools are dead time! You still have to think and do stuff in real time! Find something that you only use as your reminder system.

✓ Try to *avoid emailing* where possible and give somebody a call if you have a short question or a message.

✓ *Low-light working environments* make you depressed. There is a study that says our brains need a shock of light to help curb depression and feeling blue.

✓ Contrary to the popular belief, *don't have a clean and super-duper organized desk*! It's proven to get you depressed! A few things on your desk are more than welcome and it's even good to set them up slightly out of order. Also, get things that inspire you right there in front of you and you will feel way better!

✓ Try not the leave your office promptly every day at *the same time*. Sometimes work a little later or leave a bit earlier. I cannot explain why, but the absence of repeated time alertness is proven to lift up your spirits!

✓ *Don't be too rigid* about your planning and to-do lists. They don't dictate your life — you do. Don't expect to be problem free either. Being completely unbending about getting everything done can work against you. Being flexible in life makes you adapt better to changes! Leave some room for spontaneous decisions and make space for your exec to change his mind (even if that happens three times over, coming back to the first option after all). No finger pointing!

✓ Use *'crunch time'* only as a short-term strategy. Crunching means buckling down, eyes on the deadline or any other conscious busy period. What it also implies is that you neglect yourself, not coming up for air and burning out inside. Here's another scientific study that says: sustained periods of crunch only lead to diminishing returns. Well, we knew that, right?

✓ Practice *self-compassion*. A recent study by two physiologists proved the value of self-compassion over self-criticism. They found that a message of self-compassion helped achieving set goals. Many would think that the message of self-compassion would slow you down, but it actually helps cultivate the willpower to go on and act towards your goals. And I'm not talking about full character and situation analysis. Just a simple 'Well done!' to yourself for something small will usually do the trick. So, don't sell out on yourself. You need to love and like yourself! You're Personally Awesome by default! That is actually the essence of being impressed... you have to see your own value way above anything else.

No excuses

Be committed to make 'time off' work for you! To excel in our line of work we need to be in great shape. You need to be gentle with yourself because most of what you do is actually dependent on you as a person. Keep in mind that we are gatekeepers — so be one in full shape and form. And if that is not a clear motivation for you, think of the consequences when you're 'out of order'! What is the price you, your peers and your exec have to pay? You really don't want to cause that to happen.

I've mentioned a ratio of positive vs negative experiences before. It's a staggering ratio of 1/5, meaning you will have to work five times as hard to make up for one mess up. It was a slip up because you were too tired to check the advisory report again and that made your exec look bad in the eyes of his superiors. Not something to look forward to, right?

So be good to yourself! Cherish your super powers and take time to get your cape dry-cleaned once in a while. Be nice and forgiving to yourself, because that will make you nice to others, multiplied. Take care of yourself first so you know the effect and wonders your care does for others around you.

Love yourself before you can radiate your goodness. Be the example others follow and urge them to take 'time off' too. Remember the triangle: you need to move to be in balance. Find your way and your pace — as long as it works it doesn't matter what it is. If you are relaxed and energized you are most likely positive, and in the state of positivity we see more clearly how we can help and support others. That is science you cannot deny! If you excel others will have no choice but to follow!

Would you be rather loved or feared?
Both, I want people to be afraid of how much they love me.

Chapter 18. Community

Once upon a time, in a small country by the sea, there lived a teenage girl. Making her way through high school, she did not encounter any major setbacks in life. Having very busy parents who lost themselves in their professional lives she missed a certain degree of guidance and exploration of her true self. As graduation approached, choices had to be made about what to do next. Like most girls her age with business-oriented parents she was pushed to continue with her economics and finance majors. Being good at them anyways she didn't mind much — the world was her oyster and she would conquer life as it came.

She was raised with an extreme sense of self-sustainability and long-range survival skills. She therefore decided to take on the extra challenge of combining a university degree with a fill-time internship in a Big Four accounting firm. This would prepare her for the real business world from the very beginning. Everything looked shiny for a little while, but she quickly discovered that this was not what she liked to do. The outside world didn't notice a thing, but inside something didn't click. So she took matters into her own hands — as she was raised to do — and switched to a new job and a new course of study. They fit a little better, but still not completely. The search went on.

Over time, her duties narrowed to assisting financial executives. One gave a lot of room for personal input and made the girl flourish in terms of creative thinking. She was chasing every challenge until the end, no matter how big or new the assignments were. Others were very strict so the girl learned the importance of attention to detail and accuracy. Some were outgoing and caring. Others were distant and quiet. It didn't matter, she had no preference and she loved every bit of it all. Because she had finally found a place that felt good, where the duties matched her skills, she was looking forward to go to work in the morning and she vowed to get ever better at this new and exciting profession she grew to enjoy and be proud of. The profession of being an Executive Assistant to masterminds of this world!

Yes, that story is mine and only looking back can I see the steps that led me to where I am today. It's like the metaphor of the ship: if you stand on the front deck, overlooking the endless water desert in a *Titanic*-like posture, you will not see the path of the ship before you. There is no waterway with signs and traffic lights, but you are sure that the captain knows the right direction and steers the ship to your destination — he's a true magician! But then it gets chilly and you move to the afterdeck of the ship and there you see a majestic trail of white bubbles and waves that seem to spread all over the world. That was your travelled path. You can see it, you can sense the marks you've left and it's pretty clear where you came from. I love this metaphor! Especially when things happen in my life for which there are no clear explanations and I have to make decisions with less than enough facts to support even thinking about options.

The cool thing about faith is that when you show signs of being on a voyage, letting go of what doesn't work and trying new things over and over again, at some point faith steps in and shows you a shortcut. Unfortunately, it's never obviously clear how that route might lead to answers about your direction and purpose.

The reason why I brought this up here is to illustrate that this is only one way to become an Assistant. There are countless variations and all of us have our own story.

I think that our profession is one of few ones you can end up doing coming from totally different beginnings. There are even differences per continent and industry on how you end up being an Assistant. All that is very intriguing, but when it comes to schooling and skills growth, it's hard to find something that fits all our needs.

There is no single accepted MBA equivalent for Assistants. Every country has its own institutions, training courses and even educational budgets and guidelines. We suffer from the image of being disposable but at the same time, skilled and experienced Assistants are needed all over the place. How do they think we get to be all that without as much attention being spent on our development as any other settled profession in the company?

We get there because it's what we do, how we do it and who we are inside! Our profiles and upbringings might differ, but we all possess the same personal qualities, values and convictions. Truth be told, I was disappointed to find out that there is no university degree for Assistants (although nowadays there is more out there than five years ago, I must admit). But I was pleasantly surprised to find a huge online community. A great number of communities of like-minded Assistants with impressive numbers and origins. They are mostly represented online, as we all suffer from time deficiency disorder (TDD) and usually work in solitude. I joined all groups I could find and shortly after I experienced an overwhelming flow of great tips, articles, discussions, troubleshooting solutions and so on. You know, sometimes it's just the knowledge that there are others dealing with the same issues out there that provides a sense of comfort and motivation.

Time to improvise

If you honestly and sincerely cannot find something that you need and seek — you are lucky! Because now you can safely make exactly that and fulfill your potential by creating something that is needed.

I was on a quest to find self-improvement programs for PAs, and didn't find anything that fitted my needs back then. Most were targeting hard skills or only fractions of the soft skillset. The ones I found were usually programs meant for troubleshooting, but I wanted to be a step ahead of that!

That got me thinking. To know what we need on the educational side of personal development and get us further ahead, we need to define commonalities that every Assistant has to possess. But even here there is not one agreed set of skills or qualities. The book *Who Stole My Pen,*

Again provides a great insight into what we Assistants need to be and do. Although I don't think it's doable to have or prevail in all of those amazing areas, it is a great resource to find something that speaks to you and try to master it. Just to be crystal clear here (before I'll get all those angry emails with lists of courses and so on), I'm talking about the soft skillset here. I trust you know, learn, practice and excel in the practicalities of your job already. What we usually forget is that our soft skills are the ones that make the hard skills needed and make them work with intended results. Just like your mindset is a big but forgotten multiplier of your hard skills.

✓ If you are not *Willing* to be good at something (let's say taking minutes at board meetings), you will not try harder to produce shiny reports or join an online program to became great at minute taking. You will not grow.

✓ If it's not your priority to be *Available* to your exec whenever he needs you, you will not become technology savvy to be 'online' 24/7 and you won't find ways of making that not interfere with your personal life too much.

✓ If you are not bothered at all about how others perceive you (as *Nice*), then your communication skills will reflect that in your emails, the way you answer the phone and your tone to others, resulting in less than perfect relationships all over the place.

✓ If you don't have that *Tenacious* inner drive to keep on going when things get tough, you will quit, skip work or avoid complicated projects.

✓ If you won't strive to be result-oriented and *Effective*, you will not have 100 checklists to remind you of recurring issues or always be on the outlook for new technologies to unburden you when it comes to mundane duties.

✓ And without the noble sense of *Dedication* — well, I don't think you could hold a PA position for any sustainable period of time because your practical track record would be slim to non-existent.

In other words, without outstanding soft skills you become a robot, barely dragging yourself out of bed every morning and rushing home to more of the same. Excuse me for being so blunt, but sometimes we need to pinpoint the obvious because we don't see it. While searching for new things to do, the easiest thing you can do is enrich the present with exciting elements.

So, where do we stand on PA soft skills education? Let's do a quick '3What' analysis:

What's now?

Where do you learn? Mostly, we learn on the job. Some of us graduated from secretary programs and started at the bottom. Some of us are lucky to have a mentor (who is usually the exec himself). But all of us are loyal students of Life University, which usually results in a bootcamp kind of education. Do we like it or have any control over it? Not likely. Next...

How do we learn? When we decide to get into some new stuff we usually confide in our BFF Google first. Then we might catch up on some actual book reading or even try a physical course. The context of those training courses is usually far from ideal, but they're better than nothing.

We might ask a close colleague PA for some advice, but usually we cannot disclose too much as that might impact your image and your position within the company. Do we like it or have any control over — it's getting there. A lot of research and time is required though. The grand downer is the high costs of those training programs.

Sometimes you're lucky to get your exec to fund your development. To do that, you need to discuss your ambitions upfront and get it all incorporated into your official job performance profile. How will you otherwise get a few thousand Euros to participate in a sales program that offers a great negotiation module?

What's new?

Try to think of a way that would suit your needs to travel the path of self-mastery and improve your application of soft skills to boost your practical performance. I would love to hear your ideas, so please email me or share them in my Global PA Academy community groups (all the information is in the back of the book).

I'm sure there is already a lot going on, but it's very clustered per country or industry. To begin with, it's great to see that the concept of Internal PA Networks is growing in popularity. If you have no clue what that is, Google it and also the name Victoria Darragh. I see her as the godmother and keeper of this recently discovered treasure.

She puts it in practice and it does wonders for PAs within a company. See it as a union that fights for the rights and wellbeing of PAs within a certain industry or business!

As for courses and training — it would be great to have one place to go to. I have a dream: to be able to access the Central Education Intelligence Google database for Assisting Professionals! Aha, the CEIGAP is born! I'm joking, but the concept is intriguing, right? I'll put contacting Google on my to-do list though — you never know. I might get their PA on the line and she would love it and push for it with all her W.A.N.T.E.D. superpowers! By the way, Executive Secretary website does have a listing of a lot of related training courses and events, so if you are looking to get informed make sure to visit their website www.executivesecretary.com first.

What's next?

The main thing I have discovered on my learning journey is that I'm not alone and we all suffer from the same condition of TDD. We want a little more fun, to be able to make secretarial jokes that only PAs get, to talk freely in a safe environment without being afraid that something will bite you back, a shoulder to cry on to unload the extraordinary amount of 'bleep' and to move on relieved, energized, motivated and inspired!

To be understood is very underestimated. We provide that to others and they don't even understand what they're getting. In collusion to what can become a very long and cheesy promotional speech let me express my firm belief that PA communities is the way to go!

It's there for us online already. If we're lucky within our companies there will be an Internal Mother Ship in the form of a PA network, or even distant mastermind group conglomerates around the globe. I felt so privileged to learn about the concept of Circles which Sheryl Sandberg introduced on a global skill with her Lean In organization. Coincidently (not!) she is the COO of Facebook, so she has great insight into how communities work.

Power of people

I want to share with you now my biggest 'next'. It's a product of all the pages in this book and it has become my cherished baby — please meet Global PA Academy (**www.globalpaacademy.com**).

In the last few years I have been on an extensive search, participating in numerous events and seminars for PAs and I've read a lot of books. All of those had some amazing strong points, but in my view they were missing something. All of them together is a great combo and that gave me the idea to try something new. Based on the principals and example of the renowned TIBA (The International Butler Academy, the most prestigious institution for high-end and royal butlers) I fell in love with the concept of one place where PAs can grow personally, being educated to elevate their skills practically and be pampered at the same time in the great company of like-minded professionals.

GPA is tweaked and rephrased to suit the needs of the loners out there, bringing our great minds together worldwide. Providing the needed support to us as we go and being there for us when bleep hits the fan. A place to get motivated, relax and find our own way to excel — basically to be ourselves in safe and protected environment. High standards, a code of conduct and prestigious care and quality. We deserve it as our main task is to provide the best support to the leaders of the world today. Sounds cool right!

Well, my dream has turned into reality! The first educational event on the PA 'state of mind' was live and kicking back in 2015 and the future is big and bold! A neighbor of TIBA, this newborn has its fresh beginnings in The Netherlands. But hey, Amsterdam is known worldwide to have a great airport and you never know where life takes you...

And I can proudly share with you that Robert Wennekes, the founder and CEO of TIBA, supports the GPA concept. He is our honored keynote speaker and there is a bright future ahead of us. My hopes are high to get GPA up to the standards (or at least somewhat close!) of TIBA excellence. A global legacy for New Generation Assistants in the making!

Anyways, back to the community! The web is the medium that brings us closer. We have a Circle on LeanIn.org (GPA Dragons) for you to join whenever you please and a LinkedIn group (Global PA Academy) for your convenience. There won't be much more out there from us, as GPA will be kind of a secret sorority and brotherhood for Assisting Professionals. One place, one source — let's see if I can make it work! My skills will be tested to their painful extremes and I'm counting on it!

Also, the next baby is on its way (depending on when you read this book): the Iconic Assistants Mentoring platform (IAM&Co). After some additional research and analyzing the 'what's now' stage after the GPA launch in 2015, it came to my attention that what we need most is mentoring! But in my experience, it's difficult and expensive to get to the well-known PA mentors out there.

Therefore I came up with an idea to set up a closed and low-fee online mentoring platform led by 'younger-generation' Assistants and other outstanding experts to increase the value of the content provided. Such additional experts will be renowned NLP coaches, career and placement experts, self-made and extremely successful businessmen, TIBA counselors and many more.

I specifically choose 'new-generation' mentors as there are many young and outstanding PAs working in extraordinary environments and for awesome executives that are closer to our reality nowadays. Fresh views and fresh tips from and for the contemporary workplace.

This platform will provide quick Q&A solutions, vlogs and tips about various issues. And I don't mean technicalities, but interpersonal skills, personal development and advice for challenging situations. The mentors will all be active or former top-notch Assistants, which is different to other PA support systems. It will *not* be focused on where we work or for whom — it will be about us and what/how we do our magic.

The idea is to set up low-fee monthly memberships where members can ask any questions they have to the panel of our awesome mentors. The answers will be visible to the whole community (but within a closed setting). I plan to have about ten topics, with each mentor taking on a specific one. We will also have guest mentors, events and so 'many much more' that I get dizzy just by thinking about the possibilities — the world is our oyster. Let's serve it the way we like it!

The reason and purpose for GPA and IAM&Co is to nurture and support your Assistant 'state of mind' to make you excel in what you do! I hope to meet you, whenever and virtually, where all of us will come together to grow as one!

Well, that was my sales pitch. I hope that expensive marketing training paid off! Now, let's move on to the next thing on the menu.

Learning curve

Before I give center stage to some amazing PAs out there who set aside their precious time to answer my questions about soft skills and mindset I want to mention one last thing when it comes to education. It's all about educating our executives!

First of all, you need to make sure both of you are aware that for this relationship to work (and any other for that matter) it has to be based on a two-way stream effort. I see this as a huge point of attention when I start assisting self-made successful entrepreneurs who have not had a real PA before. It's a long and sometimes painful process, because it's about letting go. Letting go of a part they used to control and give a part of their precious treasure (the company they built with a lot of sweat and tears) to someone they don't know yet.

Three times in a row, different industries and different personalities: all of them coped with the same challenges of letting go. It's my job to prove over time that everything they give me is in good and capable hands. And it doesn't matter how often or intensely I urge them to let go — it will only happen when I prove myself to be worthy, time and again. Time is not my friend here, my soft skills and abilities are!

Also important is to agree on what you need from them. Most of you will know that it's a real learning curve for both sides. Even if you have known your exec for many years, things change, technology is sprinting and you need to update your relationship procedures as well.

I once heard a PA tell a story about how their difficult relationship with their exec flipped from bad to good by going to 'relationship counseling' together. Now, that's a very extreme and probably exceptional solution (they worked together for over 25 years) but it worked for them and she stayed to be his PA until his final hours, literally. Don't worry, he was an older gentleman and had commitment issues. But she had something that triggered his trust and he didn't want to let her go — so they made it work.

I'm not saying you need to do the same thing by any means. That proposition would surely not be in your favor when mentioned during an evaluation after your first year of service. But maybe you can use a variation of it. Any learning experience together with your exec is magically beneficial for your relationship. It has to do with our brain waves during learning — they make you connect easier with people around you. In a practical sense, propose to take notes at a training session he is attending or escort him to a conference of his preference. This step requires a certain trust already in place, so just see it as an option to try once upon a time.

In case you will be courageous enough to offer your advice on something that might impact the situation for the better (because you have just completed a training session on interpersonal dilemma problem solving techniques), the outcome will largely be dependent on the factors above. At some point I tend to spill my grains of wisdom here and there (or so I hope). Some executives listened to my advice and went straight into implementation mode with great instant results. Some of them took my pointers to the drawing board to make them fit their strategies and they too were pleased by what they generated. And some ignored me completely, didn't listen or weren't receptive to any of it. I'm fine with any outcome. What matters is that you do what you think is needed. The final decision is, at the end of the day, up to your executive. He will notice you and your contribution. It can only pique his curiosity and inspire admiration of your dedicated efforts!

Defense

In defense of your exec, hear this. Sometimes they are not responsive to your requests because they are not mind readers. Be explicit and forward in what you need to do your job to his expectations. Sometimes our execs go through rough patches in their lives and they just don't have any space in their head for you. They are masters in keeping it cool on the outside and keeping it all to themselves.

If you're a good PA you will know something is up and let them be, saving it for a later moment. Or just be very quick and to the point. The faster he can say yes or no, the better, but this requires some preparation from you. One topic, ten seconds, three sentences, seven facts tops, and only a yes/no option for an answer. You can fit anything into this construction!

One last thing: you might be the first PA he has encountered to be focused on education and personal development. For some execs it is not a given to invest in their PAs, as they don't count on you to stay forever or they don't see the added value of your progression. Whatever it is, the way to deal with it is to gradually and smoothly release the grounds for development and the obvious benefits for him if you get better at something. That's the key — talk in the form of his benefits! He cannot say no to something that would make his life easier, right? Be smart about it — it's your future you're dealing with.

Center stage rehearsal

The one thing that bothers me the most when it comes to listening to a PA is that your exec is constantly wondering: am I talking to an expert, an apprentice who's there to learn my skills and move on or just a secretarial Assistant who is good with Microsoft Office? It's important to understand that you control the answer to this question and it's your maturity of the skills that makes all the difference! It's not even what you say but how you say it.

I knew an extraordinary PA once. She looked very ordinary while sitting at her desk drumming away at her keyboard at 100 miles an hour and she was constantly glued to her phone making arrangements in four languages. It was fascinating to see her work. When she ran to the coffee corner for a cup of hot choco she smiled nicely and whispered 'Hi'. She was actually pretty timid among the team and didn't say much or speak very often.

But all that changed in a split second when her exec was nearby or she had to interact with him on any issue. She grew to be a few inches taller, her voice was one to be respected, everything she said made sense and was straight to the point. She recited a list of 364 items from the top of her head and had a stellar memory for every word her exec told her in a period of only a few minutes. It was true magic to see them together. I never saw that kind of efficiency again. And believe me — that exec was difficult and extremely demanding. They were a perfect fit. It was a hard job and she left the company about four times I believe. But she came back every time he asked her 'nicely'. She was the only one who knew how to deliver the support in the right manner! It was all about the *how*!

That is exactly the reason I want every Assistant to be on top of their abilities as that makes you an expert by definition. It's up to us to make this change and be seen as the supporting powerhouses behind the leaders. No, nobody is really irreplaceable — but we can let them believe we are indispensable! It's up to you to grow and shine in the area of what you do best.

With hard work comes responsibility, with responsibility comes expectation,
with consistent delivery on expectation comes respect,
with respect comes valuation, acceptance and dependence.

LET'S GO FOR IT AS A TEAM — GAME ON!

Chapter 19. PAs on Air!

When I started toying with the idea of writing a book I seriously questioned the need for it. No, not a very strong point of departure. So I came up with a survey to see what other professionals in this field or people that are connected to us thought about soft skills for Assisting Professionals.

Well, luckily it turned out to be a hot topic and I got many amazing answers to my questions. It pushed and inspired me to move on with this book and I'm forever grateful to the people that took time and effort to share their opinions. I could keep it all for myself, but I just cannot. It's great to see that, as scattered as we may be, we are truly like-minded professionals.

I will stop talking now and give the stage to some of the brave souls who agreed to be mentioned in this book. I have selected the highlights and respected privacy requests. It's not specifically about the person who shares it, but the content of their wisdom. Ladies and gentlemen — the stage is yours.

Case study 1:
Preliminary questionnaire on the importance of soft skills

The preliminary questionnaire sent to a selected group of professionals, both Assisting Professionals and executives. Answers are displayed in no particular order.

Which soft skills do you think are crucial for a service-minded person in assisting positions? It has to be a skill that even if s/he is not qualified enough on paper you would still recommend them as practical skills can be learned.

Public speaking. Becoming more comfortable with handling difficult situations and people.

The most important skills are listening, being friendly but not familiar, approachable, dedicated and focused on the job requirements. Loyal to the employer's needs. Have a good sense of humor. Being a good timekeeper and planner. An eye for detail is important. Resilience and understanding the needs of the job.

Open-minded, creative, flexible, pro-active, and positive.

As a business owner, having a strong work ethic and initiative are my number one required soft skills in the dream makers I hire (I call my team members dream makers, as they help me build my dream and they are extremely important in the process).

Ability to suggest/propose new tasks/assignments we assisting professionals believe that we could take on (or ways of improving how to go about them); 'walk the extra mile' as the saying goes.

A service-oriented person should first of all have great communication skills, followed by being a well-groomed person. I believe the first impression you create is a long-lasting one, especially when working in a field like this. You don't always have the time to create a memorable impact, depending on the way you interact with people. Being a charismatic person will help you thrive in your career, regardless if it is service-oriented or not.

A true 'heart of service', nurturing personality, willingness/eagerness to learn, flexibility.

Ability to organize things, to prioritize tasks, to delegate/share tasks (or parts of tasks).

Ability to plan ahead, to make general rules to go by (according to different scenarios/situations), to anticipate the needs of the people we assist and of their businesses (this includes keeping an eye out for anything that may help in the work we do: new technologies, new trends in the area of business our bosses work in etc.).

Having a very clear head, to see immediately what questions to ask (if needed) when getting a new task, how to go about them, what information details are needed now and which can wait for a little later while at the same time being of absolute discretion, choosing very carefully what information to give even inside our company, and this includes our own personal information: careful with office gossip!

Tact and diplomacy in the face of difficult situations (they will come), together with the ability of providing clear answers in a succinct manner at all times (details can be given when asked or felt there's really a need).

Anticipation, flexibility.

Empathy is very important, not only with our bosses but to an equal extent with work colleagues, clients, providers etc. Assisting professionals are a bit like the oil in the engine, we help it run smoother. This does not necessarily mean agreeing to everything they say or ask, but trying to see things from their perspective to better understand their needs and see how those needs fit with the rules of the company or person we work for so we are better able to explain eventual disagreements or different rules. Our responsibilities include saying 'no' at the appropriate times.

Ability to keep our heads and temper cool when pressure builds up. This is very important for us assisting professionals, for our positions necessarily entail having to put up with the bad temper our bosses can (and will) have when they themselves are under pressure. A very important part of our responsibilities involves taking as much of the pressure as we can off their backs and making their lives as easy as possible.

Having a very good memory is important, because assisting professionals do not always have the time to write everything down (but we must keep a track of everything, at least in our memory) and also because part of our job consists of 'connecting the dots' among the flux of information we constantly receive.

Patience and resilience.

Optimistic, cheerful attitude is at the top of the list along with an ability to quickly adapt to changes and client demands.

Diplomacy, good communication skills, ability to work under pressure.

Commitment to excellence, get it done attitude, reliable, dependable.

The mindset to think things through (consequences) and the mindset to really want to solve problems before they appear.

Energy, passion and commitment.

Proactive attitude, integrity, determination, responsibility.

Flexibility and adaptation.

Communication and interpersonal skills.

Calm, politeness, proactive thinking.

Energetic, resilience and systematic organization.

The lack of which soft skills, in your opinion, would interfere with the career of assisting professionals and will not let them excel in their profession even if they are perfectly qualified on paper?

Lack of maturity and emotional intelligence. Taking things personally and choosing to feel slighted and insulted easily are qualities that will limit success as an Assistant.

Poor attitude, lack of grooming and appearance, arrogant approach.

Not being submissive to your leader when needed and disrespecting them. For example, sarcastic remarks, back talking or ignoring their requests will only hold you back from further achievement.

I doubt someone can be perfectly qualified on paper and not have the necessary soft skills to work in this field. Usually, people are hired not for their educational background but for their attitude. It doesn't really matter if you studied mathematics and you are just looking for a temporary part-time job. As long as you have the correct attitude you will get it. Afterwards if you like it, you might even stay for a longer period of time or make a career out of it. That's the thing, you either love it or you don't so you move on.

Ego, inflexibility, lack of 'team' mentality.

Excessive empathy and/or will to please, which often leads to saying 'yes' when we assisting professionals should be saying 'no' (e.g. taking on more responsibilities than we can handle at that particular moment).

Excessive speed to do something when it would be better to take the time to plan and/or get more/better information in order to successfully complete the task.

Lack of responsibility, excuse making.

Stressing, being close-minded.

Excessive attention to details, to the detriment of getting the main task done or to lose time that would be needed when there are other tasks waiting.

Excessive tact and diplomacy, which may either lead others to not getting the message quite right or to wrongly believe they could get more.

Excessive multitasking: only if one is really very good at it can one get it right every time. A better strategy is to concentrate on the task at hand and share/delegate if and when possible. Sharing and delegation are usually more easily acceptable by others when done in a team spirit or when providing those others with the opportunity of getting credit for it.

Taking things personally, and letting comments or reactions affect you.

Bad attitude is the biggest one as well as an inability to understand that the clients wants, demands and expect nothing short of excellent results.

Poor communication skills, no emotional intelligence.

Sticking strictly to the job description.

Not being proper.

Being too polite or too nice.

Coy or shyness.

Being stubborn towards the employer, 'sitting mentality' (passiveness), underdeveloped language skills.

Overconfidence and egocentrism.

How do you value soft skills compared to technical skills/education?

I believe that tech skills are easier to teach than soft skills. If there are two candidates who have equal tech skills but one has a personality that is better suited to the culture, you know who is going to get the job. Different companies value these skills differently. The best Assistants work to hone both as they are extremely important.

Within the service industry your personal skills account for 2/3rds of your ability to do the job. Training and qualifications are fine to have but how you approach the role is key.

I can teach technical skills, but you have to adapt naturally to soft skills such as being a team player, being positive and communicating properly with your team. However, I highly value the importance of an education and encourage my team to keep up their education and set high goals for themselves.

Unfortunately, soft skills are secondary as most individuals who need administrative/personal assistance seek one who can 'hit the ground running'.

Soft skills are more important if the technical skills are met (if a PA doesn't how the technical stuff soft skills won't help).

More than anything else.

They are totally separated (I think). You can have a background education which has nothing to do with the professional environment you end up in.

A good combination of the two is best, however, if you don't have the soft skills to excel as a PA you will never succeed, no matter how qualified you are.

It's a 90/10 imbalance of skills as the technical aspects of any project are easily mastered and once understood are fixed.

Soft skills are key.

50-50.

First the soft skills, then the technical ones.

Soft skills are undervalued! Technical skills can be added but soft skills never.

Practical experience is the best experience.

Technical skills are the basis that can make everybody work on more or less the same level. The soft skills add a personal touch, personality if you like, to the worker and it is what separates us from each other. The soft skills are what makes us be liked by an employer. Or the opposite.

Both are needed but it depends on the business. I would value individuals capable of soft skill and loyalty over high tech and self-serving.

Is there a piece of professional advice/remark/quote that you received in your career (positive or negative) that supported you?

'Do one thing well, not two things badly.' Olympia Dukakis

Service is King.

The only person you should try to better is the person you were yesterday.

 Don't be selfish; don't try to impress others. Be humble, thinking of others as better than yourselves. Philippians 2:3.

It should never be about you.

What would you suggest the upcoming generation of professionals should do/be in order to get to that professional excellence they strive for?

Handwritten thank-you notes will set you apart from others. Show excellent manners. Power down your phone and devices during interviews and meetings. Show respect for others of all ages. Pick up the phone to speak with others rather than text, especially regarding sensitive matters.

Be dedicated, loyal, approachable, friendly, smart, well-groomed and dressed.

Keep developing yourself continuously by watching the world and people around you.

Step in the other person's shoes and see the world according to them.

It is important to understand that being your best takes constant work. Remember to surround yourself with others that are more experienced and excelled than you are; learn from them. Keep up your education and be multi-talented. Give back to others in need and learn from your mentors as one day you will need to be a mentor. Keep up with other professionals in your community by attending events and conferences and build your network. Find a few professionals you can go to when you need advice and also be there for them in return.

Be patient. Nowadays people are not patient when it comes to their career (including myself and many others among me). We should be patient and learn from the best, learn from life experiences, travel, meet people, get culturally connected with others. This will help you better understand other people's needs and will enhance your ability to work together with/for them. Try to gain the experience you need in other countries, especially if your own country is not fully developed in this sector.

Strive to be as high of an achiever as their principal.

As the saying goes, 'practice makes perfect', so I encourage them to practice, practice, practice their skills, both soft and hard and of course learn new ones. I also encourage them to do the following: sharing tricks, examples and stories with other fellow assisting professionals, including from different companies/areas of business/countries: they may be doing the same things we do daily, but better! Those who share will also be building up a (hopefully very) good professional reputation; not only online but more importantly by word of mouth, which may eventually give them better chances of getting that job (or of receiving a tempting job offer). Besides, s/he who always takes from others without giving will be shunned in the end.

Taking the time to think how to work better and making it more pleasant.

Take full responsibility, be totally dependable and reliable.

Know the business of the manager supported, know the organization and the partners and have, a network of professional/reliable suppliers/service partners available (to get things done).

Attend boot camp training.

Work in a service environment as a waiter or cabin crew, you gain team spirit and a high level of service as well as manners.

Get a PA diploma. Or if they would ideally like to be a PA in a particular field then definitely a degree in that field.

Each should read Gary Ryan Blair's book Everything Counts. It's a declaration of excellence and explains everything you need to be successful regardless of the profession.

Touch typing is essential!

Understand the type of business of their 'boss'.

Take a minute to breathe/live.

Listen, be punctual and strive for success.

At first, get the basic technical skills and understand them well.
Second, trial and error with the intention to learn. And third, always keep an open mind, because opportunity lies in small corners and sometimes have to be worked for. Personable and authentic, organized and technologically well educated. (Executive)

There are always people we look up to. What are the personal or practical qualities you are attracted to in your role models?

Being forthright. Speaking up about tough issues in a way that moves the work forward and leaves everyone with their dignity.

Sense of humor, business awareness.

Patience, wisdom and knowledge.

I am attracted to people who do what they say; I see it through their actions. I surround myself with those who respect me and others around them, set boundaries for themselves and respect mine in return. My role models make time for me, invest in me and make me feel important. Your role models will most likely be more accomplished, wealthy and more educated than you. However, they should encourage you, respect you, pick you up when you fail and celebrate you when you are triumphant.

I admire those colleagues who are more efficient than I am (either because they work faster, or better, or a combination of both), are better organized, or have an amazing memory. I also admire those colleagues who give a more professional result or image; and those who train themselves in something useful instead of going on Facebook when they have some spare time. All of them inspire me in my quest for excellence, and I am very thankful to them for their examples.

Humility, honesty, dedication, resourcefulness, creativity.

Are there any specific qualities of an assisting professional that you think would make it or break it if he/she would be your PA/Assistant/Estate Manager/Butler?

Rudeness, disrespect, and insensitivity about the differences between people. Not learning from mistakes and experience.

I've had some colleagues who were very keen on office gossiping, and while at the beginning it seemed flattering to be in their confidences, I quickly realized how bad that was for the general office mood, with little clans making war on each other. I can't stand that. For me, gossiping really breaks it.

Team player, friendly, approachable, good listener and able to take and accept direction.

Positive attitude and integrity.

I currently have my dream makers that I must lead on a day to day basis. They know I have their best interests in mind. Therefore I expect in return daily respect, a positive attitude and to only stay with me if they are happy, doing what they love to do. In return, I strive to be a strong leader and work hard at making daily decisions in their best interest as well as the company's.

Grooming, punctuality, striving for perfection — these are the three things that matter the most to me. The rest anyone can learn as long as they have discipline and ambition at work.

A 'true heart of service', humility, honesty, dedication, resourcefulness, creativity are always winners; a 'know it all' with no flexibility would not succeed with me.

Decisive, people of their word, 'walk their talk'.

A person's character and personality.

The ability to think outside of the box and have the belief in themselves to be as successful as they desire.

Integrity, excellence, focus and joy!

Confidence, charisma, ability to remain calm, levelheaded.

A combination of IQ and EQ.

To be the best in their field of work... (discipline).

Strong and determined minds.

They make themselves happy by working for other people. And most of all, they believe they are part of something greater than themselves and fight for a cause.

Authenticity and genuine interest in the business or professional you represent.

They take full responsibility, are totally dependable and reliable, get it done, no excuses, don't wait to be told what/how to do things but intuitively know what needs to be done.

Thinking ahead, solving problems before they understand and use the system of functional escalation.

(Lack of) flexibility.

No professionalism, no manners, too junior. A good PA must be strong, that is, have a strong personality to find her way in this particular field.

Showing initiative is extremely important, trying to stay one step ahead so I don't have to think of every detail. Professional at all times and a willingness to learn how I would like things done rather than them thinking they know better.

Poor grammar, missing deadlines, being late and unprepared are the kiss of death. They must get serious about doing the job right or with the worldwide reach of the web, your reputation will negatively proceed you.

Flexibility and adaptability.

Getting things done, honesty, integrity, no excuses, confidentiality. Being lazy or not honest will break you.

Make it: immaculate appearance (not about beauty), polite language, proactive work and eagerness to learn. Break it: the opposite of these things.

It can't be just about the money or the title... There has to be a real connection and a goal objective near or far.

Deliver results no matter what (my ideal PA is the one in The Devil Wears Prada).

Bad knowledge of language.

Missing on getting things done no matter what, no excuses.

Mutual respect is the basis for a good working relationship.

Do you think an education/training in soft skills is as important for assisting professionals? Do you think you can learn to be service-oriented/minded or is it a personal quality?

There are qualities that an Assistant is born with such as being organized and intuitive. There are also many qualities that can and should be learned. An enthusiastic willingness to learn is absolutely necessary to excel at the highest levels.

I do certainly believe very strongly that an education/training in soft skills is at least as important as in hard ones. And very often in our profession (as in others), soft skills are actually more important than hard ones. At the core of our profession is the fact that we are the interface between our bosses and the rest of the world, so our bosses can have more time to do what they have to do; that's why we assisting professionals deal with people every ten minutes and subsequently we need to have and develop strong soft skills.

Some people are born (or somehow 'raised' to be) service-oriented/minded, and some others will have to learn how to become so.

You can learn service skills but an attitude of mind to serve is key.

It is important! Training these skills is not easy for the people involved. Soft skills start with yourself, the way you look at the world. Soft skills training is touching that element in life. Out of a person's comfort zone.

My answer is to take that on a person to person and case by case basis. Some people are easily trainable and you see it in their actions. For example, I had a talk with a team member about being on time and that person immediately turned their behavior around and it has not been an issue since.

I believe it is more a personal quality rather than something you can learn. I don't doubt the fact that we can enhance someone's skills though training but there should always be something there to make it happen. Either it's the desire of learning or the striving for success but it should be there. Training is more for polishing the skills we already have and teaching us how to use them wisely and correctly.

One can always 'be trained/educated', but the true test comes when it is time to implement the material(s) absorbed and really dedicate the time required to 'assist'.

It must be a personal quality but education is necessary.

You are born with strong soft skills.

It's both a personal quality and learning from others.

I am convinced that every service-minded professional can become better and greater by getting the support and opportunity of a person or company that helps to bring these qualities out in the light. A severely frustrated and annoyed person might have a good service mind inside, but it will take a long time to get it through the emotional barriers in that person's mind.

I believe people can be trained in soft skills. It's a personal and individual decision to acquire any skill.

Yes, yes. Some Dale Carnegie-like training would be helpful.

It's a personal quality but can be trained/learned if the basic mindset is available.

Yes, absolutely. But you need to want it more than life itself.

Yes, you can definitely learn. But it also comes from your education. If it's not natural, you might find it hard to evolve quickly. It's all about your background. But still you can learn when you're young.

I think it's important to teach soft Skills, however not everyone can learn and adapt, it depends on the person.

Both. Some are more natural then others, but with enough desire all skills can be learned and mastered.

It can be taught but more often it's a skill that you either have or you do not have.

Do you think the title of an assisting professional reflects the level of their abilities and does it form a preconception regarding their qualities? (EA, PA, Estate Manager, Secretaries, Assistant to…, Office Manager, Butler, Staff Head Master)

It is a challenge to find the right definition since the responsibilities in this profession are not easy to describe. It is always a tailor-made job. The fulfillment should be the job content and not the title of the job.

Titles matter, yes. What is more important though is the written job description and the realistic expectations set between staffer and employer. Ongoing positive and respectful communication is critical.

Titles should not matter, it is the ability to do the job with the right attitude that is most important.

I think this depends a bit on the national language (e.g., a Legal Secretary in English is not quite the same as a Secrétaire juridique in French) and a great deal on the corporate/company's language. The latter should reflect as exactly as possible the reality of the position we assisting professionals occupy in the company, and in some cases this is not so.

When I hear those titles, I think 'strong, gate keeper, experienced, be nice to that person'! But as a former PA I may be biased. I do think that a lot of PAs are also EAs at the same time and sometimes others may not be aware of that.

Unfortunately, yes to those who do not have a comprehension of the diverse responsibilities of the assisting professionals' role.

Sure…

I've personally never cared about titles, but I'd want to give them a title they felt proud of.

What's in a name. It's more about the relationship between manager/business owner and the PA than about the job name.

Yes, EA is administrative, PA is discretion, and so on.

No, the title can at times have nothing to do with the level of their abilities. I think a decent title is a bonus if it's earned, however, definitely does not reflect their abilities.

Of course it does. Our job is to make our employer look like a rock star to their core audience.

The title of EA or even PA does not reflect their level.
No.

A strong title will always be noticed and listened to better.

Some of these words have a high value because of connections people make with them. Connections with status, money, widely promoted titles or even TV series. Some of the words have a negative connotation because of stereotypes created in media. A 'secretary' for example is always pictured as a female office worker that passes her time doing her nails. On the opposite side, abbreviations and titles with 'Manager' in them tend to make us think more highly of the function.

It depends on the individual's personality and character... But titles can be incentivizing.

Do you have any specific observations regarding the level of assisting professionals nowadays? Or anything else that catches your eye in the field of assisting professions?

The workplace is getting more complicated, not less. There will be an increasing need for professional education opportunities for support staff. Supplemental training in both soft and hard skills is fast becoming a necessity and not a luxury option.

I want to be a part of ending bullying in our global workplace, which is a huge problem. I want to inspire business leaders across the globe to invest in the training and education of their administrative staffs because it is a very smart business decision to do so. I want to inspire college leaders to increase leadership training for graduating students so that they enter the workplace more prepared for what they are going to face.

Absolute flexibility in mindset and action is something that needs an ongoing focus. Taking care of the other person is something you really need to like, almost love, to do. People with that passion in their heart and attitude will be the golden nuggets in our profession.

It seems to be an exciting time in today's world, where the level of assisting professionals is at its all-time high. As a recent speaker at the 'Behind Every Leader' conference, I was extremely impressed with the level of quality and educated PAs & EAs that are the backbone of some of the world's most powerful leaders.

Some assisting professionals view their positions as jobs, not careers; again, it comes back to having a 'true heart of service'.

When they step up as leaders, it is always a beneficial quality.

A good PA filters information, work and events of the manager/professional supported, so this manager/professional can use the time available effectively (delivering maximal value for the organization, for customers and for realizing goals).

In general people are not 'hands-on'.

I have noticed lately that executive Assistants do not reflect the image of their bosses. They don't dress nicely enough, they often don't know how to put their make up on, and their appearance is generally low. Lately I've been very concerned about that fact. It's like they don't care. When you have a good salary, a wealthy, known boss, you must appear at your best as you reflect his/her image in the office (and for clients). I learned that when I was part of a cabin crew.

I think when things don't go to plan and in some cases may be a disaster and tempers are high, it's important to stay calm and always know there is a solution to the problem. Even if you don't know what that solution is right there and then, it's important to reassure everyone with a temporary solution. Remain calm and professional at all times. Acting skills can seriously help too and the gift of the gab is hugely beneficial. I managed to get myself out of so many situations and deal with so much drama this way.

We don't teach Assistants enough any longer at a young age — skills need to taught early on otherwise it's too late.

Professional levels are globally rising as a whole along with our qualification levels.

Like more and more people in our trade, I too have been witnessing the slow rise of a variety of outsourcing options for our profession, the so-called 'virtual Assistants', whom are not virtual but real people with real qualifications, real experience and real jobs. Not every assisting professional is suited to become a 'virtual' one, because basically it is two positions in one: the familiar one of carrying on with our assisting professional cap, and the unfamiliar one of really putting ourselves in the boss' boots, doing our marketing, getting new clients, getting paid by them, paying the rent, the taxes and the expenses, being responsible for paying our own salaries etc.

Something what really catches my eyes from a global perspective is the nearly complete absence of male secretaries (except perhaps in some Anglo-Saxon countries). This one used to be (another) male profession until WWI, when women massively replaced the men, who were fighting the war, and (very rightfully) refused to 'return to the kitchen' at the end of it. Even now, they won't consider the profession, as it is deemed 'only for girls', despite different campaigns in the last 20 years or so promoting equality of rights for men and women alike. So we end up having thousands of potentially pretty good male secretaries who won't take up this job and will stay jobless because 'it's women's work' while at the same time more and more women take up more and more jobs in industries who were 'man-only' a few years ago.

I think that globalization means among other things that we assisting professionals should be able to be at least fully bilingual, and I have noticed that in Europe even three languages are not enough. Linguists and philologists have proved that each language carries its own, different understanding of situations and so mastering a foreign language means that one is much more able to understand the way of thinking of people with that language. I am very proud and happy of having a native level of English, French, Spanish, and Italian: they help me help my bosses and their contacts to better understand each other and work together better.

I live and work in Russia where soft skills are not yet the most strong point one can find in an office environment. However, there is a large and growing amount of young boys and girls that want to do things better, take pride in their jobs and are smiling to all people they get in touch with. I have seen a particular situation in a very famous hotel in Moscow, where a guest was very upset and was shouting quite loudly at reception. The GM of the hotel was nearby with his Assistant and he sent her into the cage of the lion. It took her about two minutes to get a small smile on the angry guest's face and have him apologize without even asking him.

People often rest on the laurels of what they were able to accomplish in the past. But technology and the worlds of contacts, organization and social media are very fluid. Professionals need to be comfortable with change and continued education in technological advancements.

Contributors
(along with those that requested to remain anonymous)

Adam Fidler	PA Guru
Andra Vachente	Guest Services Manager at Burj Al Arab Hotel
Bonnie Low-Kramen	Bestselling author of *Be the Ultimate Assistant*, who is teaching and speaking around the world. www.betheultimateassistant.com
Bridgette Bester	Personal/Executive Assistant
Damián Dell'Amico	Personal Assistant & Legal Secretary Executive Assistant ROAR Global
Ineke van de Laak	Owner, Global Courtesy
Karine	Former PA for many clients in Paris and New York. EA for different Vice-Presidents / Presidents in Monaco and Paris. www.smart1s.net
Lauretta O. Rosado	Estate Manager at Confidential Employer
Lindsey Holder	Former Celebrity PA & Style Ambassador, Author, Entrepreneur. www.lindseyholder.com @savvyassistants
Drs. Marischka Setz	Founder and Managing Director DNHS.nl
Robert Wennekes	CEO & Chairman of The International Butler Academy
Robin Greenfield	Butler and House Manager at Confidential Employer
Todd Harris	PA to Gary Ryan Blair
Tom Beal	Founder of MakeTodayGreat.com

Conclusion

All the contributions were very to the point and valuable. I don't know most of the contributors personally, but their personalities shine through their answers. That I found to be the most remarkable thing. And the fact that we do think alike, although in many variations... We do value the same things and want the same results! I found it very inspiring and heartwarming to read the answers, and I hope you do too.

The most surprising and divisive topic had to be the one about the titles. Executives don't seem to care, Assisting Professionals largely do. So what's the lesson to be learned here?

Case study 2:

Are you indispensable as an Assisting Professional?

Knowing all the above I didn't stop there. There is this amazing social media platform called LinkedIn, which I admire a lot. So I started to participate in discussions wanting to find out more about what other members of our supernatural service community think about similar topics.

The most significant one was about the alleged phenomenon of being indispensable. Luckily, some of the participating members shared their victories. But what struck me most is that most of the comments where degrading our profession, saying we are very dispensable (based on bad personal experiences) so we better not act like it....

Somebody actually said we shouldn't even try to get there! That was really shocking to me. No, it's not about acting that way, but experiencing that as a result of our endeavors. I do love the twist Felicia gives to this phrase here below, she uses it to her advantage. And I bet she makes herself indispensable this way!

Your reality reflects the state of your mind — remember that before you think another syllable.

I sense that there is a mindset issue that needs to be addressed. It's our positioning that is at stake and our PA branding that needs first aid! And as Anette states below: our position is truly indispensable! For some weird reason we think we are not. Food for thought and a war to be fought! So to keep up the spirits, here are some victorious comments I would love to share with you.

The questions I posted on most major LI groups for Assistants were:

What makes you indispensable? How would you respond if your employer asked you why they cannot do without you?

340

Linda Diergaardt
Personal Assistant at Trans Kalahari Corridor Secretariat

First and foremost is the institutional memory I have of the company. Secondly I am a great administrator and manage to handle my tasks efficiently, effectively and with finesse. I don't mind putting in extra hours to ensure things get done. Especially when we have events taking place. And although it is a cliché I really do go that extra mile to ensure that when someone presses my buttons I respond immediately. And that is how I am known in our organization. But all is not always shiny and bright. It also means I have to be on top of my game each and every time. Glitches happen but it only inspires me to work harder and be the best I can be as an administrator.

Gloria Hines
Executive Assistant at Staples

My boss paid me the best compliment ever. He wrote in my performance review 'she is irreplaceable; in other words, I would not be successful without her!' And by this he did not mean I was a wizard at Excel or PowerPoint, but more the other qualities an Executive Assistant must possess... The personality to do the job; organizational skills; sense of humor; calm under stress; reliability; confidentiality etc. It was the best compliment I ever received because I know that I am a good reflection on him, which is important in the business world for your busy Executive. Remember to stress those important qualities; you can always learn a software program but you can't change your personality and commitment values!

Angela Connell
Executive Assistant to Managing Director at PKF Lawler, Australia

We have just merged with another firm and at the first partners' meeting, my boss said of me to the other partners, 'She knows everything that's happening in the practice and I trust her because if we cannot trust Angela, we are in trouble.' That I think cemented my position even further. I never thought of trust as being a benefit to the management, but I guess that is one good word to describe indispensable.

Marguerite Breda
Executive Assistant, Manager Lending Processing

I do many major things that my boss doesn't want to do, or doesn't do well, without being asked. Without supervision. Because I understand her priorities and work style, I free up her time and mental effort so she can focus on what she wants to do and does well. The two most precious commodities: time and serenity.

I also ensure that she is always focused on the future, because today is taken care of. That way she's able to leverage her strong leadership skills on the next big thing while I handle or finish up the present. Something as simple as creating an effortless share-point file system or as complicated as a 2/6/12-month calendar of projects (ever shifting) so that at a glance she knows what needs to be done and where we are with it. So I create time, serenity and focus. And there is no app for that.:-)

Felicia Davis
Assistant to the CEO at Windstream Holdings, Inc.

'No one is indispensable, not me, not you. And as long as I realize that, I will make the extra effort to be even better at what I do, which makes you believe that I am indispensable.' The minute I believe that I am indispensable, I have failed.

Anette Rahbek
PA/EA, Project & Change Management, Denmark

True, we are not indispensable, but the work we do is. No C-suite company would hire EAs if the tasks to be managed by the EA/PA were not considered indispensable for the CEO or senior level VP to perform at their best. A gatekeeper/anchor person is one who ties together a string of separate, diverse and sometimes conflicting tasks to make one cohesive whole, where nothing is missed and no ball dropped.

In closing...

Downright amazing, we have an amazing job to do and we love it! We are all Personally Awesome!

There are no words to describe my excitement about what's to come. We will transform our profession from within and we will position ourselves as truly *indispensable*. Assistants will take a place at the table, and we have a lot to offer. We always did, but now it's time to come out of the shadows. Don't forget: we stand by and assist the world's leaders, innovators, changemakers and creators. They rely on us to be there by their side and trust our abilities. That's an honorable position and an absolutely *indispensable* one. Be proud of it! Be proud of yourself as you fit this position perfectly. We are a special super breed and we stand stronger together. But it has to be in your mind first. Start there and make your path an exciting one to travel, full of pride and fulfillment.

Thank you for reading this book. You make my day! As a final closing, I want to mention a quote from Jennifer Corcoran, who is truly out there pioneering our profession lately. She wrote a LinkedIn Pulse post on 'Social Media for Assistants' and it was very inspiring to read, especially the part below. Thank you Jennifer!

Jennifer Corcoran
Office Manager, PA / EA, Blogger, Founder of CAN, London

Administrative professionals make up a fifth of the world's working population. We are a global tribe and Personal Assistants need to recognize the value of their personal impact and how it is impossible to not have an image or presence. We are brand ambassadors for our role, boss, company and ultimately the PA profession.

Hear hear! The sky is not the limit, we know that. If we stick together and grow as one, we will become a force to reckon with. To all indispensable Assisting Professionals!

When Assistants excel, others benefit!

Invitation from the author...

I hope you enjoyed reading about ways to create, motivate and tweak your excelerating Assistant state of mind!

I'm confident you found something that will boost your branding, self-pride and bring you the much needed acknowledgement and recognition of your value. If this first volume of *New Generation Assistants* series has inspired you in some ways I would love to hear from you. You would do me and the rest of Personally Awesome Assistants around the world a great favour by writing a short review on Amazon.

Together we are stronger, together we can change our branding and advocate our amazing profession.

Stay tuned for the next publication in this *New Generation Assistants series* (volume 2), which will be all about personal positioning, resume profiling and your awesomeness branding.

Join our LinkedIn group for exciting and exclusive Assisting Professionals personal development updates and discussions:

www.linkedin.com/groups/8235338

Connect with us on Facebook for inspiring quotes, intriguing vlogs and daily 'Assistant state of mind' tips & tricks:

http://www.facebook.com/iconicassistants

And check out our groundbreaking online PA mentoring platform, *Iconic Assistants Mentoring & Co* (IAM&Co) with top-notch 'next generation' PA mentors who support world's best known and acknowledged leaders in their lives and businesses. Now, they are ready and *Willing* to do the same for you! Where ever you are, whichever Assistant title you have – this platform will be your trusted source of inspiration, industry knowledge, heartfelt support, cut through advice and a lot of personal attention: **www.iconicassistants.com**

Send me an email (mentoring@globalpaacademy.com) with your feedback, your resistance list and anything else you would like to share with me and I will give you a FREE 3-months trial membership at IAM&Co, as my thank you for your trust, time and efforts to improve and grow!

Stay Personally Awesome and may the W.A.N.T.E.D. skills be with you,

Anna Tjumina

Private & Business PA

Founder of Global PA Academy

Mentor IAM&Co

www.globalpaacademy.com

Workbook of Indispensable Assistants

✓   *Resistance List*

_____
_____
_____
_____
_____
_____
_____

✓   *Boost card – The Why*

_____
_____
_____

✓   *Superpowers & practical applications*

1. _____
2. _____
3. _____

✓ *Achievement list*

1. _____
2. _____
3. _____
4. _____
5. _____

✓ *Innovation list of (unrelated) success stories*

1. _____
2. _____
3. _____
4. _____
5. _____

✓ *Integrity values list*

Personal

1. _____
2. _____
3. _____

Objective

1. _____
2. _____
3. _____

Expected

1. _____
2. _____
3. _____

✓ *Skills role models*

1. _____
2. _____
3. _____

✓ *Action role models*

1. _____
2. _____
3. _____

✓ *Connecting factors of dedication*

1. _____
2. _____
3. _____

What's Now - Evaluation

✓ *Current pain points*

1. _____

2. _____

3. _____

✓ *100% partition split*

✓ *Limiting W.O.R.M.s*

1. _____

2. _____

3. _____

✓ *Life roles & mindsets*

1. _____ : _____
2. _____ : _____
3. _____ : _____
4. _____ : _____
5. _____ : _____
6. _____ : _____
7. _____ : _____

✓ *Frustration list*

1. _____
2. _____
3. _____

✓ *My/exec's quadrant evaluation*

Internal

1. _____ / _____
2. _____ / _____
3. _____ / _____

External

1. _____ / _____
2. _____ / _____
3. _____ / _____

✓ *Life areas, rating and weakest links*

1. _____ : _____ : _____
2. _____ : _____ : _____
3. _____ : _____ : _____
4. _____ : _____ : _____
5. _____ : _____ : _____
6. _____ : _____ : _____
7. _____ : _____ : _____

What's New – Goal Setting

✓ *Life areas and goals*

1. _____ : _____
2. _____ : _____
3. _____ : _____
4. _____ : _____
5. _____ : _____
6. _____ : _____
7. _____ : _____

✓ *Hard skills development List*

1. _____
2. _____
3. _____

✓ *Soft skills development List*

1. _____
2. _____
3. _____

What's Next – Implementation

✓ *Inspiration guide of proved strategies*

1. _____
2. _____
3. _____
4. _____
5. _____

✓ *Not to-do list*

1. _____
2. _____
3. _____

✓ *Substitute list (limiting beliefs and thought vs supportive beliefs and thoughts)*

1. _____ / _____
2. _____ / _____
3. _____ / _____

✓ *Testing situations for new skills*

1. _____
2. _____
3. _____

✓ *Me-time lists*

Happy List

1. _____
2. _____
3. _____

Jerrycan List

1. _____
2. _____
3. _____

My Happy Town

_____
_____
_____

Bucket List

1. _____
2. _____
3. _____
4. _____
5. _____
6. _____
7. _____

Recurring Want-To-Do List

1. _____
2. _____
3. _____

✓ *Daily relax rituals*

1. _____
2. _____
3. _____
4. _____
5. _____

Resources of Indispensable Assistants

✓ *Books*

Lean In by Sheryl Sandberg
The Trust Equation by Charles H. Green
Who Took My Pen ... Again? by J. Burge, N.Fraze and J. Freeman
The Third Wave by Alvin Toffler
Difficult Conversations by Douglas Stone, Bruce Patton and Sheila Heen
Brain Rules by Dr. John J. Medina
Getting Things Done by David Allen
Think and grow rich by Napoleon Hill
How to win friends and influence people by Dale Carnegie
Working on Yourself Doesn't Work by Ariel and Shya Kane
The Mindfulness Code by Donald Altman
The Whole Brain Business Book by Ned Hermann
Winning From Within by Erica Ariel Fox
The One Minute Millionaire by Mark Victor Hansen and Robert G. Allen
Elements of Success by Nisandeh Neta
Happiness by Matthieu Ricard
The Art of War by Sun Tzu

✓ *Websites*

www.trustedadvisor.com
www.communication-styles.com
www.executivesecretary.com
www.globalpaacademy.com

.

51931351R00201

Made in the USA
San Bernardino, CA
06 August 2017